THE SOCIAL LIFE OF
CHILDREN
IN A CHANGING
SOCIETY

THE SOCIAL LIFE OF CHILDREN IN A CHANGING SOCIETY

Edited by
KATHRYN M. BORMAN
University of Cincinnati

LAWRENCE ERLBAUM ASSOCIATES, PUBLISHERS
1982   Hillsdale, New Jersey   London

ABLEX PUBLISHING CORPORATION
1982   Norwood, New Jersey

Lawrence Erlbaum Associates, Inc., Publishers
365 Broadway
Hillsdale, New Jersey 07642

Library of Congress Cataloging in Publication Data
Main entry under title:

Social life of children in a changing society.

Includes bibliographical references and indexes.
1. Socialization. 2. Children and adults. 3. Children
—Language. 4. Social change. I. Borman, Kathryn M.
HQ783.S565   1983   303.3′2   82-11557
ISBN 0-89859-187-2
ISBN 0-89891-130-5 (Ablex)

Printed in the United States of America
10 9 8 7 6 5 4 3 2 1

Contents

This volume is dedicated to Greg and Geoff, two children of a changing society.

Preface

This book developed from a symposium in which participants examined childhood socialization from a number of perspectives and with several disciplinary lenses. The major purpose of the symposium and thus of this volume is to provide an integrative, multidisciplinary discussion of the social development of preschool and young elementary school-aged children. As a result, there are contributions to this volume from anthropologists (Leacock, Ogbu), psychologists (Lippincott, Mueller, Ramey and Snow), sociologists (Borman, Denzin) and scholars who have self-consciously adopted an interdisciplinary framework to inform their work (Gideonse, Green, the Kretschmers, Sutton-Smith, Wallat).

Four propositions serve as organizing components for the contributions to this volume. First, childhood socialization is importantly dependent upon agents of socialization, specifically, parents, teachers, and peers and, in addition, is highly contingent upon language and processes of interaction. Also, children who are developmentally delayed through conditions of either social or physical handicap may require special consideration in their socialization needs. Moreover, both the processes of socialization and the social lives of children are cross-culturally varied.

In view of these considerations, I have organized volume contents into four major sections: (1) Parents and Others: Those who Influence Children's Lives; (2) Language as a Primary Socializer: Normally Developing Children; (3) Language as a Primary Socializer: Developmentally Delayed Children; and (4) The Cross-Cultural Perspective. The Introduction and Endnote serve as a framework, emphasizing on the one hand, the evolutionary and social change contexts and, on the other, the political dimensions of childhood socialization.

The chapters included here are original contributions, and, in some cases, major new formulations of old notions about childhood socialization. All chapters contain significant insights drawn by each author from his or her ongoing research.

In Chapter 1, Denzin places heavy emphasis upon the "essences" of childhood experiences recalled in adulthood and recorded in intimate detail in autobiographical materials including letters, diaries and the like. His "notes" range over the insights of Mead, particularly Mead's emphasis on the early appearance, by age 3, of the fully developed self and extend to the autobiographical data of Proust, A. A. Milne and the Henry James, Sr. family.

In Chapter 2, Leacock examines school experience that, taken as a whole, socializes children to continue in the class and caste positions to which they were born. Classroom socialization hinges upon expectancy effects broadcast to children by teachers whose differential behaviors toward children are shaped by institutionalized systems of race and class bias. Leacock marshalls evidence from recent case studies of classroom life to explore the subtle ways teaching style and the curriculum shape children's lives.

In Chapter 3 Sutton-Smith carts away the baggage of an older theory of peer retentions in childhood. Instead, Sutton-Smith's performance theory of peer relations highlights children's social life as intense, dramatic, difficult and rambunctious. Play and games are the primary vehicles children employ both to transform reality and to mimic social relations.

The next section of the book concerns language as a socializer of normally developing children. In Chapter 4 Snow examines the role in children's language acquisition taken by parents, particularly by mothers, the most frequent caretakers. Early language "instruction" by parents, as Cross has illustrated, consists not of talking in a certain way but of talking about certain things. As Snow's research with children under 3 illustrates, semantically related utterances are provided by caretakers in particularly propitious contexts, without the presence of an older sibling and during periods of meal preparation, general caretaking and play. It appears that parents are in fact language teachers but only when conditions are right.

Wallat and Green in Chapter 5 use highly detailed microanalyses of classroom communication to discover how the kindergarten child learns to show his or her membership in classroom society. According to their research, the most revealing period in the classroom day is transitional time, the period when the classroom group moves from individual work to the group circle meeting. Classroom norms and conventions are visible in both verbal and non-verbal signals. Interactional skills acquired during the first year of schooling allow the child to recognize and practice the construction of social events in common with others.

In Chapter 6 Borman and Lippincott consider the dynamics of social cognitive development within the context of the culture of urban Appalachian children's games. The authors' argument provides a link between social structurally-based theories of socialization and the cognitive developmental perspective of Piaget, both of which center on the importance of children's spontaneously organized play and peer interactions.

The third section of the book is concerned with language as a socializer of developmentally delayed children. Ramey, McGinness, Cross, Collier, and Barrie-Blackley in Chapter 7 outline the Abcedarian program developed by Ramey and his colleagues to provide a language enriched curriculum for infants and very young children. Intervention begins before the child's birth for children identified as at high risk for school failure. Program emphasis is placed upon improving and strengthening task-oriented behavior, improving peer relationships and interactions and improving adult-child interactions.

In Chapter 8, the Kretschmers analyze the differential socialization systems among parents and children who are language-delayed. They describe a number of studies in which language-delayed children are compared with younger, developmentally normal and comparably skilled children. Although language-delayed children apparently suffer from an inability to connect the spoken language systems to a system of cognitive knowledge, once the process of language use is activated, these children soon begin to use highly developed adverbial constructions, etc., consonant with their relatively greater cognitive maturity. Thus, the Kretschmers conclude that socialization occurs under conditions of mutual respect and sensitivity regardless of the symbol system used in the process.

Mueller and Bergstrom in Chapter 9 stress the importance of peer relations in early childhood for the development of social intelligence, particularly cooperativeness, playfulness and friendliness. Although Mueller and Bergstrom urge that adult caretakers allow even quite young children (under 18 months) to settle their own disputes, adults are urged to construct physical environments which foster positive peer interaction. Toys, play equipment and materials are important in the structuring of peer relations among both normal and special needs children as analyzed in several studies reviewed in this chapter.

The last section of the book examines the cross-cultural perspective on children's social life. In Chapter 10 Gearhart and Hall's central concern is to examine cultural variation in vocabulary use as this variation has implications for children's cognitive development and school performance. School-related tasks, particularly those involved in learning to read, and specifically, to infer the thoughts, feelings and intentions of story characters, are dependent upon meta-cognitive skills. Gearhart and Hall assert that children's meta-cognitive abilities, self-consciously organized and coordinated mental routines, are related to the use by parents and teachers of internal state words. Moreover, the considerable cross-cultural variation in the production of internal state words may be detrimental to specific racial and social class groups.

In Chapter 11, Ogbu takes a careful look at cross-cultural studies of childrearing and concludes that a cultural, ecological model, one that takes the influences of society as well as interpersonal influences into account, is badly needed to reformulate childhood socialization concepts. This model stresses that competencies inculcated in children depend on the requirements of their future positions in their society's social and economic systems. To flesh out the model, researchers will need to gain native formulations of the ways individuals become successful in their particular environments. Thus, researchers must acknowledge that societies are dynamic, culturally pluralistic settings.

In considering the full set of contributions to the volume, I am struck with the persistence of several themes:

1. *Competency by Age 3.* Children are not viewed as passive recipients of adult socialization. Rather, children are seen as linguistically, imaginatively and interpersonally competent by 3. By that age, children successfully negotiate peer interactions, express complexity in their verbal utterances and exact considerable power in their relations with adults, peers and siblings.

2. *The Role of Adults.* Far from being omnipotent socialization agents, adults are seen, however, as necessary to children's social development by virtue of their superior knowledge and experience in the world. Adults are particularly necessary in constructing favorable milieus for social experience including providing adequate time and space for close, emotionally supportive interactions. Caretaking rituals allowing the adult and child to establish and maintain dyadic synchrony seem critical to the lives of *all* children including the very young child and special needs child. Thus, adults are important mediators and clarifiers of experience. Moreover, by using language that addresses their self-aware cognitive processing of immediate, shared experience, teachers and parents create a context for interpreting the world.

3. *The Role of Peers.* Although the role of adults in shaping children's lives is beyond dispute, the importance of peers on their own terms is only now being acknowledged. Peers, especially close friends who are age mates and the same sex, are vigorous, highly salient foils against whom the child can bounce a wide range of feelings, interpretations and actions. Especially important in shaping the child's personality, peer relations allow joyous, spontaneous expression of closely shared activity. This is especially the case because children close in age and in shared experience have developed more or less equivalent cognitive structures enabling them to establish literally more meaningful interaction among themselves than between themselves and an adult.

4. *The Importance of the Social Milieu.* The time for considering children's social lives and social development as though they occur in a vacuum is over. Although not all contributors agree on how children might best be served (for example, Ramey et al. advocate an interventionist model while Ogbu calls for radical social change) most are actively aware of the impact the social setting has upon children's lives. Rather than concentrating only upon the intrafamilial and interpersonal aspects of child rearing, the developmentalist, policy maker, parent, teacher and others concerned with children must be keenly aware of the full

set of societal influences impinging upon children. The cultural, historical and economic contexts all define the child rearing milieu and shape patterns of child rearing in subtle and potentially harmful ways for large numbers of children in this and in every changing society.

A number of individuals provided support for the symposium held at the University of Cincinnati, April 26–28, 1979. I am particularly grateful to Patricia O'Reilly who negotiated funding and to Adele and Harold Goldstein and to Dan Ransohoff of the Martha B. Ransohoff Fund of the Greater Cincinnati Foundation for providing support. Jane Shreve, Theresa Berwanger, Walter C. Borman, and Greg and Geoff Borman provided all manner of help throughout the period that the symposium and this volume were in production. Thanks to you all.

Kathryn M. Borman

THE SOCIAL LIFE OF
CHILDREN
IN A CHANGING
SOCIETY

INTRODUCTION

Introduction: Evolution, Culture, and Social Change

Kathryn M. Borman
Harold D. Fishbein
University of Cincinnati

The children's lives studied in this book are embedded in the social structure of children's immediate experiences in families, peer groups, and school settings. These settings are in turn situated in time, the late 20th century, and place, the highly urbanized, industrialized West. Further, the cultural trappings of our society are located in an evolutionary framework, at a point only a relatively short distance from our species' first major cultural revolution, the shift from a technology, social organization, and pattern of communication based upon hunting and gathering to a design based upon farming. The cultural landscape against which children's social lives unfold must be understood in terms of these perspectives.

This introductory chapter serves a single major purpose: to provide a conceptual framework for the contributions to this volume. This will be done by embedding contemporaneous views of child development and children's social life in an evolutionary context. Three major evolutionary themes are initially explored: biological evolution and the individual; evolutionary culture change; and the evolution of the family as a human organization. The authors believe that these perspectives, primarily taken by the disciplines of biology and anthropology, are required for a thoughtful analysis of studies exploring the social life of children in a changing society.

BIOLOGICAL EVOLUTION AND THE INDIVIDUAL

The logical starting point for this discussion is the evolutionary context of human development. Fishbein (1976) following Rensch (1959) and Lorenz (1969) has referred to evolution as an experiment in design. The design of a species is best seen as a developmental system keyed to certain significant sequences of interaction with the physical and social environment which each member of that species is normally expected to encounter. The design is coded in the genotype and the experiment is carried out as the developing individual—the phenotype—interacts with a sequence of environments. If the experiment is successful, then the particular developmental system is viable, and the genes responsible for the system are transmitted to the next generation. What this usually means is that successful individuals survive and reproduce. If offspring develop in similar sequences of environments, it is likely that their developmental systems will also be successful. However, if offspring develop in very different sequences of environments than those of their parents, then their designs may be unsuccessful, and they may not transmit their genes to the next generation. If the sequence of environments all offspring encounter is markedly different from those of their parents, then the species as a whole may not survive.

Evolutionary designs should not be seen as rigid templates for development that occur independently of the ecology of the individual. Rather, there is both "openness" (flexibility) and "constraint" in the design, and indeed, these characteristics are aspects of the design. In general, the "higher" the animal, the greater the openness and the lesser the constraint regarding behavioral development. Thus, humans probably have more flexibility in their behavioral development than chimpanzees, who in turn probably have more flexibility than monkeys. The degree of openness in behavioral development of a species is indicated by the learning capacities of the members of that species. From the viewpoint of species adaptation, the greater the learning capacity, the lesser the "need" for genetic change as a response to ecological crises. For example, during the last ice age members of our species survived cold, snowy climates by learning to use skins of other animals to keep warm rather than by growing furry skins themselves. Of course, it is unlikely that genetic change would have occurred rapidly enough for the latter to have occurred in time to save the species from extinction.

Although humans have large learning capacities, our designs are heavily constrained, some aspects more than others. Fishbein (1976), following Waddington (1962) and Piaget (1971), has described these constraints as "canalized." Canalization involves:

> . . . a set of genetic processes which ensure that development will proceed in normal ways, that the phenotypic targets will be attained despite the presence of minor abnormal genetic or environmental conditions. Canalization processes operate at each point in development to correct minor deflections from the sought-for phenotypic targets. Presumably canalization processes ensure that important phenotypic constancies will occur in all members of a species, e.g., in humans the presence of two eyes, one nose, two hands, language, bipedal locomotion. Canalization is a *collusion* of genes to keep the developing organism in balance. Not all characteristics of an individual are canalized, nor are those which are, equally canalized. (p. 7)

In a later section of this chapter we shall provide a more detailed discussion of the canalization model. For the present purposes it is important to note the linkage between canalization processes and learning processes. Fundamentally, learning processes are set into motion when we contact our environment, and have the effect of progressively organizing our future perceptions, thoughts, feelings, and behaviors. The changes that occur have the long-term effects of producing a better coordination between our behavior and the environment. It is remarkable that what and how we learn is similar across a wide range of cultures. The role canalization plays is straightforward—it shapes the interaction between the person and the environment. Washburn and Hamburg (1965), two leading scholars of the evolution of behavior, have put the matter as follows:

> What is inherited is ease of learning, rather than fixed instinctive patterns. The species easily, almost inevitably learns the essential behaviors for its survival. So although it is true that monkeys learn to be social, they are so constructed that under normal circumstances this learning always takes place. Similarly human beings learn to talk, but they inherit structures that make this inevitable, except under the most peculiar circumstances (p. 5-6).

When the evolutionary record is looked at from the view of the human behavioral design, three broad classes of behavioral canalization appear. The first is mammalian, which is likely strongly canalized, and involves the emergence of mother-infant bonding. The second is primatological, which is probably moderately canalized and involves the emergence of the social group. The third is human (i.e. the genus Homo), which is also probably moderately canalized, and involves the emergence of a particular kind of family (Fishbein, 1979).

About 200 million years ago the placental mammals evolved from our reptilian ancestors. Apart from a physiological heritage, our most important enduring characteristic is extensive and long-term nurturance of the young. Up until very recent times all infant mammals required a lactating mother in order to survive. The mother was her infant's sole source of food and a major source of its protection and socialization. Long-term maternal care required that mothers stay very close to their nursing offspring, often in physical contact with them. Close proximity and physical contact still appear to be the essential conditions for infant bonding to occur. It is thought by John Bowlby (1969) and others that among mammals unless infants form close bonds with one or more adults, their development will be markedly disturbed.

The primates evolved about 75 million years ago from some common mammalian ancestors, probably resembling contemporary tree shrews. Apart from obvious anatomical and physiological similarities, the key common denominator of nearly all the "higher" Old World primates (monkeys, apes, and humans) was membership in long-duration subsistence groups. Like their counterparts among other primates, human subsistence groups provided opportunities for food, protection, reproduction, and socialization for their members. These groups had several important attributes:

1. Mother-infant dyads were the core of the group. Relative to other mammals mother-offspring involvement was very long, nearly always extending beyond the period of infancy. Thus, not only did this produce strong mother-child bonding, but often strong bonding between siblings.

2. Members of these groups were well-known to one another and, relative to outsiders, had strong bonds with each other. Group cohesiveness was essential in order for subsistence groups to carry out their essential functions.

3. Socialization occurred primarily by play, observation, and imitation. "Teaching" as we know it was uncommon. Play was typically most intense during the juvenile period of development and occurred among similar-aged, same sex individuals. Socialization by observation and imitation occurred throughout the life-span.

It is likely that 3 to 5 million years ago, our immediate ancestors, the Australopithecines, evolved in environments in which relative food scarcity was a regularly occurring event. That is, at times during the year there was not enough food in the nearby regions to support a moderately-sized subsistence group, e.g. more than 25 adults and children. The solution to this periodic scarcity involved a marked change in the social organization of these groups. That is, smaller conclaves of adult male/female offspring subunits formed which in time of food scarcity temporarily left the main group for days or weeks to fend for themselves. It cannot be stated with any assurance whether these groups consisted of nuclear families, as we know them today, or as mother-offspring units in the company of adult males to whom they had affectional ties. If these groups consisted of two or more adult males, it is likely that these males formed closer ties to one another than they did to other males in the main group.

The above mammalian, primate, and Australopithecine social adaptations set the stage, and were probably a necessary condition, for the next period of human evolution. It is highly likely that about one to one and a half million years ago the species' male ancestors started to engage in the collaborative hunting of large game for part of the group's subsistence. This form of hunting required substantial cooperation among the hunters. But in order to cooperate, other changes had to occur. Male-male aggressiveness had to decrease, but bonding had to increase. A second major social change brought about by collaborative hunting of large game was that male/female role differentiation increased regarding food seeking activities, tool making activities, and tool use. In most environments a hunter-gatherer group would starve if it exclusively depended on hunting success. In order for the males to have the opportunity to hunt, they had to depend on the food gathering success of the females, and the sharing of food among males and females. Sharing of food now became obligatory.

If at this point in human evolution, subsistence groups were already comprised of single male/single female/offspring units, it is highly likely that this family structure was strengthened. If the family "design" was not yet in existence, then it probably came into existence then. The family was special in that greater bonding and reciprocity among its members occurred relative to other members in the group.

Given that future hunters and toolmakers had to be trained, this period in human evolution brought about increased adult male involvement in offspring, especially with the male children. Fathers were identified as such, and were differentiated from "uncles" and male non-relatives. Fathers became heavily responsible for their own offspring, but nevertheless had responsibility to the offspring of their collaborators. Related to increased paternal involvement in offspring was the strengthening of cross-generational cooperative activities. Thus, parent/child reciprocities emerged such that parents were responsible for their young children and children became responsible for their old parents.

The hunter-gatherer behavioral design has been with us for at least one million years. Thus, for 99% of human existence all of our ancestors were hunters and gatherers. This was the sole human design until about 10,000 years ago when agriculture and domestication began to be consistently practiced. It is only in the last 5000 years with extensive urbanization that these and other activities became widespread and highly differentiated as described in the following section.

EVOLUTIONARY CULTURE CHANGE

Cultural ecology has been described by social anthropologist Julian H. Steward (1977a) and others as the study of processes by which human societies adapt to their environments. Human biology and psychology serve both to constrain and to liberate human behavior including the development of major cultural institutions: technology, language, and social organization. However, it is often difficult to distinguish cultural adaptations from the very biological and psychological factors which shape and delimit them. It is apparent that the biological requirements for cultural evolution were an erect posture, specialized hands, a throat and mouth structure permitting speech, stereoscopic vision, and areas in the brain for the functions of speech and association (Steward, 1977a).

Oppotunities to create and expand cultural institutions interacted with biological and psychological structures over time in complex ways. One manifestation of these interactions was the development of "multilinear" patterns of cultural evolution which have succeeded in ensuring that there is considerable variation across cultures in basic human institutions such as the family, a concept to be expanded in the next section of this chapter. Within societies, child rearing practices, the roles of each parent in child rearing, and assignment to household tasks and responsibilities by age and gender of the young are widely variable and are dependent on variation in culture forms. The expansion and contraction of the social life of children reflects expansion and contraction of opportunities within society. Societies such as our highly urbanized and industrialized setting are undergoing continuous change which has implications for children's development.

Cultural ecology does not involve a one to one correspondence between ecosystems and human behavior primarily because this equation ignores what Bennett (1975) has termed the key variable in understanding cultural evolution—namely, the human social system. The social system is comprised of "human needs, skills, anxieties and population—all of which are not narrowly determined by particular subsistence systems, but rather, can push these systems to produce at varying rates" (Bennett, 1975, p. 280). Human action, in other words, can and does stretch, modify, and change ecological systems. This view is extremely important for an understanding of cultural evolution as a "consequential process" and not merely as an anthropological or biological puzzle. Bennett sees the tendency for anthropologists to take an academic approach tied to systems theory rather than an activist position linked to social policy as rooted in anthropology's "preoccupation with a particular type of society: the relatively isolated relatively slow to change, low energy society—microsystemic community" (p. 296). Societies of this kind more often than not are viewed in a systems analysis as in equilibrium with their ecological settings. In order to plan social policy relevant for a complex society a far more inclusive analysis is needed. Specifically, a global perspective focused upon urbanized emergent societies and a cross-disciplinary vehicle for analysis are required. Both need to be informed by a view of individuals in human groups as dynamic, exploitative, and often unpredictable. Although it is ironic that the species' behavioral design is tied to a pattern that evolved in hunting-gathering societies, the fact of the matter is that for the widest segment of humankind, this behavioral design is now implanted in truly complex social and cultural arrangements. It it is for this reason that we as a species often have the sense that events guide us and not the reverse.

In the course of outlining major demographic shifts in an evolutionary context, Steven Polgar (1975) has offered a summary of the major cultural alterations associated with our species' gradual transitions (1) to hominization, (2) to agriculture, (3) to feudalism, and (4) to colonialism and industrialization. Although Polgar stresses the ecological components of these transitions, particularly the altered relationships between human populations and natural settings, we wish to point up the social and cultural transformations accompanying these epochal changes.

First, although hunting-gathering societies during our species' first 2 million years lived under relatively homeostatic conditions in a way not much different from most other animal species, "biological and cultural inventions" considerably important to later human development served to differentiate human social organization from that of other mammalian groups. These human adaptations included "the establishment of home bases for migratory bands, sexual division of labor in subsistence activities, incest rules, the transition through at least three successive species, periods of large game hunting, development of better tools, emergence of true language and expansion into all continents" (Polgar, 1977, p. 3). Particularly in the later periods of the epoch, these achievements accompanied the extinction of a number of species and the reduction of forested lands to the status of grassy plains.

The transition to cultivation from gathering introduced the largest scale alteration of the relationship between human beings and supporting ecological systems. Population anthropologiests including Polgar have concluded that the change from a relatively low utilization of resources set the stage in an alarmingly dangerous way for future generations of human social organization and culture change.

Although the relationship between the species and its supporting ecosystem was based upon the principle of control of one system (the ecological system) by another (human micro-societal systems) during the period of agricultural development, the principle of social exchange persisted in governing interactions *within* human groups. Indeed, these small societies were associations of close and near kin. Polgar (1975) argues that the "central feature in the transition to feudalism is the change from reciprocal systems of exchange to major reliance upon redistribution and the associated development of power differentials between kin groups" (p. 7). Increasingly centralized political and economic power arrangements became critical to the maintenance of processes of redistribution of goods. Thus, Polgar sees the evolution of feudal society as a progression from the corporate kin group with rights of ownership extending over the productive resources of its blood-related members to networks of multilineage kin groups and finally to highly differentiated, non-lineage societies. Correspondingly, social organization based on family lines was altered by the gradual decrease of family control in "juridicial matters" and the parallel increase in a remote, centralized authority's control over these concerns.

Centralized authority based upon either appointed or inherited power held by a single (usually male) individual allowed for the "rational" control of production and ultimately resulted in the stockpiling of a surplus of goods. The paleoanthropological record protrays the social and cultural features of these arrangements. Power was centralized and housed in large buildings that dominated feudal settlements. Numbers of children increased, insuring a large domestic labor supply and land use intensified (Polgar, 1975). Social differentiation in the form of class identification emerged, and in fact, was the salient feature in this period. Accompanying centralization of power and populations were early forms of urban blight. Concentrations of relatively large numbers of people with an inadequate medical technology contributed to a "deterioration in average health status" (Polgar, 1975, p. 12) leading to waves of destructive plagues throughout the feudal period.

The principal cultural achievement of the subsequent period of colonialism and industrialization was the economic reorganization of the primary colonizing nations of western Europe. This accomplishment was rooted in technological advances in warfare which were in full circle tied to expansionist mercantile ventures. Although at first only capital investments were marketed, the nineteenth century witnessed the development of land and human labor as marketable commodities (Polgar, 1975). Relying on Polanyi (1957), Polgar places the national origins of these latter developments in England where "the combination of enclosure, the revised poor laws and fluctuations in the economic success of foreign trade and manufacturing created a large 'reserve army' of the underemployed which in turn helped the final transformation of labor into a market commodity" (Polgar, 1975, p. 12).

Rational planning which had taken a foothold during the feudal period now became increasingly centralized under the control of nation-states. Planning extended not only to mercantilism but also to more fundamental economic concerns—population change for example. Polgar argues the state's key concern here has been and continues to be encouraging or discouraging population growth as growth is regulated by market needs. Thus, as the "rapid growth of urban populations . . . exceeded labor requirements and over-burdened the service sector, rural development and the building of new towns have become prominent issues in policy discussions. And family planning is now promoted in many countries as an instrument of 'population control,' instead of being genuinely offered to improve family health and welfare." (Polgar, 1975, p. 13)

Colonialism and industrialization, while expanding the opportunity structure for some human groups, have together exacted a terrible ecological price. Polgar concludes his summary by pointing to the current rapid deterioration of resources, widespread pollution and rush to extinction by a large number of species hastened by humankind's expansion. His conclusion is not hopeful for, although he does not see humanity's passionate courtship with its own possible demise as a collective death wish, he *does* judge that these ecosystemic nightmares are directly the result of "the power imbalance favoring nation-states and industrial enterprises over communities and humankind as a whole." (Polgar, 1975, p. 14). The species' evolutionary design, shaped and sustained by long-term existence in hunting-gathering enclaves, seems woefully inadequate to cope with the social organization that characterizes the highly industrialized West.

THE EVOLUTION OF THE FAMILY AS A HUMAN ORGANIZATION

Interdependence of family members within a household composed of two or more persons increases as each person takes on more specialized roles. Put another way, as the division of labor becomes more intricately patterned (e.g. mother performs only nurturant, expressive functions; father performs only instrumental functions) the family is more likely to be set adrift if one of its members fails to perform his or her usual tasks. Over time, role specialization in the family has tended to increase, leaving contemporary Western families vulnerable to disruption if a family member, weighted with specialized burdens, dies, departs, or becomes incapacitated. Indeed, the history of the family as a human organization is characterized by several careers or major evolutionary trends. F. L. W. Richardson (1975) in describing the progression from relatively simple to increasingly complex family organizational arrangements draws comparisons to the corresponding increase in societal structures from individual efforts at food gathering to complex arrangements of trading nations in industrialized societies. Likewise, Richardson parallels the increased biological complexity of the species and its immediate forerunners over the course of the past 100 million years. Thus, social arrangements for procreation and rearing the young have developed from mating pairs among insect eating mammals to the disrupted family-community nexus in current industralized societies. The correspondence among biological, family organizational and societal structures should not to be seen as abstract or reified. These interacting systems are dynamic and dialectical and are not necessarily emblematic of large-scale evolutionary "progress" of which humanity is the beneficiary. Indeed, Richardson concludes that although individuals have become increasingly interdependent, this interdependence is more characterized by hostile exchanges than by cooperative interactions among nation-states.

Richardson's typology of the family as a human organization to a point parallels that of Fishbein's (1979) perspective on the individual design described earlier. However, although Fishbein also argues that the human behavioral design is interwoven with the technological base of the human group, his analysis concludes with discussion of hunter-gatherer societies and does not extend to examination of subsequent societal forms. Richardson's stage-related typology extends backward and forward from this social form, although he, like Fishbein, regards the pattern of family organization in hunting-gathering societies as ideally suited to the human behavioral design. Richardson sees the family as having its roots in the temporary relationship between mother and litter that characterized the "family" group in insect-eating mammals from which primates later evolved. According to Richardson's account, "These early small mammals lived largely alone except for brief periods when a mother with her litter formed a temporary family-group. Each animal gathered its own food, which was limited in kind" (Richardson, 1975, p. 308).

The second major evolutionary shift was to permanent "family" groups or loosely organized "tribal" bands. This configuration characterized early social arrangements of our immediate predecessors. Some form of specialization existed among these affiliations of closely related individuals such that females largely took on child nurturing functions while males specialized in protection of juveniles from intruders.

The third stage in the development of organizational arrangements saw the emergence with early human groups of what Richardson terms the family-community pattern. Unlike the loose configurations of related individuals at stage two, these groups were continuously affiliated clusters of related family groups who orchestrated fairly elaborate episodes of hunting, gathering, and food preparation. These subsistence functions were distributed among individuals in the group and were carried out cooperatively. The establishment of the continuity of a larger community was apparent in the seasonal gathering of various affiliated tribes.

At the fourth stage, the family-community nexus was broadened to include large scale "chiefdoms and preindustrial trading and military states . . . totaling from perhaps ten thousand to several million members" (Richardson, 1975, p. 309). Congeries of military, religious and civic institutions exacted membership, creating more complex systems of specialization and interdependence.

Finally, over the period of the past 200 years, contemporary family organization has become embedded in a complex national-global system. The family-community relationship has been weakened by "the expansion of institutions and cities" and altered by increasing rural to urban migration, rapid enlargement of nation states, and increased bureaucratic complexity and specialization. Indeed, these processes have likely accelerated beyond the capacity of our species to control them.

In the remainder of this section we briefly discuss some specific ways family household composition and child rearing practices are related to the "maintenance systems"(Le Vine, 1973, Whiting & Whiting, 1975) or ecological elements (Berry, 1976) of contemporary society. In an analysis similar to Richardson's, Berry's review of this literature protrays four aspects of social structure as having important influences on the family and on child rearing: (1) the ways people exploit their enrivonment for food; (2) the ways people form settlements; (3) the extent to which food is stored; and, (4) the typical population of the local community.

Our discussion of patterns of family composition is based primarily on research of Blumberg and Winch (1972) who examined data from several hundred contemporary societies. These investigators underscore the strong relationship between family composition and the technological base of society. They make a distinction between societies in which 80% or more of all households consist of a nuclear family i.e. mother, father (if still married) and their children (if still unmarried), and those societies in which more than 20% of households consist of more complicated family types e.g., polygomous, two or more married brothers, parents and one or more married children. For convenience, we shall refer to these two types as "nuclear" and "non-nuclear." The basic findings are as follows: Gathering, hunting, and urban-industrial societies are primarily nuclear; pastoral, fishing, horticultural, and cereal cultivation societies are primarily non-nuclear; and intensive agricultural societies are primarily nonnuclear, but less so than the above groups. Two social structures are strongly correlated with these arrangements. First, if the average population of the local community is either very small or very large, nuclear families predominate. Second, if social complexity, i.e., number of different social roles, is either very low or very high, nuclear families predominate. Whether or not a society tends to be nomadic or sedentary has no strong relation to family composition.

How do we understand interelationships between societal complexity and size and the domestic arrangements of families? One partial explanation is that if the economic activities of a family require the long term commitment, cooperation, and involvement of several adults, then families will tend to be non-nuclear, composed of networks of interrelated mutual dependencies. On the other hand, if the husband and wife can support themselves and their children by their own work, without continuous involvement of the same group of adults, then family households will likely be nuclear arrangements. The latter are typical conditions of hunter-gatherer, and industrial societies, and the former are the typical conditions of most of the remaining societies.

The two major contemporary studies with child-rearing emphases are by Barry, Child, and Bacon (1959) and Whiting and Whiting (1975). When we speak of child-rearing emphases, we mean the kinds of behavior that parents want to encourage in their children by reward, or discourage by punishment. In a wide range of societies that have been studied, it has been found that obedience training and responsibility training for household tasks go together, and self-reliance training and achievement training go together. Societies which reward obedience/responsibility, tend to ignore or punish self-reliance/achievement, and vice versa. There are obviously a huge number of other child-rearing emphases, but these two pairs have been most widely studied. The data refer to children between the ages of 4 and 12.

The basic findings of the child rearing studies we have briefly reviewed strongly parallel those for family household composition. Hunting-gathering, fishing, urbanizing, and industrial societies place strong emphases on self-reliance and achievement. The herding and the agriculture and band societies underscore obedience and responsibility. Le Vine (1973) suggests that these findings are related to family size: small families produce self-reliant/achievement oriented people and large families produce responsible/obedient people. We know from the previous discussion that with the exception of the fishing societies, hunting-gathering and urban societies are comprised primarily of nuclear families which are usually much smaller than non-nuclear families. Levine also supports this explanation by noting that within our own culture, children from large families are less achievement-oriented than those reared in small families.

These results seem to imply that social structure and culture rigidly and uniformly determine developmental trajectories. This is not the case overall, since some societies provide alternative forms. In indistralized societies where the division of labor is complexly structured and specialized, social class divisions create differential socialization milieus, some more optimal than others. In the United States, working class families seem especially burdened by an isolation from roles other than those associated with their own jobs (Piotrkowski, 1979). Children in working class families experience socialization characterized by their parents' stress upon conformity to a value code governing appearances. Working class parents stress cleanliness, neatness and obedience to authority, whereas middle class parents stress individual achievement and authority (Kohn, 1977). Occupational choices in later life may be limited for working class children. They have little exposure to knowledge of work roles other than those held by their parents in combination with a parental socialization pattern emphasizing conformity. Moreover, they experience a system of schooling organized in vocational and "academic" tracks with usual placement in the former.

In conclusion, as we consider Richardson's stages of family organization, we see a divergence of hunter-gatherer socialization patterns in the urbanindustrial societies located in a national-global system. In the latter societies there is a further differentiation related to social class membership. In every society and social class within a society, there remains a fair amount of flexibility in individual developmental outcomes owing to the biological, technological and social idiosyncracies characterizing all human groups.

CHILD DEVELOPMENT

In this and in a concluding section, the discussion is keyed to the contents of the remaining chapters as these contents implicate children's development in our rapidly changing society. Several of the chapters in this book analyze issues concerning the speeding up or slowing down of cognitive, linguistic, or social emotional development as a function of handicap, teacher attitudes, peer influences, and the nature of parental involvement. We believe that one useful framework for child development in which to understand these issues is the canalization model mentioned earlier. Figure 1 is a drawing of the image Waddington uses to describe the way canalization works. The image primarily derives from his research in embryological development. The rolling ball represents the child's development of some characteristic e.g. attachment to a caretaker. As the ball approaches a decision point, the characteristic (for example, attachment) must move along one of two or more pathways. In the attachement example this means that a potential attachment figure must be present and that a bond will develop between the infant and that person. The distance traveled and the depth of the pathway indicate the strength or degree of canalization of that characteristic. So, the greater the time spent in appropriate (evolutionary-designed) ways with the caretaker, the more secure will be the infant's attachment to that person. If an attachment figure is not present when the ball has reached the attachment decision point, then development will be abnormal and the child will be anxiously or insecurely attached or unattached, as was apparently the case with institutionalized children observed by Dennis and Najarian (1957) and Spitz (1945).

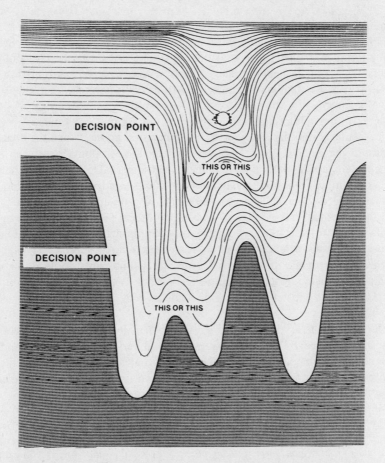

FIG. 1.1. The epigenetic landscape. The rolling ball represents the development of some canalized characteristic. At each "decision point" the characteristic is required to move onto one of at least two divergent pathways. As development proceeds along one of those pathways, the more difficult it becomes to move it into the alternative pathways (Drawn by Alex Fraser from Fishbein, H. D., *Evolution, Development and Children's Learning,* 1976).

What this drawing implies, then, is that at each decision point, the developing individual "looks for" some particular environmental stimulation so that development can proceed normally. For strongly canalized characters, relative to more weakly canalized ones, either the decision point is more extended in time or wider varieties of environmental stimulation will satisfy the requirements of the character. Increases in the variation of acceptable environmental stimulation means that there is a great deal of redundancy in the system thus accounting for the apparent normality of children with severe handicaps, as shown in the Kretschmers' paper on the learning of language by deaf and hard of hearing children. In an analogous way, by extending the time of the decision, the developing individual has more opportunities to find a suitable environment. For infant attachment the decision point extends from about 6 weeks to 6 months. If the infant has not had appropriate contacts with a caregiver during this time period, then it is unlikely that he or she will develop normal infant attachment behaviors.

There are other important implications of this figure. The times of greatest developmental instability are at or near the decision points. Once the character has passed the decision point and has proceeded well along a pathway, it is difficult to disrupt its normal development. These periods of relative instability are called "critical periods". They are periods where appropriate stimulation is absolutely necessary in order for development to proceed normally.

If the individual has gone well past the critical period without appropriate stimulation, then in all likelihood previously appropriate stimulation will not be adequate for normal development of that character. An appropriate caregiver experienced for the first time at one year of age will probably not lead to normal attachment. The model indicates that the further in time and space from the critical period, the greater will be the difficulty in bringing development back to a normal sequence.

John Paul Scott (1968) a leading researcher in the area of socialization of mammals has come to the conclusion that critical periods play an important role throughout development, and not just during infancy and childhood. We quote at length the following from him to illustrate the pervasiveness of this phenomenon:

> . . . a critical period is one in which rapid organization of some kind is taking place. While this is going on, it is easy to change the nature of the organization. However, organization in itself has a tendency to produce stability. *Therefore, any period in life when rapid organization is taking place is a critical period,* since the changes which are easily and often accidentally produced at that time become a fixed and relatively permanent feature of the stabilized organization. In the case of primary socialization, the young animal is organizing its first social relationships. By extension we can reason that *any period in life when a major new relationship is being formed is a critical one for determining the nature of that relationship.* Such a period would occur in later life during courtship and mating and the resulting formation of the first sexual relationship. . . . The period of primary socialization is an unusually critical one in that it may indirectly affect the formation of these later relationships. (p. 142)

Despite the pervasiveness of critical periods, as noted by Scott, if the individual has not reached a decision point for a particular canalized character, then environmental stimulation will have essentially no impact on how that character will develop. It does not make much sense, for example, to attempt to teach a one-year-old how to read or write. Although one cannot initiate the onset of a canalized sequence, within limits, once it has started, part of the sequence can be accelerated. As an illustration, once a child starts talking, enriching the language environment will speed up the acquisition of spoken language (see Snow's chapter in this regard). Developmental characteristics are interrelated; hence one must wait for the normally developing aspects to catch up with those accelerated, before the system as a whole progresses. Thus, development of logical thinking may place limits on the extent to which language acquisition may be moved ahead.

Intimately related to critical periods are "readiness" periods. With the exception of some behavioral characters canalized in infancy, most human decision points involve lengthy time periods, e.g., learning to speak grammatically. In these cases, it makes most sense to talk about periods in which environmental stimulation has greater or lesser effectiveness in producing the sought for behavioral development. For example, some motor skills involve canalized components which the individual may not be ready to learn until he or she is about 6 years old, e.g., the complementary use of two hands. Attempting to "teach" a 3-year-old to use the hands in a complementary fashion may have some positive effects, but not nearly as great as attempting to teach the child at 6.

When we think about decision points, critical periods, and periods of readiness, we almost automatically are led to the conclusion that development proceeds in a succession of stages. A large number of psychologists, such as Freud, Piaget, and Erikson hold this view. It should be emphasized, in light of our discussion about the interaction of biology and culture, that to some extent both the number of stages and their contents will be determined by the society in which the person is socialized. When we look at contemporary Western culture it seems to us that three age-related developmental stages and two transitions can be identified.

The first stage is infancy. This is the period from birth to approximately 2 years of age. The major tasks here involve forming social bonds to both parents, developing what Erikson (1963) calls a sense of "basic trust," and completing the development of sensory-motor intelligence (Piaget, 1970). The first transition period involves a forceful separation from the mother, produced by weaning and in many families by the birth of a sibling. The second stage is childhood, a stretch of the individual's life extending from about age 4 to 12. During this time the child develops strong same sex peer relations, strong sibling bonds, and important relationships with teachers. Socialization influences shift from home to neighborhood and school. Cognitively, the child is completing the development of concrete operations (Piaget, 1970) as well as acquiring a vast array of academic skills. The second transition period in this sequence is early adolescence. During this period dramatic hormonal and physiological changes occur which influence both self-evaluation and evaluation of others, especially those of the opposite sex.

The third stage is late adolescence, a span in the individual's development incorporating the period from about age 14 to age 18. These are the senior high school years. Same sex and different sex peer relations are strengthened, child-parent relationships are weakened, and work involvement and career planning get started, or get actively under way, depending on social class. Cognitively, formal operations often get completely developed (Piaget, 1970); however, some individuals, depending on genetics and social experiences, never complete this cognitive stage.

It is difficult to say conclusively whether stimulation leads development of biologically-based, stage-dependent characteristics or whether the reverse is true. For example, it seems clear that children during the period of middle childhood in our society invest an enormous amount of time in keeping company with their peers. Interaction in the course of organizing and playing games has special importance in connection with anticipatory socialization into work and social roles (Borman & Barrett, 1981). Children gain at least a rudimentary mastery of abstract conceptions such as power, roles, and strategies through participation in games. Lev Vygotsky (1978) has argued that play at games *leads* development because of the necessity in games for children inevitably to recognize the "implicit rules governing the activities they have reproduced in their games" (1978, p. 129). Cognitive processes based upon both concrete operational and formal operational thought in Piaget's terms or upon "higher mental functions" in Vygotsky's language are grounded upon social, historical and cultural foundations. Since higher mental operations are socially formed and culturally transmitted, "it follows that if one changes the tools of thinking available to a child, his mind will have a radically different structure" (1978, p. 126). Vygotsky's emphasis upon the significance of the material milieu in the development of abstract thinking is extremely important for a careful consideration of the properties and likely significance of environmental stimulation as an interacting force with decision points, critical periods, periods of readiness and stage-like progression of individual development.

SOCIAL LIFE OF CHILDREN IN A CHANGING SOCIETY

Characteristics of Group Life

The term "social life" in the context of the contributions to this volume defines the interaction experienced by children in the groups in which they regularly participate and have membership. The social lives of individual children vary considerably with social class and culture since children, relative to adults, may have either reduced or expanded opportunities for membership in a variety of groups. For example, low income families characteristically participate in fewer community-based groups than middle class families (Fried, 1973). Groups themselves vary according to characteristics such as size, ratio of adults to children, and ratio of boys to girls. They also differ in function since a play group composed of peers differs from a child's family group and from the school learning group. The fundamental feature of group life as described throughout this volume is the emphasis in each case upon the importance of mutuality to the cooperative achievement of group goals.

In our society outside the context of the family most grouping of children are relatively homogeneous according to age. Although this is strikingly clear in the case of school-aged children, it is also true in the case of preschoolers' play groups. This pattern strongly contrasts with the social organization of early human hunter-gatherer subsistence groups and contemporary nonhuman primate groups such as the great apes and chimpanzees. Melvin Konner (1976) has recently written about peer groups from an evolutionary and cross-species perspective. He has concluded that in all the apes and with nearly all the monkeys, same-age, same-sex, pre-adult peer groups are absent. As with early human social groups, primate infants, juveniles, and adolescents are reared with and are involved with group members of both sexes and a wide range of ages. Typically the young spend their time in play and observation, usually preferring to be with those of the same sex. Konner argues that from the viewpoints of protecting the young, modeling rituals, traditions, and skills, and integrating members into the social group, such adult-young, multiage, mixed-sex, informal groups are superior to same age peer groups.

Yet, age-segregated peer groups appear to be the norm in most contemporary societies, even those in not-yet industrialized societies. Enid Schildkrout's (1978) observation of Hausa children in urban Kano stresses the point that even though institutional fragmentation (i.e., the separation of traditional family functions across an array of age-segregated schools, nursing homes for the elderly and the like) is less marked than in Western societies, the interaction of people of different ages is still severely limited. In Moslem Hausa society where rapid social change is accompanying rapid industrialization, children in the northern Nigerian city of Kano "enjoy a freedom that no other group in the society commands—the right to wander in and out of peoples' homes" (Schildkrout, 1978, p. 124). Although this privilege affords children opportunity for traditional forms of informal learning through the observation of adult friends, neighbors and relatives, the important point is that age is a principle of social differentiation among the Huasa as it is among virtually all contemporary human groups. Age groups are characterized by their own systems of rights, privileges, duties and obligations.

The Roles of Adults

The social life of contemporary American children is highly dependent upon the efforts of adults, siblings, and peers for its organization and quality. Adults who are particularly important in this regard are parents and teachers. Although both figure prominently in children's lives, the roles they play are varied, with parents assuming importance in the earlier-occurring processes of attachment formation, habit training, and communication skills transmission in the context of informal and often playful exchanges. It is the latter process that is of particular interest to the work of Denzin, the Kretschmers, Snow, and Ogbu in this volume.

The social organization of instructional interactions between parents and their young at some level reflects both the constraints and objectives of human adaptation. The achievement of at least some level of independence from the family of origin and the capacity to establish one's own household is a major developmental task in Western societies. Critical in the child's early social life within the family is the opportunity to be mentored by a warmly attached adult. The interactional format followed by parents and children reflects mutuality, for example, as in the work carried out cooperatively in maintaining conversational turn-taking. Adult leadership is especially clear in the role parents take in establishing the affective tone and purpose of the exchange. The importance of mentoring by an adult is clear in a study of deaf infants recently reviewed by Maccoby (1980). When trainers were used an hour a day to teach sign language to the infants, infants became attached to their trainers. Later, attachment bonds in the context of learning signaling skills grew between these same infants and their mothers when the experimenters involved parents as tutors in sign language to their own children.

Parents who stretch the limits by providing provocative, often incongruous and generally playful episodes of interaction may be demonstrating to children the importance in both contingent and later learning of taking risks. We earlier remarked that human behavior is, if not erratic, certainly far from predictable. It may be that novel, even outrageous forms of interaction help to set the stage for later responses to issues, dilemmas and circumstances encountered as adults. Human adaptability demands a capacity to consider the widest range of possibilities. During the course of their interactions, parents and children work out mutually understandable signal systems. Jerome Bruner (1972) sees this parental role as both universal and necessary for the child's exploratory behavior. As Catherine Snow illustrates, parents *can* be language *teachers;* however, skill transmission in the household is carried out informally, incidentally, and often when parents and children are engaged in activities which momentarily intersect and affort the opportunity for parental "instruction."

Although teachers of young children may have curricular goals that anticipate elementary school learning tasks in reading and other subject matter areas, their interactions with children are strongly colored by affect nurturance similar to that displayed by parents. Playfulness and incongruity as a general rule do not, however characterize these exchanges. Teachers of preschool and kindergarten children have a strong commitment to inculcating social norms, including the rules governing school group membership. And as Wallat and Green (in this volume) make amply clear, this is a serious business.

The Role of Other Children

Peers have generally been regarded as significant forces in children's lives in industrial societies. Peer groups are relatively unimportant and have little impact in those societies in which the family and kin group adequately prepare members for social adulthood, occupational and parental "fitness," and ensure that this stage of functioning is reached by a reasonable age (Eisenstadt, 1956). Traditional societies where distribution of roles and rewards is primarily based upon membership in a kin group rather than upon individual achievement depend upon often complex modifications of rules governing rights of primogeniture and intermarriage to provide avenues to adulthood.

In our society peer groups in early childhood function as play groups affording opportunities for friendly, equalitarian exchanges, especially if they are relatively free from adult intervention and control (see especially Mueller and Vandell in this volume). Other aspects of group life among children include the opportunity for older children to acquire and rehearse game strategies (see Borman and Lippincott in this volume) and to be caught up in the joy of the exchange itself (as described by Sutton-Smith in this volume).

The peer group or age group in modern societies differs in at least two ways from those in non-Western agrariarian societies: there are age groups for females, and the age groups for males and females are not organized in a given society in the same formal ways with common initiation rites and traditions. Most modern societies contain three main kinds of age groups: those of the school; those of adult-sponsored agencies such as Girl Scouts, YMCA, and Little League; and those which are spontaneously organized by individuals based on common needs and interests. The latter pre-adult groups are often not under direct adult supervision (indirectly they are in the sense that they must be law-abiding); and in some societies the group goals and activities are anti-social or rebellious. S. N. Eisenstadt (1956) suggests that two of the factors which determine whether the spontaneous groups will be rebellious are: the extent to which the family norms and values deviate from those of the larger society; and the extent to which the family is unable to influence the attainment of full social adulthood by its members.

Eisenstadt summarizes the impact of age groups on the individual members as follows:

> In all societies age groups are formed at the traditional stage between adolescence and adulthood, and are oriented toward the attainment and acknowledgment of the full status of their members. Through participation of the group its members develop their identity and self-evaluation, and it is in terms of such evaluation that the common identification and solidarity (cohesiveness) of the group is evolved and maintained. This strong emphasis on common experience is found in every type of age group, and serves as the essential driving power for its individual members. (p. 183-184)

Social Change

The primary focus of this volume upon the social life of children in a *changing* society directly leads to a consideration of the concept of social change. It is often difficult to distinguish purposive social change from "crescive" social change described by Roland L. Warren (1977) as change occurring independent of goal-directed human efforts. For example, it is clear that societal notions about the importance to social development of play (as opposed to wage labor) in the lives of children have fundamentally changed in the last hundred years. It is more difficult to attribute these alterations in societal thinking to social change factors, although there are institutional changes (child labor laws, compulsory schooling) that reflect purposive human action. Both an evolutionary and a developmental perspective in addition to an emphasis upon institutions such as the family, peer group and school which organize children's experience suggest that is is purposive, adaptive change itself at both the institutional and individual levels that is critical and not merely growth, maturation, or acquisition of increasing amounts of knowledge and experience.

Social structures, like cognitive structures, are not stable. They are altered by human efforts, primarily through social interaction. The problem of the relationship between social structure and social interaction and resultant patterns of social change is a major theoretical problem in social psychology and will not be debated here. Currently in this society, major structural and ideological shifts have resulted in an altered set of orientations to self and social institutions. The primary structural change has been the increased participation in employment outside the home by women, particularly women with young children. The primary ideological shift has been toward a positive valuing of personal freedom, personal rights, and conceptions of fairness and reciprocity with a parallel devaluation of social institutions, including the school and the family (Lueptow, 1980).

Structuralists such as Steward (1977b) and Richardson (1975) are persuasive in arguing that both evolutionary stages and less dramatic variation in culture forms are linked to shifts in the technology supporting a society's economic organization. Thus, epochal changes in human social organization, i.e., the descent from arboreal environments to the savannah; the movement from the savannah to agricultural settlements and the passage from farming communities to industrialized towns and cities as well as less dramatic social differentiation tied to changes in family structure, i.e. current patterns of increased illegitimacy rates and increasing rates of divorce and remarriage, depend upon altered work arrangements. To put it another way, smaller scale societal changes are nested within large scale evolutionary stages and both are contingent upon alterations in technology.

The cultural ecology of child rearing in families has been illuminated by ethnographic studies of family interaction and serves to illustrate the link between technology, culture forms and socialization outcomes. In particular the work of field researchers under Beatrice and John Whiting (1973, 1975) established the importance of social structural factors in determining the patterns of childrearing observed in different settings and seen as independent of biological and psychological (including psychoanalytic and personality) factors. As summarized in Maccoby (1980) the factors associated with cooperative, altruistic behavior in children were rooted in the family's technological system. That is, family household work patterns featured the assignment of numerous tasks characterized by the demand for the child's increased responsibility (with increased age of the child) in the areas of child care and food production, preparation and serving. The delegation of these responsibilities was lodged in a situation in which the mother had considerable work responsibilities outside of the home (Maccoby, 1980). In addition, children expressed high levels of respect for their parents' authority which in turn was rooted in parents' "consistent and strict enforcement of . . . demands for obedience" in connection with children's responsibilities. The outcome of those patterns seems clear:

> The Whitings believe that children become more helpful to others when they live in cultures in which 1) their work makes a genuine contribution to the family's welfare, 2) these tasks *must* be done, and 3) parents and children are aware of the importance of the tasks to the family's safety, health and comfort. When this situation prevails, parents (often assisted by others in the culture) will see to it that the child learns a helpful way of life, and this helpfulness will show itself in spontaneous altruism when no authority figure is present. (Maccoby, 1980, p. 335)

As we have concluded in earlier sections of this chapter, altruism and cooperative behaviors are important components of our species' successful social organization. Ensuring the socialization in children of these responses should be a primary goal of the group-life children experience. Operating against this attainment are the strongly rooted norms in our society of individual achievement and success. In the family these often work in combination with a high degree of role specialization and together serve to structure and justify a sharply delineated division of labor within the household. Opportunities for socialization to altruism are likely to be reduced in such settings. However, there is some reason for hope. Offering the potential for this socialization outcome is the major structural change mentioned above currently transforming American families: the increased labor force participation of mothers with young children. Although these same working wives and mothers now spend more than twice the time engaged in household chores than their spouses, increasing rates of maternal employment outside the home may begin to lead major shifts of responsibilities *inside* the household. However, more equitable distribution of housework *and*, let us not forget, the attendant socialization of altruistic behaviors in children will only be accomplished if self-consciously supportive planning and provisions are forthcoming. If these social changes take place we can indeed be optimistic about children's lives.

ACKNOWLEDGMENTS

The authors share equally in writing this chapter. The statement of authorship indicates the alphabetical ordering of the authors' names. The first author gratefully acknowledges the Ohio Program in the Humanities under the grant OPH-80-015 and the Department of Educational Leadership, University of Cincinnati, in providing support.

REFERENCES

Barry, A., Child, I. L., & Bacon, M. K. Relation of child training to subsistence economy. *American Anthropologist,* 1959, *61,* 51–63.

Bennett, W. Ecosystem analogies in cultural ecology. In S. Polgar (Ed.), *Population, ecology, and social evolution.* The Hague: Mouton Publishers, 1975.

Berry, J. W. *Human ecology and cognitive style.* New York: Wiley, 1976.

Blumberg, R. L., & Winch, R. F. Societal complexity and familial complexity: Evidence for the curvilinear hypothesis. *American Journal of Sociology,* 1972, *77,* 898–920.

Borman, K. M., & Barrett, D. E. Study three: Negotiating playground games. In K. M. Borman (Ed.), *Children's interpersonal relationships, playground and social cognitive skills.* Final report submitted to the National Institute of Education, May, 1981.

Bowlby, J. *Attachment and loss* (Vol. 1). New York: Basic Books, 1969.

Bruner, J. Measure and uses of immaturity. *American Psychologist,* 1972, 27.

Dennis, W., & Najarian, P. Infant development under environmental handicap. *Psychological Monographs,* 1957, *71,* No. 436.

Eisenstadt, S. N. *From generation to generation.* Glencoe: Free Press, 1956.

Erikson, E. H. *Childhood and society* (2nd ed.). New York: W. W. Norton, 1963.

Fishbein, H. D. *Evolution, development, and children's learning.* Pacific Palisades, California: Goodyear, 1976.

Fishbein, H. D. An evolutionary perspective of the family. *The Behavioral and Brain Sciences,* 1979, *2,* 384–385.

Fried, M. *The world of the urban working class.* Cambridge, Mass: Harvard University Press, 1973.

Kohn, M. L. *Class and conformity.* Chicago: University of Chicago Press, 2nd ed., 1977.

Konner, M. J. Relations among infants and juveniles in comparative perspective. *Social Science Information,* 1976, *15,* 371–402.

LeVine, R. A. *Culture, behavior, and personality.* Chicago: Aldine, 1973.

Lorenz, K. Z. Innate bases of learning. In K. Pribram, (Ed.) *On the biology of learning.* New York: Harcourt, Brace and World, 1969.

Leuptow, L. B. Social change and sex-role change in adolescent orientations toward wife, work, and achievement: 1964–1975. *Social Psychology Quarterly,* 1980, *43,* 48–58.

Maccoby, E. E. *Social development.* New York: Harcourt Brace Jonanovich, 1980.

Piaget, J. Piaget's theory. In P. H. Mussen (Ed.) *Carmichael's manual of child psychology* (3rd ed.). New York: Wiley, 1970.

Piaget, J. *Biology and knowledge.* Chicago: University of Chicago Press, 1971.

Piotrkowski, C. *Work and the family system.* New York: the Free Press, 1979.

Polgar, S. Population, evolution, and theoretical paradigms. In S. Polgar (Ed.), *Population, ecology, and social evolution.* The Hague: Mouton Publishers, 1975.

Polyani, K. *The great transformation: The political and economic origins of our time.* Boston: Beacon Press, 1957.

Rensch, B. *Evolution above the species level.* New York: Columbia University Press, 1959.

Richardson, F. L. W. Organizational evolution from mating pairs to trading nations: Spontaneous and competitive striving with interacting individuals all regulating each other. In S. Polgar (Ed.), *Population, ecology, and social evolution*. The Hague: Mouton Publishers, 1975.

Schildkrout, E. Roles of children in urban Kano. In J. S. La Fontaine (Ed.), *Sex and age as principles of social differentiation*. London: Academic Press, 1978.

Scott, J. P. *Early experience and the organization of behavior*. Belmont, Ca.: Brooks/Cole, 1968.

Spitz, R. A. Hospitalism: An inquiry into the genesis of psychiatric conditions in early childhood. *Psycho Analytic Study of the Child*, 1945, *1*, 53–74.

Steward, J. H. (Ed.) The concept and method of cultural ecology (1968). *Evolution and Ecology*. Urbana, Ill.: University of Illinois Press, 1977. (a)

Steward, J. H. (Ed.) Cultural Evolution in South America. In *Evolution and Ecology*. Urbana, Ill.: University of Illinois Press, 1977. (b)

Vygotsky, L. *Mind in society*. Cambridge: Harvard University Press, 1978.

Waddington, C. H. *New patterns in genetics and development*. New York: Columbia University Press, 1962.

Washburn, S. L., & Hamburg, D. A. The study of primate behavior. In I. Devore. (Ed.), *Primate behavior: Field studies of monkeys and apes*. New York: Holt, Rinehard and Winston, 1965.

Warren, R. L. *Social change and human purpose: Toward understanding and action*. Chicago: Rand, McNally College Publishing Company, 1977.

Whiting, B. B., & Whiting, J. W. Altruistic and egoistic behavior in six cultures. In L. Nader & T. W. Maretzki (Ed.), *Cultural Illness and Health: Essays in Human Adaptation*. Washington D.C.: American Anthropological Association, 1973.

Whiting, B. B., & Whiting, J. W. *Children of six cultures*. Cambridge: Harvard University Press, 1975.

PARENTS AND OTHERS: THOSE WHO INFLUENCE CHILDREN'S LIVES

1 The Significant Others of Young Children: Notes Toward a Phenomenology of Childhood

Norman K. Denzin
University of Illinois, Urbana

Childhood is a unique social world, one that is cut off from, yet a part of, the adult, taken-for-granted world of everyday life. Children are a fact of the human condition, and all societies must ultimately address the question of childhood socialization. That is, "how will these raw products called infants and children be transformed into workable human beings who will have a human nature suitable to the society at hand?" Phrasing the question thusly, we can argue that there is nothing intrinsic to the object called child that would make it more or less human-like. Children, like adults, are social productions. Some societies don't have a concept of childhood (American Amish), some have children who remain children for a protracted period of time (the American middle class); others dislike them (Parisian French), and many seclude them in nurseries and private training and boarding schools (Great Britain).

Despite conflicting definitions of children and of childhood, human infants nonetheless are transformed into social interactants—into individuals who have selves with levels of self awareness and into persons who have social and intimate relationships with others. These others, the significant others of children, constitute the topic at hand. Who are the child's significant others, when do they

Presented to the conference on "The Socialization of Children in a Changing Society," April 26–28, 1979, University of Cincinnati, Cincinnati, Ohio. This conference participated in the City of Cincinnati's observance of the International Year of the Child and was held in cooperation with the Cincinnati Area Teacher's Center.

enter into the child's world, what relationship do they have with one another, how do they structure and mold the child's world of experience?

I turn first to the topic of significant others in childhood, and then, secondly to a phenomenology of childhood. By a phenomenology of childhood is intended a return to the essences, or essential remembered experiences, of childhood that children have, experience, and remember about themselves as children. (The term phenomenology references the study of human behavior from the standpoint of the feeling, thinking human organism. See Bateson, 1979, Denzin, 1980). In particular, I shall address, as did Proust and Halbwachs, the memories of childhood that children and adults recollect, showing that these memories and recollections constitute essential features of the person.

Empirically I shall draw upon a wide body of autobiographical materials which reference remembered childhood experience. I will, in particular, place heavy emphasis on the collective letters of the Henry James [Senior] family, including the correspondance among his children: William, Henry, Alice and Robertson. These letters, I will suggest, offer directly remembered experiences of childhood, and they suggest that families pass their experiences forward, on to one another.

THE CHILD'S NETWORK OF SIGNIFICANT OTHERS

Infants, as Mead and Cooley observed, are born into ongoing networks of social relationships, most typically the primary group of the family. These relationships constitute social worlds of meaning, symbolization, intimacy, routine, and ritual. These relationships are filled with individuals who will later become significant others to the child, and the child will come to view these people as influential and meaningful in the organization of his own behavior. Feelings of intimacy, friendliness, warmth, closeness, hostility, anger and ambivalence will be built up towards the significant others (Wiley, 1979). Infants first experience their humanness in the context of the primary group, often in interactions with the mothering figure. As Wiley (1979) observes: [the infant's] first awareness, then, that humans are subjects, as well as activities and bodies, is in encountering and being trusted with this subjectivity in the mothering one (p. 13). Merleau-Ponty (1964), in discussing the child's relations with others, establishes the primacy of the significant other as follows:

> ... recent studies have tended to show that even external perception of sense qualities and space—at first glance the most disinterested, least affective of all the functions—is profoundly modified by the personality and by the interpersonal relationships in which the child lives ... there is no moment at which you could grasp, in a pure state, his way of perceiving, completely apart from the social conditioning that influences him. Inversely, you can never say that the way in

which the child structures... his environment is unrelated to the hereditary or constitutional dispositions of his nervous system. He himself is the one who structures his surroundings. (p. 99–100; 108)

Six categories of significant others can be identified. The child is likely to confront and interact with these various classes of others at predictable times and in predictable places. I paraphrase Lindesmith, Strauss and Denzin (1977):

The first are those termed *sociolegal,* and they are the child's parents or guardians, his or her siblings, and other members of the kinship system. Second are *socio-others,* drawn from the sociability network that surrounds the primary group of the family. These individuals assume fictional "kinship" in the family and may be called "aunts" and "uncles." Baby-sitters also fall in this category. Third are the *coequal,* or *compeer,* significant others. These include siblings, but also playmates and children in the neighborhood and at school who come to assume a high degree of socializing influence over the child. By the age of three or four, compeers rival parents and other sociolegal significant others in their influence over the child. Certainly by the first grade, and by seven or eight, he or she may have moved nearly entirely into a peer-oriented world of social control. The fourth class of significant others are *child care experts.* These persons have attained some legitimate authority over child care and child evaluation. Physicians, pediatricians, child psychologists, and psychiatrists, teachers, lawyers, politicians, professors, presidents, and social workers dictate and shape the broader process by which a society produces its children. A fifth class of child caretakers and significant others is drawn from the mass media. *Media others* enter the child's world through television, the radio, record players, the movie theatre, storybooks, and nursery rhymes. These others may view themselves as experts on childhood; but more importantly they staff and populate the child's world of fantasy and entertainment. Captain Kangaroo, Mr. Rogers, and the Big Bird and the Cookie Monster on "Sesame Street" represent such fictive and real others who daily enter the child's world of interaction. Media others may have more contact with the child than do any of the above classes of individuals. The last major class of significant others comes from the world of public places. *Public place others* include policemen, firemen, mailmen, clerks and strangers in stores, and individuals normally met by the children or their caretakers when in the public arena. These ideal-typical others fall into a residual category and their influence on the child is likely to be specific to particular situations or services. These six categories of significant others constitute what may be termed the child's interactive world. The two most important categories of significant others will be drawn from the sociolegal and compeer sectors of the child's social world. These persons make up the child's primary group and they provide the sources of self-worth and self-awareness that the child first experiences. They are, as M. Kuhn noted *orientational significant others.* They shape conceptions of self, provide vocabularies of motive, furnish symbolic environments, and promote a sense of "we-ness" and solidarity. Depending on the stances that these others take toward the children, their rate of social development will be hastened or retarded. (p. 356–358)

The Significant Other's Influence

The child acquires a sense of self, subjectivity, and objectivity through interactions with significant others. There is a great deal involved in this assertion, for it assumes that the child must be transformed into a speaking, feeling, thinking, gesturing, responsive and responsible organism—into, that is, an interactant. The forementioned categories of significant others are *ideal types* and do not reference the actual lived experiences of a child who builds up a repertoire of behaviors and relationships with actual persons who represent these types. That is, the child has an interpersonal history with the significant other. This history constitutes the experiential web of the child's remembered childhood.

Consider the following recollections from A. A. Milne's (1939) autobiography. Milne and his brother Ken construct a story about a toad. They were 9 and 10 years old at the time.

> Well, now we were on the ground, and both looking, with Brownie's help, for anything we could find, and there was this toad, and it seemed suddenly of enormous importance that we should have a stuffed toad to live with us. Was it already dead, or did we kill it? I cannot remember. But there and then, the little girls and their mother having gone home to tea, we cut it open and removed its inside. It was astonishing how little, and how little like a toad, the remnant was. However, we took it home and put it in the mineral drawer, where gradually it dried, looking less and less like a toad each time we considered it. But a secret so terrific, a deed so bloody, had to be formulated. The initial formula was Raw Toad (as you would have believed, if you had seen what we saw). Raw Toad was R.T., which was 'arte,' and Latin for 'by with or from art.' Artus was a limb (or wasn't it?) and the first and last letters of limb were L. B. Lb. was pound; you talked about a 'pig in a pound'; pig was P. G. and (Greek now, Ken had just begun Greek) πηγη was fountain. So, ranging lightly over several languages, we had reached our mystic formula—'FN.' Thumbs on the same hymn-book in Dr. Gibson's church, we would whisper 'FN,' to each other and know that life was not all Sunday; side by side in the drawingroom, hair newly brushed for visitors and in those damnable starched sailor suits, we would look 'FN' at each other and be comforted. And though, within six months (the toad still unstuffed and crumbled into dust), we were sharing some entirely different secret, yet, forty years later, the magic letters had power to raise sudden memories in two middle-aged men, smoking their pipes, and wondering what to do with their sons. (p. 47-48)

Milne and his brother display a wealth of self-reflexivity in this situation. As two brothers, they turned the dead toad into an abstract concept, meaningful to and understood by both. They influence one another and, in the process, together build a common experience. Their thinking evidenced reciprocity, relativity and non-egocentrism. They were in a true social relationship with each other (Merleau-Ponty, 1964). They were displaying, in George Herbert Mead's (1934) terms, fully developed selves. Mead states:

.... There are two general stages in the full development of the self. At the first of these stages, the individual's self is constituted simply by an organization of the particular attitudes of other individuals toward himself and toward one another in the specific social acts in which he participates with them. But at the second stage in the full development of the individual's self that self is constituted not only by an organization of these particular individual attitudes, but also by an organization of the social attitudes of the generalized other or the social group as a whole to which he belongs. These social or group attitudes are brought within the individual's field of direct experience, and are included as elements in the structure or constitution of his self, in the same way that the attitudes of particular other individuals are; and the individual arrives at them, or succeeds in taking them, by means of further organizing, and then generalizing, the attitudes of particular other individuals in terms of their organized social bearings and implications. So the self reaches its full development by organizing these individual attitudes of others into the organized social or group attitudes, and by thus becoming an individual reflection of the general systematic pattern of social or group behavior in which it and the others are all involved—a pattern which enters as a whole into the individual's experience in terms of these organized group attitudes which, through the mechanism of his central nervous system, he takes toward himself, just as he takes the individual attitudes of others (p. 158)

Mead's fully developed self has been observed to appear in the child's behavior repertoire at around 3 years of age. Merleau-Ponty (1974) remarks:

At around three years the child stops lending his body and even his thoughts to others.... He stops confusing himself with the situation or role in which he may find himself engaged. He adopts a proper perspective or viewpoint of his own—or rather he understands that, whatever the diversity of situations or roles, he is *someone* above and beyond these different situations or roles. (p. 151–152)

Prior to the development of a fully organized sense of self and self-awareness, the child is largely *dependent* on significant others for the generation, organization, and interpretation of their on-going experiences. That is, they experience themselves through the experiences of the significant other. When self-hood is established, the child generates and gives meaning to his own social experiences. Accordingly, it is necessary to move back in chronological time and chart the emergent character of the child's relationship to the significant other.

Chronicity and the Other

Central to the socialization process is the acquisition and use of language. Language provides the link that connects the child to the primary group. It is through a continual conversation of gestures with the significant other that the child comes to acquire a sense of himself, his body, and the bodies and selves of others. The languages of childhood mediate, yet produce, the socialization process, and children are active participants in this on-going event (Denzin, 1977).

Children, in fact, produce languages and conversations of gestures which may be unique to them, or special only to their families. Children produce special ways of socializing themselves, and they develop unique ways of interacting with others. Still, initially at least, the child is dependent on the caretaking activities of the significant other.

The social structure of the family makes a place for the child before and upon birth, and children are *temporally marked* as the first born, the last born—the youngest—or the one in the middle. Their temporal standing in the family's social structure establishes an obdurate fact which their socialization hinges on. They will always be the first, second, or third born child, no matter how old they become. Even if they are an only child their temporal place in the family is a permanent marker which they will carry throughout their moral careers as persons. Their temporal ranking in the family thus attaches itself to recurring emotional experiences regarding such matters as jealousy, envy, pride, hate, disgust, derogation, selfishness, sharing, and pride. Children are who they are, after all, through their relationships to the other individuals who make up this social structure.

Henry James (1913) offers the following remembrance of one of his early childhood perceptions. It involves his temporal standing in the James family, behind his older brother William.

> . . . One of these, and probably the promptest in order, was that of my brother's occupying a place in the world to which I couldn't at all aspire . . . as if he had gained such an advance of me in his sixteen months' experience of the world before mine began that I never for all the time of childhood and youth in the least caught up with him or overtook him. He was always round the corner and out of sight, coming back into view but at his hours of extremest ease. We were never in the same schoolroom, in the same game, scarce even in step together or in the same phase at the same time; when our phases overlapped, that is, it was only for a moment—he was clean out before I had got well in. How far he had really at any moment dashed forward it is not for me now to attempt to say; what comes to me is that I at least hung inveterately and woefully back, and that this relation alike to our interests and to each other seemed proper and preappointed. (p. 9–10)

In Henry James' case, he, the novelist, was always the *younger* brother of William, the psychologist and philosopher.

This lasting sense of standing below William is bitterly conveyed in the following letter (H. James, 1920):

Devonshire Club, St. James's, S.W.
Nov. 14th, '78

My dear William,
. . . I was much depressed on reading your letter by your painful reflections on *The Europeans;* but now, an hour having elapsed, I am beginning to hold up my head a little; the more so as I think I myself estimate the book very justly and am

aware of its extreme slightness. I think you take these things too rigidly and unimaginatively—too much as if an artistic experiment were a piece of conduct, to which one's life were somehow committed; but I think also that you're quite right in pronouncing the book 'thin' and empty. I don't at all despair, yet, of doing something fat. Meanwhile I hope you will continue to give me, when you can, your free impression of my performances. It is a great thing to have some one write to one of one's things as if one were a third person, and you are the only individual who will do this. I don't think however you are always right, by any means. As for instance in your objection to the closing paragraph of *Daisy Miller,* which seems to me queer and narrow, and as regards which I don't seize your point of view. J'en appelle to the sentiment of any other story-teller whatsoever; I am sure none such would wish the paragraph away. You may say—'Ah, but other *readers* would.' But that is the same; for the teller is but a more developed reader. I don't trust your judgment altogether (if you will permit me to say so) about *details;* but I think you are altogether right in returning always to the importance of the subject. I hold to this, strongly; and if I don't as yet seem to proceed upon it more, it is because, being 'very artistic,' I have a constant impulse to try experiments of form, in which I wish to not run the risk of wasting or gratuitously using big situations. But to these I am coming now. It is something to have learned how to write, and when I look round me and see how few people (doing my sort of work) know how (to my sense,) I don't regret my step-by-step evolution. I don't advise you however to read the two last things I have written—one a thing in the Dec. and Jan. *Cornhill,* which I will send home; and the other a piece I am just sending to Howells. They are each quite in the same manner as *The Europeans.* I have written you a letter after all. I am tired and must stop. Blessings on Alice. Ever your

H. J. jr. (p. 65–66)

The Minds of the Child and the Significant Other

The infant has no access to the mind of the significant other. While infants' sensory apparatuses permit them to see, hear, touch, and smell the other, they lack the neurological capabilities of entering into the thoughts and feelings of their significant others. Conversely, the significant other cannot enter the child's mind because presumably there is nothing in there. This sets the stage for a curious pattern of interaction in the first 12 months of the infant's life. Since the infant cannot be interacted with, they are interacted at; they are manipulated, dressed, undressed, cooed to, yelled at, stroked, rocked, carried to and placed in situations where they are observed, studied, or ignored. Anthropomorphic motives are attributed to them, and they are given personalities as well as names.

The other cannot experience the child's body; they can only observe it and make inferences about what is going on inside it. Hence, while the infant is very much an object and focus of interaction for the caretaker, it is so in a very curious and highly limited manner.

At a very early age (2 weeks) infants display a sensitivity to the actions of others. They smile if smiled at, and their eyes follow the movements of others who come into their presence. Merleau-Ponty (1964) terms these smiles "motor smiles.'' The child who smiles after someone smiles at him has simply imitated the gestures of the other. He has not constructed a point-by-point correspondence between the visual action of, say, the mother, and the meaning of the smile to them. The infant is incapable of so doing. Yet, the infant has smiled and has thus connected a portion of his body to the body of the other. Such infants are in the first phase of development which Merleau-Ponty (1964) calls pre-communication, or as we might say, pre-conscious communication. However, and more critically to the point, the infant's pre-conscious communication is realized in relation to the world of the significant other (Merleau-Ponty, 1964); that is, in relationship to the conduct and actions of an other in the immediate here and now of the situation.

At first the child imitates the conduct of persons, not persons per se (Guillaume, 1925). The infant thus learns about or discovers his own body through the importation of aspects of the other's conduct into a "behavioral schema" that references his body (including its various parts) in relationship to other bodies. The body begins by being introceptive. As Merleau-Ponty (1964) notes, in the earliest stages of life "external perception is impossible . . . for visual communication and muscular control of the eyes are insufficient" (p. 121-122). The body begins as a respiratory body. The respiratory apparatus gives the infant an experience of space. The mouth, the lungs and then the other regions of the body come into prominence. Between the third and fourth months the internal domain of the body begins to interact with the external elements of the child's environment. Myelinization is taking place; nerve fibers are becoming more complex and elaborate. Around the fourth month the child may be observed to pay attention to its right hand, exploring one hand with the other. The infant's consciousness of his own body is thus fragmentary and only gradually becomes integrated. With experience and consciousness, the behavioral schema becomes more precise and undergoes restructuring. *Syncretic sociability* underscores the character of the interactions that transpire between the infant and the adult. There is an indistinction between the me of the infant and the me of the adult. As yet there is no firm partition between the two bodies and the two minds. Non-thetic awareness is the mode (Wiley, 1979; Sartre, 1939).

The child displays an awareness of the other by fixing his eyes on the particular parts of the other's body—their hands, their eyes, their feet, their mouths. The child cries when other infants cry, and the cry is the first firm signal of a definite reaction to the other (Markey, 1928). The scrutiny of the other's body enriches the child's growing conceptions of his own body. There is, then, a correlation between the infant's consciousness of his own body and his perceptions of the body of the other. The infant has, however, more experiences with his own body; the other remains an indissociated form, in the first 6 months of life.

Children under one year of age seldom interact with persons of their own age, although this pattern may be undergoing change. As Merleau-Ponty (1964) observes: "Still at five months there is no fraternization with children of the same age. At six months, at least, the child looks the other child in the face, and one has the impression that here, for the first time, he is perceiving another." (p. 125)

A rapid turn of affairs occurs after the first 6 months. The infant and the significant other become persons to one another. They enter into a "we-relationship" with one another (Wiley, 1979). Infants acquire an awareness of themselves as a body, and they see images of themselves in mirrors. These embodied pictures provide perceptions of themselves as wholes, pictures they could not otherwise gain by the mere inspection of their bodies. These mirror images—experiences the child gains from inspecting his images in mirrors—become part of the image the child holds and builds toward himself. Concommitant with the building of a picture of himself appears a heightened period of intensified interaction with the other; there is an outburst of sociable interaction. The infant enters an exploratory-interactive phase; crawling, babbling, moving, touching and disrupting are common behaviors. From mirrors and the response of others, the child is learning how to be self-reflective; he is gaining new pictures of himself. Affect and emotion, jealousy and spite become familiar experiences in the second 6 months of life. Temper tantrums are thrown, although in the experiencing of the negative emotion the child also displays desires for the positive feelings of love, attachment, security and sympathy. The caretaker's attentions toward the child during the second 6 months very much influence the interactive patterns and body-self reflections that are established. Indeed, in families with multiple children, the attention other siblings do not receive often defines the emergent character of the newborn's self-image. In the second 6 months the child is building up and building upon a behavior repertoire that will become a part of him, as self-reflexivity emerges and becomes a part of him. Merleau-Ponty (1964) observes:

In the period of pre-communication . . . the personality is somehow immersed in the situation and is a function of the child himself or the other beings with whom he lives. . . . The child confuses himself with his situation. One recalls the example of a child who had a glass in his hand (against his father's wishes), put it down and, on hearing the sound of breaking glass five minutes later, started and became just as agitated as if he still had the glass in his hand. He created a sort of magic link between the forbidden thing he had done several minutes earlier and the breaking of the glass, far away from him. In a case like this one, there is in the child no distinct conception of moments of time, nor is there any distinct conception of causal relations. The child confuses himself with his situation. (p. 146)

The child's speech patterns during this time period are holophrastic word-sentences, and he often confuses self (of child) with the other. The first-word sentences often confuse references to the child's conduct with the conduct of the other. Merleau-Ponty (1964) notes:

When the child (even the very young child) says "hand" (hand-hand), this means his father's hand as well as the hand represented by a photograph or his own hand. This seems to presuppose a kind of abstraction, a recognition of the same object in a plurality of cases. And in fact the object identified is greatly different (for example, there is not a great resemblance between a child's hand and the photograph of an adult's hand). In reality, however, there is no abstraction here. There is simply no radical distinction in the child between his own hand and that of another. . . . This allows us to understand why the use of the word *I* comes relatively late to the child. He will use it when he has become conscious of his own proper perspective, distinct from those of others, and when he has distinguished all of the perspectives from the external object. In the initial state of perception there is consciousness not of being enclosed in a perspective and of guessing—picking out across it an object which is outside—but of being in direct touch with things across a personal-universal vision. The *I* arises when the child understands that every *you* that is addressed to him is for him an *I;* that is, that there must be a consciousness of the reciprocity of points of view in order that the word *I* may be used. (p. 150)

Merleau-Ponty sets this knowledge of self as a distinct object at or around 3 years of age. Elsewhere (Denzin, 1978) I have suggested that emergent self-awareness can be observed by the fifteenth month. Interactional age, not chronological age, I suggested, determined levels of self-reflexivity and abilities to distinguish the body and the self of the child from the body and the self of the significant other. With self-awareness comes use of the personal name. The name becomes a hook around which the child comes to hang identities, experiences, and recollections. Names, too, reference others that the child has relationships with. Among a group of mothers at a preschool, young children recognize *their* mother; among a group of fathers walking home they recognize *their* father. In short, at least by the age of 3 the child has acquired a sense of interpersonal history, a sense of time, a sense of himself and a sense of the relationships he is embedded in. Furthermore, he has built up a behavior repertoire that distinguishes him from his significant others. He has a corporeal scheme which registers and records his bodily experiences, and he can now talk to himself and enter into the organization of his own behavior.

THE CHILD'S HISTORY AND ITS RECOLLECTIONS

By the age of three the child is on the edge of producing, on a self-reflexive basis, his own history. He is the images he sees in mirrors; his body in fact has empirical status in the real world of his everyday life. His body has a name and experiences. Most importantly, he and his body have experiences with others and, as the child reflects on those experiences, he not only constructs but reconstructs "remembrances of things past" (Proust, 1934). The 3-year-old, then, is in touch with, and a constructor (and reconstructor) of the very experiences in his life-world that makes him more human-like. He is the narrator of his own life-history, the teller and doer of his own story. His story, life, and history are played out inside his locations in the social structure of his significant others. Consider the following, one of the final requests of a 5-year-old male dying of leukemia (Bluebond-Langer, 1978):

(Jeffrey is lying in bed. The TV is on, without the sound, but he is not even looking at the picture.)

Myra: Hi, Jeffrey. Can I come in?
Jeffrey: (Nods almost imperceptibly from the bed.)
Myra: (Puts on a mask and gown and washes her hands.)
                                         (Myra enters the room.)
Myra: Are you comfortable, Jeffrey?
Jeffrey: (In a slow whisper) Yeah. Will you read me the part in *Charlotte's Web*, where Charlotte dies. The book is over there.
Myra: Sure (goes over to the night table and gets the book and sits down. Shows Jeffrey the chapter entitled "Last Day.")
Jeffrey: (Nods.)
Myra: Can you see OK?
Jeffrey: (Nods.)
Myra: (Begins to read aloud.)[1] . . . "Next day, as the Ferris wheel was being taken apart and the race horses were being loaded into vans and the entertainers were packing up their belongings and driving away in their trailers, Charlotte died. The Fair Grounds were soon deserted. The sheds and buildings were empty and forlorn. The infield was littered with bottles and trash. Nobody, of the hundreds of people that had visited the Fair knew that a gray spider had played the most important part of all. No one was with her when she died." (Closes the book.)
Jeffrey: (Dozes off.)
Myra: (Places the book by his bed, leaves him a note on the end of the bed.)
                                         (Myra leaves the room.)
Later that afternoon, at 5:15 p.m., Jeffrey Andrews died. (pp. 128–134)

Jeffrey orchestrated the final passage of his own death. A 5-year-old confronted, defined and dealt with an ultimate reality.

Consider now, the perhaps less dramatic recollections of a 53-year-old male postal clerk on the wearing of dresses as a child (Stone, 1962):

I can remember back in the South, forty-five years ago, the children—boys—always wore dresses up to the time they were three or four years old. When I was about five, six, seven, or eight, they wore those little Fauntlerory suits. God damn! I hated those. Then knickers came. I wore those until I was about fifteen years old. I was fifteen and a half when I had my first long pants suit. (p. 107)

---

[1] I quote from Bluebond-Langer's text, which reproduces the conclusion to *Charlotte's Web*.

Adult memories of childhood run deep. In another vein, Proust (1934) recalls his mother kissing him at bedtime when he was a child:

> My sole consolation when I went upstairs for the night was that Mama would come in and kiss me after I was in bed. But this good night lasted for so short a time: She went down again so soon that the moment in which I heard her climb the stairs, and then caught the sound of her garden dress of blue muslin, from which hung little tassels of plaited straw, rustling along the double-doored corridor, was for me a moment of the keenest sorrow . . . Sometimes when, after kissing me, she opened the door to go, I longed to call her back, to say to her "kiss me just once again," but I knew that then she would at once look displeased . . . to see her displeasure, destroyed all the sense of tranquility she had brought me a moment before, when she had bent her loving face down over my bed . . . (p. 10)

Proust's remembrances of his mother are vivid in detail and rich in emotion and feeling. The going-to-bed ritual clearly had a significant impact upon his childhood experiences; the transitions from wakefulness to sleeping were very much contingent on his mother's "good night" kiss.

Ritual is crucial to family social structure, and children appear able to recollect family rituals as the following suggests (Bossard & Boll, 1950):

> Each night before Dad would retire, there would be placed on the stand beside his bed a tall glass of orange juice. No one in particular was designated to perform this task, but as each of us came home or went upstairs to bed we would check on this "must." Forgetfulness on our part shamed each of us. The only mention of Dad's part would be a reluctant, "Missed my orange juice last night, everyone must have been tired." That hurt us because we hurt him. (p. 66)

In ritualizing a set of behaviors family members lend elements of emotion and meaning to everyday conduct. These meanings are conveyed to the child. An act as superficially trivial as reading the evening paper can be assigned ritual significance and remembered by the child. Bossard and Boll (1950) report one such instance:

> The morning paper is always read first by my father, and then the other members of the family in order of age. After all the family has finished, the servants can read it if they wish . . . On returning home from school or work, the newspaper is broken up into three sections, the funnies taken by my youngest sister. I take possession of the sport page. Mother takes the pages on household hints and women's items. The paper is rearranged by me to its original condition and left at the arm of the easy chair which father always occupies after supper. Thelma, my oldest sister, takes possession of the paper after father has finished reading it. (p. 73)

This ritual clearly reifies the place and standing of each member of the family. Gender socialization, as well, is clearly at work in this childhood remembrance.

The following episode, from the autobiography of Katherine Du Pre Lumkin (*The Making of a Southerner,* 1947) suggests another segment of childhood experiences that becomes a part of the child's collective memory.

> At the club-forming age we children had a Ku Klux Klan. It was a natural thing to do it, offspring of our warm Southern patriotism. We were happy in it for the aid and blessing it won from our adults. Our costumes, while made from worn-out sheets, were yet cut to pattern with help at home; they had fitted hoods, also, with tall peaks, and emblazoned across the front of the robes were red cheese-cloth crosses. Constitution, by-laws, and ritual were something out of the ordinary. They were written, not on paper, but transcribed, as we supposed the original had been, on a long cloth scroll, at the top of which was a bright red cross. Our elders helped us write the ritual and rules and, true or not, we firmly believed that our laws and oaths were in some sense an echo from the by-gone order. It was certainly a game and fascinating as such. But it was much more besides. Its ritual rolling off our tonges with so much happy gusto, was frequently interlarded with warm exhortations to white supremacy . . . A chief topic of business when ceremonies had ended was the planning of pretended punitive expeditions against mythical recalcitrant Negores. And while in one sense it never was real, in another it went far beyond pretense. We vented our feelings . . . These were read. We felt patriotic; so was this read—this warm, pulsing feeling of Southern loyalty. (p. 136)

This remembrance demonstrates how childhood memories maintain both actual social structures and a sense of a remembered social structure.

Finally, consider a "turning point" (Strauss, 1959) in a child's life. Dylan Thomas (1955) provides an instance. He describes Samuel Bennet, leaving home, early one morning in January of 1933.

> If only he could shout at the ceiling now . . . Come and look at Samuel Bennet destroying his parent's house in Mortimer Street, off Stanley's Grove, he will never be allowed to come back . . . He opened the door to the china pantry. The best plates shone in rows, a willow tree next to an ivied castle, baskets of solid flowers on top of fruits and flower-coiled texts. Tureens were piled on one shelf, on another the salad-bowls, the finger-bowls, the toast-racks spelling Porthcawl and Baby, the trifle-dishes, the heirloom mustache-cup. The afternoon tea-service was brittle as biscuits and had gold rims. He cracked two saucers together, and the horn-curved spout of the teapot came off in his hand. In five minutes he had broken the whole set. He would have to be quick now . . . His sister's crochetwork was too difficult to destroy, the coilies and the patterned tea-cosies were as hard as rubber. He pulled them apart the best he could, and wedged them up the chimney . . . He burnt the edge of his mother's sunshade at the gas-mantle and felt the tears running down his cheeks and dropping onto his pyjama collar. (pp. 7–10)

This is an event that is not likely to be forgotten, and it points to a key feature of adult and childhood recollections of childhood; namely, the lodging of the child's self in the experience. Whether it is leaving orange juice for one's father, wearing dresses as a child, kissing one's mother goodnight, sorting out the evening paper, belonging to a Ku Klux Klan group, or leaving home, the child's self is embedded in a recurring experience, or in an experience that separates him from the family social structure.

Records of the Child's History

Families keep histories on their shared and significant experiences. As Halbwachs (1925, 1950) suggests, certain childhood memories are recaptured through recourse to these family artifacts. Photo albums, mementos from vacations, souveniers from port cities and gifts brought back from trips mark moments in historical time and lodge the child's self in the remembrance of the event in question.

In a similar event, memorable events, whether embarrassing, turning-point in nature, or even as consequential as the death of a pet parakeet or turtle, are themselves memorialized in the child's memory. Those events become a part of children's biographies, and they carry those memories with them into adulthood, find that who they are as adults is in large measure a result of who they remember themselves being as children.

The James Family. Family members often write letters to one another. These letters, when taken together, often yield collective remembrances and portraits of the family's shared history. The James Family Letters provide a valuable illustration of this point (see Matthiessen, 1947; Henry James, 1920; Henry James, 1913, 1914, 1917; Gunn, 1974; Burr, 1934; Edel, 1964; and William James, 1884). Mathiessen (1947) suggests that the James family, including Henry James, Senior, his wife Mary Walsh, and their five children: William Henry Junior, Garth, Robertson, and Alice, may "constitute one of the most vivid and varied groups that our American nineteenth century produced . . . William James and Henry James, Junior . . . touched upon nearly all the major cultural interests of their age." (p. v) The James family was certainly unusual. The father had radical views on education and raised his children, for a period of time, in Europe. His was a theory that valued individual experience, individual expression and emotional turning points. During their early childhood the James family was constantly on the move, throughout Europe, from Geneva to London to Paris. The James children "complained they had had an 'hotel' childhood" (Edel, 1964, p. 4). The father's philosophy was very much shaped by the following experience, which he was later to report to his five children (Wm. James, 1884):

> In the spring of 1884 I was living with my family in the neighborhood of Windsor, England, much absorbed in the study of the Scriptures . . . One day . . . towards the close of May, having eaten a comfortable dinner, I remained sitting at the table after the family had dispersed, idly gazing at the embers in the grate, thinking of

nothing, and feeling only the exhilaration incident to a good digestion, when suddenly—in a lightning-flash as it were—"fear came upon me, and trembling, which made all my bones to shake." To all appearance it was a perfectly insance and abject terror, without ostensible cause, and only to be accounted for, to my perplexed imagination, by some damned shape squatting invisible to me within the precincts of the room, and raying out from his fetid personality, influences fatal to life. The thing had not lasted ten seconds before I felt myself a wreck, that is reduced from a state of firm, vigorous, joyful manhood to one of almost helpless infancy. The only self-control I was capable of exerting was to keep my seat . . . this ghastly condition of mind continued with me, with gradually lengthening intervals of relief for two years, and even longer. (p. 55-56)

Henry James, Senior came to define this experience as a "vastation," a grand emotional experience that marked a major turning point in his life. His eldest son, William, recorded the following experience, probably during the winter of 1869-70 (H. James, 1920):

I went one evening into a dressing-room in the twilight, to procure some article that was there; when suddenly there fell upon me without any warning, just as if it came out of the darkness, a horrible fear of my own existence. Simultaneously there arose in my mind the image of an epileptic patient whom I had seen in the asylum, a black-haired youth with greenish skin, entirely idiotic, who used to sit all day on one of the benches, or rather shelves, against the wall, with his knees drawn up against his chin, and the coarse grey undershirt, which was his only garment, drawn over them, inclosing his entire figure. He sat there like a sort of sculptured Egyptian cat or Peruvian mummy, moving nothing but his black eyes and looking absolutely non-human. This image and my fear entered into a species of combination with each other. *That shape am I,* I felt, potentially. Nothing that I possess can defend me against that fate, if the hour for it should strike for me as it struck for him. There was such a horror of him, and such a perception of my own merely momentary discrepancy from him, that it was as if something hitherto solid within my breast gave way entirely, and I became a mass of quivering fear. After this the universe was changed for me altogether. I awoke morning after morning with a horrible dread at the pit of my stomach, and with a sense of the insecurity of life that I never knew before, and that I have never felt since. It was like a revelation; and although the immediate feelings passed away, the experience has made me sympathetic with the morbid feelings of others ever since. It gradually faded, but for months I was unable to go out into the dark alone. (p. 146)

Robertson James, the youngest James' son (Burr, 1934) said of himself in a fragment of an autobiography:

I was born in the year 1846, in Albany, N.Y. I never remember being told anything extraordinary about my babyhood but I often like to contemplate myself as a baby and wonder if I was really as little appreciated as I fully remember feeling at that time. I never see infants now without discerning in their usually solemn countenance a conviction that they are on their guard and in more or less hostile surroundings. However that may be, in my own case, at a very early age the problems of life began to press upon me in such an unnatural way and I developed such an ability for feeling hurt and wounded that I became quite convinced by the time I was twelve years old that I was a foundling. (p. 25)

Henry James, Junior (Dupee, 1974) had an experience similar to William's, also in the late 1860's, and Alice during this period was described by the father as "much more than half the time on the verge of insanity and suicide" (Edel, 1964, p. 6).

A father's experience, in this case, is remembered by his sons and reexperienced by them. Against this backdrop, Alice James:

> . . in adult life, warned William against repeating the same pattern with his children. "What enrichment of mind and memory can children have without continuity and if they are torn up by the roots every little while as we were? Of all things don't make the mistake which brought about our rootless and accidental childhood." She urged William to leave Europe for his children "until they are old enough to have the Grand Emotion, undiluted by vague memories" (Edel, 1964, p. 4).

The following excerpt from a letter written by William James in 1892 suggests that he did not take his sister's advice (H. James, 1920):

> It seems to me that the most solemn duty *I* can have in what remains to me of life will be to save my inexperienced fellow beings from ignorantly taking their little ones abroad when they go for their own refreshment. To combine novel anxieties of the most agonizing kind about your children's education, noctural and diurnal contact of the most intimate sort with their shrieks, their quarrels, their questions, their rollings-about and tears, in short with all their emotional, intellectual and bodily functions, in what practically in these close quarters amounts to one room— to combine these things (I say) with a *holiday* for *oneself* is an idea worthy to emanate from a lunatic asylum. The wear and tear of a professorship for a year is not equal to one week of this sort of thing. But let me not complain! Since I am responsible for their being, I will launch them worthily upon life; and if a foreign education is required, they shall have it. Only why talk of "sabbatical" years?— there is the hideous mockery! Alice, if she writes to you, will (after her feminine fashion) gloze over this aspect of our existence, because she has been more or less accustomed to it all these years and *on the whole does not dislike it* (!!), but I for once will speak frankly and not disguise my sufferings. Here in this percipitous Alpine village we occupy rooms in an empty house with a yellow-plastered front and an iron balcony above the street. Up and down that street the cows, the goats, the natives, and the tourists pass. The church-roof and the pastor's house are across the way, dropped as it were twenty feet down the slope. Close beside us are populous houses either way, and others beside *them*. Yet on that iron balcony all the innermost mysteries of the James family are blazoned and bruited to the entire village. *Things* are dried there, quarrels, screams and squeals rise incessantly to

Heaven, dressing and undressing are performed, punishments take place— recriminations, arguments, execrations—with a publicity after which, if there *were* reporters, we should never be able to show our faces again. (p. 321-322)

Here, a father's observations of family behavior suggest that the world of childhood can get out of control, at least for the adult. Yet James and his wife had structured a set of experiences that surely became a part of their children's remembered childhood.

Finally, we are led to consider the nature of what children remember from their childhoods. Alice James (Edel, 1964) considers the question:

I wonder what determines the *selection* of memory, why does one childish experience or impression stand out so luminous and solid against the, for the most part, vague and misty background. The things we remember have a *firsttimeness* about them which suggests that may be the reason of their survival . . . I remember so distinctly the first time I was conscious of a purely intellectual process. (p. 127-128)

One's remembered childhood may hinge, then, on the experiencing and the cataloguing of first time, significant events. In between these first time events are chains of repetitions, habitualized routines and daily doings. One establishes the credibility of their childhood by remembering it well and in vivid detail.

Conclusion

I have suggested that children have access to their own histories by at least the age of 3 years. This makes them direct participants in the construction of their own lives. The James family letters suggest that one generation's experiences often become the basis of the next generation's childhood. The letters also suggest that families have intertwined biographies that cross generational lines. Rivalries in childhood continue as rivalries in adult life. Emotional, turning-point experiences are passed from fathers and mothers to sons and daughters. Sons and daughters, in turn, pass these experiences onto one another, and even on to their own children.

As students of socialization, we must learn to take children seriously and we must study how children go about attaching significance and meaning to their everyday lives. The study of family letters, biographies, and autobiographies appears highly worthwhile in this regard.

REFERENCES

Bateson, G. *Mind and nature: A necessary unity.* New York: E. P. Dutton, 1979.
Bluebond-Langer, M. *The private worlds of dying children.* Princeton, N.J.: Princeton University Press, 1978.

Bossard, J. H., & Boll, E. S. *The sociology of child development*. New York: Harper & Row, 1950.

Burr, A. R. *Alice James: Her brothers—her journal*. Cornwall, N.Y.: Dodd, Mead & Company, Inc., 1934.

Denzin, N. K. Childhood socialization. A phenomenology of emotion and defiance. San Francisco: Jossey-Bass, 1981. *Zeitschrift für Soziologie,* Jg. Heft 3, Juli 19 S., 1977, 251-261.

Dupee, F. W. *Henry James*. New York: William Morrow & Company, Inc., 1974.

Du Pre Lumkin, K. *The making of a southerner*. New York: Alfred A. Knopf, 1947.

Edel, L. *The diary of Alice James*. New York: Dodd, Mead & Company, 1964.

Guillaume, P. *L'imitation chez l'enfant*. Paris: Universitaires de France, 1925. University of Chicago Press, 1973. (Trans. Elain P. Halperin)

Gunn, G. *Henry James, senior: A selection of his writings*. Chicago: American Library Association, 1974.

Halbwachs, M. *Les cadres sociaux de la memoire*. Paris: Presses Universitaires de France, 1925.

James, H. *A small boy and others*. London: Macmillan and Company, 1913.

James, H. *Notes of a son and brother*. New York: Charles Scribner's Sons, 1914.

James, H. *The middle years*. London: W. Collins Sons & Company, 1917.

James, H. (Ed.) *The letters of William James in two volumes*. Boston: The Atlantic Monthly Press, 1920.

James, W. *The literary remains of the late Henry James*. Boston: Houghton Mifflin Co., 1885.

Lindesmith, A., Strauss, A. L., & Denzin, N. K. *Social psychology, 5th edition*. New York: Holt, Rinehart and Winston, 1978.

Markey, J. F. *The symbolic process and its integration in children: A study in social psychology*. London: Harcourt, Brace and Company, 1928. (Reissue, Chicago: University of Chicago Press, 1979.)

Mattiessen, F. O. *The James family including selections from the writings of Henry James, Senior, William, Henry, and Alice James*. New York: Alfred A. Knopf, 1947.

Mead, G. H. *Mind, self and society*. Edited with an Introduction by Charles W. Morris, Chicago: University of Chicago Press, 1934.

Merleau-Ponty, M. *The primacy of perception*. Edited with an Introduction by James M. Edie, Evanston, Ill.: Northwestern University Press, 1964.

Milne, A. A. *It's too late now*. London: Curtis Brown, 1939. (Reprinted by permission).

Perry, R. B. *The thought and character of William James as revealed in unpublished correspondence and notes together with his published writings*. Boston: Little Brown and Company, 1935.

Proust, M. *Remembrance of things past, Volume 1*. Trans. by C. K. Scott Moncrieff. New York: Random House, 1934.

Satre, J. *Sketch for a theory of the emotions*. Paris: Hermann, 1939. English trans. by Philip Mairet, preface by Mary Warnock, London: Methuen & Co., Ltd., 1962.

Stone, G. P. Appearance and the self. In Arnold M. Rose (Ed.), *Human behavior and social process*. Boston: Houghton Mifflin Company, 1962.

Strauss, A. *Mirrors and masks*. Glencoe, Ill.: The Free Press, 1959. (Reissue, San Francisco: The Sociology Press, 1969).

Thomas, D. *Adventures in the skin trade*. New York: New Directions, 1955. (Reprinted by permission).

Wiley, N. The genesis of self: From me to we to I. In Norman K. Denzin (Ed.), *Studies in symbolic interaction, Vol. II*. Greenwich, Conn.: JAI Press, Inc., 1979, pp. 87-105. (Reprinted by permission).

2 The Influence of Teacher Attitudes on Children's Classroom Performance: Case Studies

Eleanor Leacock
City College, City University of New York

Research into the complexities of classroom life indicates that the critical factor influencing children's performance is neither a particular teaching method as such nor the background of the children in and of itself. A fair number of studies now show instead that the critical factor is the teacher's expectation that children either will or will not learn what is being taught. To say this does not mean that the process whereby teacher attitudes are projected onto children is simple. Teacher expectations for children are in part expressed in direct and consciously formulated goal-setting statements, but they are also incorporated into curriculum content, teaching style, and classroom management practices in subtle ways of which teachers are often unaware.

Before reviewing studies on the effects of teacher attitudes on children's performance, it is important to state emphatically that the behaviors of teachers, as individuals, are not the *basic* cause for children's success or failure *as groups*. To be sure, a committed teacher can make a critical difference to individual children. Autobiographies of people who have contended successfully with the liabilities of poverty sometimes express appreciation for the support of a particular teacher, and the awareness of being able to help individual children can certainly be a major gratification for a teacher. Furthermore, recent studies have supported the common sense assumption that individual teachers vary in their degree of success with their classrooms as wholes (Carew & Lightfoot 1979; Pedersen, Faucher, & Eaton 1978). However, the ability of individual teachers is constrained by the structure of their work; it would be unfair to give a new teacher the illusion that she or he could go into a school where overall standards have deteriorated and single-handedly demonstrate success in *substantially* raising performance levels in one classroom.

Socially speaking, teachers are the *agents* who mediate the success or failure of children as groups; they are not the ultimate *reason* for success or failure. The basic reason why children *as groups* succeed or fail in school has been well stated by anthropologists, sociologists, and political economists. Ogbu's (1978) *Minority Education and Caste* and Bowles and Gintis's (1976) *Schooling in Capitalist America* are foremost examples of a literature that documents ways in which the structure and function of educational institutions mesh with and reinforce socioeconomic distinctions by class and race. Both parents and teachers know that success and failure are thoroughly institutionalized in a double-track educational system whereby overcrowded and underequipped elementary schools in poor neighborhoods lead into inadequately equipped and staffed intermediate schools and thence into trade schools or dead-end high schools, while "good" schools in medium income or affluent neighborhoods lead to college-bound intermediate and secondary schools. Parents move in or out of neighborhoods in order to send their children to good schools, and teachers commonly try to work in such schools in response both to the better work conditions and to the class and race biases of our society. In short, children are not being educated in school for "equal opportunity," but are being socialized to continue in the class and caste status into which they were born.

Teachers' roles as socialization agents are shaped by a series of constraints, Some of these are direct, such as problems arising from inadequate physical plants and limited teaching materials that plague schools in low income and non-white neighborhoods despite individual examples to the contrary. Some are indirect, such as the influence exerted on performance demands by the fact that the next school in line for most poor children has low standards for entry and graduation. Interpersonal relations also enter in; a young teacher with innovative ideas is in effect challenging older established teachers who may respond with pointed unfriendliness that threatens the novice with social isolation.

Bias against children who are poor and/or nonwhite is also built into teaching materials, and despite attention to this problem, the bias has been but superficially corrected. And finally, in keeping with the attitudes of class snobbery and racial inequality that are prevalent in our society, a rationale for failure with children who are poor and non-white is provided by the "culture of poverty" concept whereby failure is expected and is blamed on children's family backgrounds. So tightly interwoven is the entire nexus of structural and attitudinal relationships that affirms differential school performance by class and race, that the differentiation which reveals itself most sharply in segregated schools and neighborhoods recurs within the structure of "fast" and "slow" classes on the same grade, or "fast" and "slow" learning groups within a classroom in heterogeneous schools as Rist (1973) has so ably documented.

It is important to remember that only recently has the ideal of education for equal opportunity been put forth as a public policy statement. It was long taken for granted that schools would have higher standards for affluent children, who were to be trained to become professionals and social leaders, and lower ones for children from working class homes, who were seen as needing no more training than necessary for blue-collar jobs. The assertion that children should not be differentiated from the start by their class and race backgrounds, but that schools should offer all children opportunity to realize and build on their individual interests and talents, is scarcely a half century old. A publicly stated admission that something should be done to realize the ideal of schooling as enabling equal opportunity dates from the post-World War II protest of the black community over segregated and unequal schooling.

The discrepancy between an ideal of education for equal opportunity and the structural reality whereby schooling keeps all but a handful of children in the socioeconomic category into which they were born, is not only a failing of schools in the United States; it is a world-wide pattern. Perhaps no one has commented more cogently and angrily on this pattern than Everett Reimer and Ivan Illich, who collaborated for a number of years in an exploratory seminar on education held in Cuernavaca, Mexico. In a seminar report, Reimer wrote, "Schools, we found, keep two thirds of the world's children out, and make early dropouts of most lower class children who manage to get in" (Reimer nd:1). The result, Reimer goes on to say, is more profound than differential access to the learning of skills. "A dropout from a general school system . . . has learned that the good things of his society are not for him—and probably also that *he does not deserve them*" (Reimer nd:4; italics his). Illich (1969) expands on the point, writing, "The higher the dose of schooling an individual has received, the more depressing his experience of withdrawal. The seventh-grade dropout feels his inferiority much more acutely than the dropout from the third grade" (p. 32). Illich's elaboration in relation to Third World countries is relevant for industrial nations as well:

> As the mind of a society is progressively schooled, step by step its individuals lose their sense that it might be possible to live without being inferior to others. As the majority shifts from the land into the city, the hereditary inferiority of the peon is replaced by the inferiority of the school dropout who is held personally responsible for his failure. Schools rationalize the divine origin of social stratification with much more rigor than churches have ever done. (p. 32)

All of this is not to excuse individual teachers who are either indifferent and sloppy or arrogant and punitive in their relations with poor and/or nonwhite pupils. Nor is it to suggest that such teachers should not be criticized and held accountable for their incompetence. It is rather to emphasize that the findings on teachers' differential behavior towards children of different backgrounds that I am about to review reflect, not the individual incompetence of a minority, but an institutional system of race and class bias that patterns the practices of the vast majority. The distinction has important implications for policy making and I shall consider these in closing.

THE CLASSROOM PROCESSES STUDY

In 1958, I embarked on a comparative study of urban classrooms along with colleagues mostly from the field of anthropology but also representing psychology and education. We studied a second and fifth grade classroom in each of four schools selected with respect to contrasts in income level and race of the student population: low income black, low income white, middle income black and middle income white. The study was part of a National Institutes of Mental Health project carried out by the Bank Street College of Education.

Study data included four and a half hours of detailed running records on classroom life; two extensive teacher interviews, one conducted before and one after the observations by a person who did not share in discussions of classroom data until the preliminary interview analysis was complete; and a brief interview with each child in the observed classrooms. The research team analyzed these data along qualitative as well as quantitative lines in order to define for comparison both formal (overt) and informal (covert) aspects of teacher attitudes and behavior, and to ascertain something of children's attitudinal responses.

The research team was looking for differences in the school experiences of low and middle income, black and white children, that would explain differences in their scholastic performance. In accord with one hypothesis being put forward at the time, we were expecting to find that a clash in values between teachers who represented "white middle class" or "mainstream" views and pupils from working class and/or black homes was alienating these children. However, we found that matter was not so simple. Systematic differences in teacher attitudes and practices startled us in the extent to which they were undermining already disadvantaged children. The primary "middle class value" we observed was hardly the motivation for success stressed in the literature, but a basic lack of respect for people who are poor and nonwhite coupled with the expectation that their children would not succeed.

As would be expected, the most extreme contrast in practices and attitudes was that between the black low income and the white middle income schools and it was clearer in the fifth than the second grades. The following figures on the black low income and the white middle income fifth grades show the lower number of teacher-initiated interactions with children concering curriculum and the greater number of negative evaluations their work received in a 3-hour period:

	Low Income Black	Middle Income White
Number of teacher remarks to individual children concerning curriculum:	82	174
Percentage relative to total number of teacher remarks:	44%	60%

	Low Income Black	Middle Income White
Average per child:	2.7	4.8
Evaluative statements to individual children regarding curriculum:		
Positive:	5	28
Negative:	15	21
Ratio positive to negative:	1:3	4:3
Evaluative statements to groups regarding curriculum:		
Positive:	0	5
Negative:	3	1

These figures cannot be explained in terms of behavioral problems that demanded the teacher's attention in the low income black classroom, for the children were cooperative and orderly during the observation periods. Neither can they be explained in terms of a greater number of child failures. Instead, in a number of instances children's correct answers in this classroom were evaluated negatively on trivial grounds, such as the failure to add a ¢ sign to the correct answer on an arithmetic example. Nor did the negativism expressed follow from simple racism, for the teacher was hard working and well meaning and was herself black. Instead they have to be understood as part of the overall pattern whereby the double-track structure of schools, in keeping with the employment structure of the society, exerts its influence on teachers by lowering their goals for working class black children.

Analysis of the teacher interviews revealed in quantitative terms the relatively negative affect with which working class and black children were regarded by their teachers. The teacher interview was designed to elicit information about individual children in the classroom, and those not mentioned in the first interview were inquired about in the second. All statements about specific children were collated and rated as positive, negative, or neutral in feeling tone (as distinguished from content—a teacher could refer to a child's problems either empathetically and positively or disparagingly and negatively). A sample was rerated separately to insure reliability. The percentages of statements that were negative for fifth-grade children in the four schools were as follows:[1]

	Black	White	Mean
Low Income 5th Grades	50%	30%	40%
Middle Income 5th Grades	36%	3%	20%
Mean	43%	17%	

[1]I am indebted to Robert Rosenthal (1974) for the form in which these figures from my study (Leacock 1969, pp. 194, 195, 198) are presented.

Carrying the analysis further, we looked at the average IQ scores of teacher-favored and disfavored children. Although IQ tests do not afford a measure of children's multifaceted abilities, they do yield an approximate index of school-oriented test-taking skills. Furthermore, the built-in cultural biases of IQ tests match those of the schools generally. Therefore, they are willy nilly fair predictors of children's future academic achievment in statistical terms (that is, they give probabilities for groups but not predictions for individuals, which is the good reason why their use in the records of individual children has been so heavily criticized). Examinations of the relation between positive teacher affect and IQ scores obtained from the school showed that, while high-scoring children were favored by the middle income white fifth-grade teacher, this was not the case for low income black children. The average scores were as follows:

	Negative Teacher Affect	Positive Teacher Affect	Difference
Middle Income White	112	123	+ 11
Middle Income Black	93	103	+ 10
Low Income White	99	97	− 2
Low Income Black	93	84	− 9

Again, the sharpest contrast was between the white middle income and the black lower income fifth grades, where the children had both class and color working for or against them. I have elsewhere documented in full some of the complex ways in which teacher expectations for success or failure were projected onto the children in these classrooms (Leacock 1969, 1970), so shall only summarize them here.

The experiences of working class and black children were virtually absent from school texts and materials, an absence that has since been but superficially and spottily corrected. The white teacher in the low income black second grade saw this as an asset—the suburban Dick and Jane family gave her charges a model to aspire to. Both she and the fifth-grade teacher in the low income black school failed to build on the life experiences of their students, but instead ignored or even denigrated them in classroom discussion. Nor were the children's lives or work more than perfunctorily honored on classroom walls. Epitomizing the difference between the black low income and the white middle income fifth grades in this respect was the posted list of free lunch children in the former in place of the list of class officers in the latter.

Both teachers referred to behavior primarily and work secondarily in their stated goals for teaching. However, the teacher of the low income black fifth grade defined behavior in terms of discipline, answering the question as to what kinds of things children should be getting out of school, ''First of all, discipline.

They should know that when an older person talks to them or gives a command that they should respond. . ." By contrast, the other teacher responded, "As I say to the children, the most important thing is to be able to get along with one another and to have acceptable standards of behavior. In other words to develop into a good human being. . ." The former teacher was clearly training the children for blue collar jobs structured along authoritarian lines. Students reporting on a project stood, reported, were questioned and evaluated by the teacher, sat down. There was no cross discussion. In comparison, in the middle income white classroom, student reporting was elaborately organized with a committee structure, a student chairing the session, and with questions and cross discussion from the class. The pattern of socialization was in keeping with the formal leadership and initiative expected in professional occupational settings.

As the research team reviewed these and other data, we saw how fully teacher goals and expectations for children's learning and behavior reflected the double-track structure of both schooling and employment. Children from low income black homes were not so much failing as being taught that they were failures. That children were resisting to some extent was evidenced by a further contrast between the white middle income and the black lower income fifth classrooms. In the former, there was a match among higher average IQ scores, higher average reading achievement, teacher favor, and child popularity as measured by a sociometric question in the child interview. In the latter classroom, this was not the case. Not only did the teacher not favor children with higher average IQ scores, but the higher scorers were not on the average the higher achievers, and higher IQ-lower achieving children were the most popular on the whole with other children. Detailed analysis, then, supported the view expressed in critical descriptions of the educational system, that the basis for the underachievement and rebelliousness of able children lies, not in a clash of values, but in the structure and content of schooling.

HARVEY'S STUDY OF THE DIFFERENTIAL TREATMENT OF SCHOOL CHILDREN

Using a carefully constructed quantitative research design, Mary Ruth Harvey (1972) studied teacher attitudes and behavior toward children differentiated by income and race. Harvey found teachers to be negative in their attitudes toward low income children, to criticize them more often than they did middle or high income children, to be more directive in teaching them, and to be prone to give them "negative feedback . . . for behaviors ordinarily regarded as appropriate" (p. 117). Noting that low achievement levels correlated with low income throughout grades 3–7, she wrote, "The treatments to which low-income children seem subject are predictive of school failure and seem able to account for the widening of school achievement differences between themselves and their high-income counterparts during the course of their elementary school years" (p. 158).

Harvey studied eight second grades, two low income black, two low income mixed black and white, one low income white, one middle income white, and two high income white. The Flanders Minnesota Interactional Analysis (1960), applied by classroom observers who were kept ignorant of the study hypotheses, revealed that teachers relied more upon criticism than praise in low-income classrooms, whereas the reverse obtained in high income classrooms (p. 84). The mean for praise and encouragement for low-income children was 2.51% and for high-income children 9.11% with little overlap between the ranges (from .09% to 6.47% for low-income classrooms and from 5.46% to 16.25% for high income).

Negativism toward low-income children obtained despite the fact that most of their teachers "had specifically chosen to work with low-income and minority children" (p. 106) in specially programmed schools. By comparison with the teachers in the middle- and high-income schools, they had more experience, more specialized training, better pay, smaller classroom sizes, more assistance from professional and paraprofessional paid and volunteer assistances, and upgraded facilities. However, they "revealed little belief in the ultimate academic capabilities of their pupils and/or in their pupils' chances for future school success" (p. 113). By contrast, teachers in middle and high income classrooms were generally optimistic and "mentioned fewer negative traits of their pupils, and specifically identified them as characteristic of but one or two children in their classrooms" (p. 114). Problems at home were specified with respect to particular children in upper income classrooms, but were generalized in low income classrooms, where teachers ascribed children's academic difficulties "to cognitive and social inadequacies which they attributed to the pupils' families and sub-culture" (p. 118).

Harvey's study documented the projection of teacher expectations upon pupils with respect to both curriculum and behavior. Using the Teacher Reinforcement Matrix, she found that teachers of low income children engaged in the "extraordinary practice of rewarding inappropriate and punishing appropriate classroom behaviors" (p. 101). The finding was so extreme, that Harvey tested and confirmed it in 13 additional classrooms in seven of the eight sample schools. Children in low income classrooms commonly received praise for "passive but inappropriate" behavior such as quiet non-attention, and negative response to "active and appropriate" behavior such as waving hands too enthusiastically, reading a story at home, or helping each other during independent work periods, all behaviors which were praised in high income classrooms. For example, a boy in a high income classroom "who had jumped in front of three others was praised for being first in line," while two children who were quietly helping each other during an independent work period in a low income classroom were told to "stop playing around" (pp. 96-7).

Teacher actions reflected their differential perceptions of children's behavior. Coded observations taken over an extented period of time "revealed few, if any, differences between the behaviors of low-income and high-income pupils," Harvey wrote. Nonetheless, "the teachers of low-income children perceived their pupils as more physically active and aggressive, less cooperative with one another, less attentive, less mature, and generally less socialized than their high-income counterparts" (p. 117). Teachers in low income classrooms frequently commented that their pupils were "hyperactive," "too active," "unable to sit still," "too mobile," etc. Harvey wrote:

> Pupil behavior data . . . for Whole Class, Small Group, and Independent Work situations do not bear out these perceptions of low-income children, yet every teacher in the low-income classrooms observed made reference to an inordinately high activity level among her pupils. Each saw this high activity level as a severe handicap to classroom learning and each indicated that she spent much time and effort attempting to control and minimize highly active, mobile behaviors. (pp. 113–114)

With respect to curriculum, teachers in low income classrooms stressed "language usage" by contrast with "creative writing" in high income classrooms. High income children had more and better science sessions. Since low income classrooms were more regimented and the children were allowed less autonomy, they spent no more than 20 minutes per day in pupil-led and participatory discussion sessions, by contrast with from 40 to 60 minutes a day for high income pupils. In short, the curriculum was "demanding, skills-oriented, (and) essentially monotonous." It was "largely devoid of stress upon Creative Writing, Artwork, Scientific experimentation, and particularly pupil-led activities," Harvey wrote, and "to whatever extent that these activities are relevant for academic progress and cognitive growth, low-income children were being prepared for other routes" (p. 118). Her findings, Harvey concluded, "seem clearly incongruent with a clinical view of school failure among the poor" (p. 158). Instead they suggest "that race, class and ethnic biases encouraged by educational institutions themselves teach teachers how to fail low-income children" (p. 161).

THE PYGMALION AND OTHER QUANTITATIVE STUDIES

While studies like Harvey's and mine documented the differentiation of teachers' expectations for and behavior toward children, the well known study of Rosenthal and Jacobson (1968) demonstrated the effect such differentiation can have on pupil performance. In the "Pygmalion" study, the researchers administered a largely nonverbal intelligence test to all children in a low income school consisting of three classes on each of six elementary grades. The test was disguised as predictive of inellectual "blooming," and the teachers were given the names of those children—some 20% of each class—that were supposedly likely to make remarkable gains during the course of the school year. The children were, however, randomly chosen; as Jacobson pointed out, "the difference between the experimental group and the control group . . . was in the mind of the teacher" (Rosenthal, 1974, p. 6). When retested at the end of the year, the experimental group had gained 4 points more in total IQ than had the control group, though mostly in reasoning (7 points) rather than verbal IQ (2 points).

The Rosenthal and Jacobson study has been widely criticized and the criticisms in turn rebutted (Rosenthal, 1974). More germane to the present discussion than a summary of arguments pro and con, however, is Rosenthal's review of other research that has demonstrated the reality of the self-fulfilling prophecy. Rosenthal's own inquiry into researcher effects on the observation of and/or behavior of rats predated his Pygmalion study, and he reviewed over a hundred other studies of human and animal behavior conducted in laboratory settings. Fifty seven additional studies were made in every day settings such as schools, offices, and factories. They pertained to adults as well as children and included effects of mentor attitudes on such wide ranging groups as girl offenders, children learning to swim, enlisted airmen learning mathematics, and disadvantaged workers learning on the job.

In some cases clear-cut differences in the sheer amount of teaching were noted. For example, one of the studies summarized by Rosenthal concerned the behavior of 60 teachers, each of whom was to teach the meaning of certain symbols to a child enrolled in a summer Headstart program (Beez, 1968). Half the teachers were led to expect the children to learn well while the other half were led to expect poor pupil performance. Seventy-seven percent of the children taught by the former learned five or more symbols by comparison with only 13% of those taught by the latter. The sheer amounts of teaching in the two situations, as observed by a researcher unaware of what each teacher had been told, were dramatically different. As summarized by Rosenthal, "Eight or more symbols were taught by 87% of the teachers expecting better performance, but only 13% of the teachers expecting poorer performance tried to teach that many symbols to their pupil" (1974, p. 8).

In both this and other studies, however, teacher expectations were projected onto learners through more than the sheer difference in amount taught. On the basis of his review, Rosenthal concluded that more effective teaching also involved the creation of "a warmer socio-emotional climate," "more differentiated feedback" on performance, and greater opportunities for response from students who were expected to succeed (1974, p. 15).

As an important factor mediating teacher behavior, Rosenthal found in the Pygmalion study that while teachers reported positive feelings towards the experimental children who gained during the year as they expected, they expressed negative feelings towards those children in the control group who also made good progress. When asked to describe the children, teachers described the former as significantly more interesting, curious, and happy,'' and to some extent as ''more appealing, adjusted, and affectionate.'' By contrast, ''the more the control group children gained in IQ the more they were regarded as less well-adjusted, as less interesting, and as less affectionate.'' Nor was this all. The negative affect was stronger if the successful children were in the slow track of a threefold grouping within each classroom. Furthermore, ''the greater their IQ gains, the more unfavorably they were rated, both as to mental health and as to intellectual vitality.'' In fact, slow track children in the experimental group expected to gain ''were not rated as favorably relative to their control group peers as were the children of the high or medium track'' (1974, pp. 11–12). Rosenthal wrote, such findings ''suggest rather strongly that there may indeed be hazards to a child showing unexpected intellectual potential or development'' (p. 13).

As a dramatic example of the negative effect race bias has on teacher expectations and behavior, Rosenthal summarized an experimental study by Rubovits and Maehr (1972). A group of white female undergraduates were asked to teach a lesson on television to groups of four junior high school students, two black and two white. One black and one white student in each group was reported to their prospective teacher as high scoring on an IQ test, or gifted; the other two were said to be low scoring, or nongifted. Observations of the teaching situations made by researchers unaware of these designations revealed that ''white children alleged to be gifted were praised two-and-a-half times for each criticism they were administered,'' while allegedly gifted black children ''were praised less than once for every three criticisms they were administered'' (1974, p. 13). The observation paralleled the findings of the Classroom Processes Study of negative teacher attitudes towards black low income children whose IQ scores on the average were higher than those of their peers.

ANYON'S QUALITATIVE COMPARISON OF FIVE SCHOOLS

An ethnographically oriented study of five schools by an anthropologist, Jean Anyon (1980, 1981) adds another dimension to the negativism and lowered goals that the Harvey and other studies show are experienced by working class and nonwhite school children. Anyon explored what is often called ''the hidden curriculum''—the content of what children are being taught about themselves, their work, and their society in the course of their school day. In the Classroom Processes Study we noted that contrasts in the ways work was structured in the middle and low income classrooms paralleled differences in the structure of work relations in middle and working class occupations. Anyon's study reveals similar types of contrasts, although analyzed and documented in far greater variety and specificity.

Anyon conducted her research in three schools in a northern New Jersey city and two in a nearby suburb. She spent 10 3-hour periods observing fifth-grade classrooms in each school; interviewed students, teachers, principals, and administrative staff members; and examined texts and other school materials. Her study focussed on the following dimensions: the nature and source of knowledge as defined both by the "hidden curriculum" and the "curriculum in use;" the definition of work and purpose of schooling; the use and functions of language; the handling of constraints and authority; and conceptions of the individual and of society.

The schools in Anyon's sample represent the full class range served by public schools. Two schools were working class; some of the children's fathers were relatively well paid skilled workers, but many were extremely poor, marginally employed, and living in deteriorated housing. The schools were 85% white. One school was "middle class," that is the children's parents included a mix of skilled workers, white collar workers, professionals and managers, and small store owners. One of the suburban schools was designated by Anyon as "affluent professional," and the other as "executive elite." Parents of children in the latter school were top executives in major corporations and financial firms with incomes ranging from $100,000 to $500,000. While from 10 to 15% of the children in the other schools were nonwhite, no minority children attended this school. On the basis of her comparative study, Anyon wrote:

> Differing curricular, pedagogical and pupil evaluation practices emphasize different cognitive and behavioral skills in each school setting, and thus contribute to the development in the children of certain potential relationships to physical and symbolic capital, to authority, and to the process of work. (1980, p. 90)

The curriculum in the working class schools was sparse and formal. Anyon noted that there was so little teaching that she had to increase her observation time in these schools in order to collect adequate data on teaching style. Work consisted in following mechanical procedures and involved little decision-making or choice. School knowledge amounted to "fragmented *facts,* isolated from context and connection to each other" as well as "knowledge of 'practical' rule-governed *behaviors*—procedures by which the students carry out tasks that are largely mechanical" (1981, p. 12, italics in the original). As an example of math teaching in terms of "often unexplained, fragmented procedures," a teacher led her students through the steps of making a one-inch grid without first telling the children what they were doing. When a child, catching on, volunteered that she had a faster way to do it, the teacher responded, "No, you don't; you don't even know what I'm making yet. Do it this way, or it's wrong" (1980, pg. 74). Another teacher, explaining his method of writing out on 3 × 5 cards the one or two science projects he assigned each year explained to Anyon, "It tells them exactly what to do, or they couldn't do it" (1980, p. 75).

Social studies also entailed mechanical rote work, such as copying a teacher's notes from the board. As in the Bank Street study, the curriculum content bore no relation to the children's own life experiences. The fifth grade focus for social studies was United States history, yet there was no reference to the working class and "its long history of dissert and struggle for economic dignity" (1981, p. 32).

Work in language arts was limited to teaching rules for capitalization and punctuation without discussion of their significance for a sentence's meaning. There was no creative writing. Assignments such as writing an "autobiography" involved answering questions duplicated on ditto sheets. As experienced by the children in the classroom, language was an instrument of control and belittlement. Only three times during the observation periods was a teacher order prefaced with an unsarcastic "please," "let's" or "would you."

In the middle-class school, knowledge was "less a matter of fact and skills and more a matter of traditional bodies of 'content.'" Such content was treated as a "possession," something of value that could be "accumulated and exchanged for good grades and college or a job... if one has 'enough' of it" (1981, p. 17). Teachers explained the content of the curriculum to the children, and elaborated on it, though they did not *analyse* it or call on the children to think creatively or critically about it. Language arts still dealt primarily with grammar, but also included an emphasis on learning how to "speak properly" and how to write business and social letters.

The affluent professional school stood in sharp contrast to the previous three. In this school, Anyon wrote, "Work is creative activity carried out independently. The students are continually asked to express and apply ideas and concepts. Work involves individual thought and expressiveness, expansion and illustration of ideas, and choice of appropriate method and material" (1980, p. 79).

Teachers and principals spoke of creativity, personal development, learning from experience, and learning to handle ideas as goals for the children in their charge while all four of the fifth-grade teachers in the working class schools simply referred to their students as dumb and lazy. One of these teachers stated her preference for teaching such children; it was easy compared to teaching in the district school for "gifted children" where one had to work hard and go in early every day. Another said she would never teach in the suburbs: "The parents there think their kids are God's gift. Although some parents *here* are beginning to think they have rights, too" (1981, p. 7, italics in the original).

In the affluent professional classrooms, the individuality of children's work and the value of their ideas was emphasized and their own evaluation of their work was treated as important. The children were involved in a great many projects; they discussed news events, produced editorials, radio plays, and the like, and had ample room for self-expression in creative writing. Punctuation was taught in relation to how it affected meaning. Control was constantly negotiated; direct orders were used only as a last resort when classes became too noisy.

Knowledge in this school was not treated as a "given" but as conceptual, analytical, and "open to discovery, construction and meaning-making" (1981, p. 23). Knowledge has personal value and can also be used as "a resource for social good" (1981, p. 23). In a brief child interview, Anyon asked, "Can you make knowledge?" and it was only in the affluent professional school that the children predominantly answered yes (1981, pp. 10, 16, 21, 29):

	Yes	No	DK or other
Working class schools	1	15	4
Middle class school	11	9	0
Affluent professional	16	4	0
Executive elite	10	9	1 "That's a ridiculous question"

In the executive elite school, knowledge was "academic, intellectual, and rigorous." The children were taught more difficult concepts than in any other school, and there was an emphasis on rationality, on reasoning, and on "understanding the internal structure of things: the logic by which systems of numbers, words, or ideas are arranged and may be re-arranged" (1981, p. 31). In response to the question as to what knowledge is, children in this school spoke less of creative independent thinking than in the affluent professional school, and more of "the need to know *existing* knowledge, and to do well; to understand, explain, and answer correctly (and quickly)" (1981, p. 29, italics in the original).

Anyon wrote that the executive elite school offered "cultural capital" to children:

> ... whose families as a class have the major portion of available physical capital in society. These children are taught the history of "ruling" groups, and that rule by the wealthy and aristocratic is *rational,* and natural—going back, for example, to the Ancient Greeks. Such knowledge is, for them, symbolic capital. They are provided with other kinds of symbolic capital as well: practice in manipulating socially prestigious language and concepts in systematic ways. They are told the importance of controlling ideas, and given some insight into controlling ideas in their own (Western) culture (1981, p. 37, italics in the original).

Work in this school was "developing ones analytical intellectual powers." Children were asked to reason through problems and "to conceptualize rules by which elements may fit together in systems" (1980, p. 83). They were encouraged to check each others work, to evaluate, and to disagree. Social studies involved independent research and children were asked to make up their own questions. Language arts emphasized language as a complex system to be mastered, and research reports and essays, rather than creative writing, were stressed. Children received training for management situations; in one instance a teacher told a pupil who was acting as student teacher, "When you're up there, you have authority, and you have to use it. I'll back you up" (1980, p. 86).

Teachers treated the children politely, always addressing them by name rather than as "honey" or "dear," and they expected to be available to the children before or after school hours as needed. Themselves from middle and upper middle class backgrounds, the teachers spoke with respect of their pupils' families as successful, as having "breeding," as at the top, as running the town. Said one teacher of her pupils, "They'll go to the best schools, and we have to prepare them" (1981, p. 31). Said another, "These children's opinions are important—it is important that they learn to reason things through" (1980, p. 84). For their part, the children were under enormous pressure to excell; "Although highly privileged, many of these children are working *very* hard to keep what they have" (1981, p. 31, italics in the original).

In sum, Anyon's study revealed ways in which fifth-grade children in the two working class schools she observed were being socialized for mechanical and routine labor; in the middle class school for white-collar bureauocratic jobs— "the paper work, the technical work, the sales and social service in the private and state bureauocracies"; in the affluent professional school for artistic, intellectual, legal, and scientific achievement; and in the executive elite school for ownership of and control over the means of production in society. "The foregoing analysis of differences in school work in contrasting social class contexts suggests the following conclusion," Anyon wrote, "the 'hidden curriculum' of school work is tacit preparation for relating to the process of production in a particular way (1980, pp. 89–90).

CONCLUSION

Further studies could be cited to show ways in which low expectations for poor and minority children are embedded in teaching styles and classroom management practices attuned to replicating existing class relations in our society, rather than to educating for equal opportunity. For example, R. Timothy Sieber, who studied a public school and two parochial schools in an economically and ethnically heterogeneous neighborhood wrote of "the school's dual functions as an organization that at once educates children formally through instruction in 'the three R's,' and socializes them informally in the basic modes of behavior appropriate to bureaucratic settings" (1979, p. 274). Paralleling Anyon's findings, Sieber documented a marked contrast between the standardized work assignments most children were receiving in the public school, and the high degree of "individual autonomy and leadership" children of professionals and managers in the private Episcopal school and the "top" classes in the public school were allowed. Sieber (1978) wrote:

> While the basic features of bureaucratic behavior are learned by these children, the heightened emphasis on individual autonomy, initiative, "creativity," and leadership, and the provision for expression of these traits in classroom life, well prepare the children to assume roles at the higher levels of bureaucratic organizations—as managers, professionals, and leaders. (p. 92)

Furthermore, as Reimer and Illich stated and as Carnoy (1974) and Ogbu (1978) have described, the pattern is international. Consistent variations in schooling for upper and lower class children enable the former to maintain their class status and prevent the latter from acquiring the skills necessary for achieving upward mobility.

These are hard facts to face for educators, parents, and community groups who wish to improve the quality of schooling for working class and minority children. Indeed, the very documentation of the consistency with which education is differentiated for children of different classes might encourage defeatism and apathy rather than invoking anger and resistance. Apple, who has himself contributed to such documentation (1979), has pointed out that "overly deterministic and economistic accounts of the hidden curriculum are themselves elements of the subtle reproduction, at an ideological level, of perspectives required for the legitimation of inequality" (1980-81, p. 8).

Apple's enormously important point is one that has bothered me considerably. Researchers have the responsibility of making their studies meaningful and useful. Apple stresses the need for researchers to give attention to ways in which teachers and students resist conformity with the system of which they are a part. To carry this line of thought further, I would say it is critical for researchers to analyze and describe the struggles that have taken place around schools and the results of organized actions. Analyses of the New York City battle for community control of schools afford excellent examples (Fuchs, 1966; Rubinstein, 1970). It is also important to supply those teachers who are dedicated to overcoming the limits of their situation with material on successfully innovative teaching. A wide range of examples is available. For instance, in 1965, Janet Castro (1971) became intensely interested in using children's games in her classroom, thereby changing her role from one of "enriching" culturally deprived children to one in which she became "the eager listener" and the children became "the eager communicators" (p. 84). A decade later "Innovative Project Amsterdam" got underway in the Netherlands (Kandell, 1978). As the result of an alternative school set up by a few individuals, some 80 schools in working class neighborhoods became involved in a program whereby lessons were matched to everyday life and the children's flow of language was not constantly being corrected, and where reading and writing levels were raised and fewer children fell behind. Such instances of success too often get noted and buried, as embarrassing examples of how possible it is to teach poor children when the effort is made. Instead they should be searched out, reviewed, and made available.

Parents and community groups, teachers and administrators, and students themselves, at various times and places, continue to work or fight for equal educational opportunity, and the better informed their efforts are, the more effective they can be. Study findings such as those I have cited make clear why innovations in teaching techniques make so little difference unless they tackle the basic questions of curriculum content in relation to children's life experiences and interests, and teacher respect for these experiences and interests. They indicate that administrative attempts to introduce reforms have to take into account the structure of a school district—are children in inferior schools literally being held back because there is no decent intermediate or high school for them to attend, hence no pressure on teachers to prepare them for one? The study findings also show why attempts to reach parents fail so often, for they are fundamentally authoritarian and patronizing. And they reveal for parent groups the necessity of linking battles around specific teachers, principals, or schools with parallel fights in other school districts, and with other community groups that are fighting on the larger issue of job discrimination.

In discussing student resistance to accepting negative teacher attitudes, Apple (1980–81) cites Gramsci's statement that we are engaging in a war on many fronts and continues. "And each of these fronts—including the struggle over culture and education, . . . is essential if we are to create more non-exploitative social and economic relations" (p. 17). Studies of the intricate relations among teacher attitudes, children's performance, and the structure of schools within the larger society, if they are to be useful, should focus more clearly than they now do on sources for change.

REFERENCES

Anyon, J. Social Class the Hidden Curriculum of Work, *Journal of Education*, Vol. 162, No. 1, Winter 1980, pp. 67–92.

Anyon, J. Social Class and School Knowledge, *Curriculum Inquiry*, Vol. II, No. 1, February 1981, pp. 3–42.

Apple, M. W. The Other Side of the Hidden Curriculum: Correspondence Theories and the Labor Process, *Interchange*, Vol. II, No. 3, 1980–81, pp. 5–22.

Beez, W. F. Influence of Biased Psychological Reports on Teacher Behavior and Pupil Performance, *Proceedings of the 76th Annual Convention of the American Psychological Association*, 1968, pp. 605–606.

Bowles, S., & Gintis, H. *Schooling in Capitalist Society: Educational Reform and the Contradictions of Economic Life*. New York: Basic Books, 1976.

Carew, J. V., & Lightfoot, S. L. *Beyond Bias, Perspectives on Classrooms*. Cambridge, Mass.: Harvard University Press, 1979.

Carnoy, M. *Education as Cultural Imperialism*. New York: David McKay, 1974.

Castro, J. Untapped Verbal Fluency of Black School children, in Eleanor Leacock, Ed. *The Culture of Poverty: A Critique*, New York: Simon and Schuster, 1971.

Fuchs, E. Pickets at the Gates. New York: Free Press, 1966.

Harvey, M. R. *Differential Treatment of Upper-Income and Lower-Income Children by the Public Schools*. Unpublished dissertation, University of Oregon, 1972.

Illich, I. Outwitting the 'Developed' Countires, *New York Review of Books*, Nov. 6, 1969, p. 32.

Kandell, J. Dutch School Uses Working-Class Speech to Help Pupils, *New York Times*, May 9, 1978, p. 2.

Leacock, E. *Teaching and Learning in City Schools*. New York: Basic Books, 1969.

Leacock, E. Education, Socialization, and 'The Culture of Poverty,' in Annette T. Rubinstein, Ed.

Schools Against Children: The Case for Community Control. New York: Monthly Review Press, 1970.

Leacock, E. At Paly in African Villages, *Natural History Magazine,* Dec., 1972, pp. 60–65.

Ogbu, J. U. *Minority Education and Caste: The American System in Cross-Cultural Perspective.* New York: Academic Press, 1978.

Pedersen, E., Faucher, T. A., & Eaton, W. W. A New Perspective on the Effects of First-Grade Teachers on Children's Subsequent Adult Status, *Harvard Educational Review,* Vol. 48, No. 1, February 1978, pp. 1–31.

Reimer, E. *Second Annual Report of the Seminar on Alternatives in Education.* Cuernavaca, Mexico: Centro Intercultural de Documentacion, Doc. 69.167, n.d.

Rist, R. C. *The Urban School: A Factory for Failure.* Cambridge, Mass.: MIT Press, 1973.

Rosenthal, R. *On the Social Psychology of the Self-Fulfilling Prophecy: Further Evidence for Pygmalion Effects and their Mediating Mechanisms,* MSS Modular Publication #53, 1974.

Rosenthal, R. & Jacobson, L. *Pygmalion in the Classroom.* New York: Holt, Rinehart and Winston, 1968.

Rubinstein, A. T., Ed. *Schools Against Children: The Case for Community Control.* New York: Monthly Review Press, 1970.

Rubovits, P. C., & Maehr, M. "The Effects of the Labels 'Gifted' and 'Nongifted' on Teachers' Interaction with Black and White Students, Unpublished ms., University of Illinois, 1972.

Sieber, R. T. Schooling, Socialization, and Group Boundaries: A Study of Informal Social Relations in the Public Domain. *Urban Anthropology,* Vol. 7, No. 1, 1978, pp. 67–98.

Sieber, R. T. Schoolrooms, Pupils and Rules: The Role of Informality in Bureaucratic Socialization. *Human Organization,* Vol. 38, No. 3, 1979, pp. 273–282.

3 A Performance Theory of Peer Relations

Brian Sutton-Smith
University of Pennsylvania

INTRODUCTION

My approach to children's social relations has been through my own research in their play and games. I find therefore a considerable contrast between the ideas that I have about children's social life and those which are typical in "socialization" theory. For me, child social life is a rambunctious, difficult, intense, and dramatic pursuit of mutual peer excitement as this is to be found in traditional past-times, opportunities afforded by the ecology, by toys or by the recreational opportunities organized by adults. This leads me in this chapter first to set down what seem to me some of the contrasting and prevailing notions in more "orthodox" socialization research, and then to move on to an alternative view of peer relations based on what we know of the way children "perform" when together in play and games. I will take the unorthodox position that because children choose to spend as much as possible of their free social time in play and games that, therefore, this should be the primary kind of understanding that we seek to have about them.

Orthodox Socialization Assumptions

The overarching assumption of educators and child psychologists for the past 100 years has been that children learn in diverse ways, and that their learning can be organized for the good of society. In the 19th century most emphasis was placed

Paper delivered at the Conference, "The Socialization of Children in a Changing Society." University of Cincinnati, April 26–28, 1979.

on what the schools would do for children's character and enlightenment. In this century, more emphasis has been given to the importance of organized leisure, games and sports, and since the 1920's there has been a focus on the values of peer interactions, although one notes here a puzzled ambivalence about the virtues and vices of peers as socializing agents. One has to take as the basic economic nexus in the 18th and 19th centuries the shift from a family based economy to a factory based economy, the displacement of the father from the home and the increased importance given to mothering. At the same time there arose the problem of unapprenticed youth roaming the streets in large numbers. According to Katz (1975), when about 50% were on the loose, a public school was likely. As most of those arguing about schools in those days were in favor of some sectarian form or other, the emergence of public schools was something of a miracle, except perhaps that the fear of urchins was greater than the fear of God! (Sutton-Smith, 1981). According to Cavallo (1981), the late 19th century was a time for reconceptualizing the character of children. Hitherto the child had been defined in largely moral or occupational terms. He or she was now defined in terms of stages in development, with physical development having priority in the evolutionary sense. Although Hall (recapitulation), Baldwin (imitation), Dewey (instrumental action) and Thorndike (reward) disagreed (as indicated) about which processes they thought most important in child development, they all agreed that peer relations, particularly in team sports, were central. Their themes were taken up by the leaders of the playground and recreation movements and between 1900 and 1920, a hundred million dollars was spent on playgrounds for children. What psychologists and playground enthusiasts (Gulick, Lee, Curtis) had in common was the belief that through their own advocacies civilization could be saved from the anarchy and unamericanism of the street children. *Child saving* was a dominant note of the time. I think it is fair to argue that ever since a major concern of 20th century thinking about peer relations has been in such child saving. There is not much difference in emphasis between the 1900 statement of Jane Adams that "organized sports . . . will be the only agency powerful enough to break the cycle of crime and poverty in slum worlds" (Cavallo, 1981, p. 59), and the more recent statement of Campbell (1964) that "Peer relations in childhood can be a major force in delinquency rehabilitation or can be used to alter the motivational structure of secondary education" (p. 317).

Thus, although modern attention is to the intricacies of the peer group, their roles, their cohesiveness, popularity, attachment, aggression, friendships, cooperation, etc., these structural concerns are usually combined with a concern for function in an adultcentric sense. That is, it continues to be asked what the distinctive socializing function of the peer group may be? How does it compare with the family? How does it operate differently across different societies? Socialization in this theoretical context means into the group itself or into the kinds of values and controls of which the larger society approves. What we have is another example of the structural-functional analyses that have dominated anthropology until recently. As has been said many times this was a sociologically conservative theoretical stance. It took for granted the social structure as found and asked only how it was maintained and furthered. It did not question the social order, nor did it imply the possibility that social regulation might be inherently a more chaotic, perhaps dialectical process (Murphy, 1971). The essentially child saving point of view is illustrated in the continuing reviews of this field by W. W. Hartup, in which he sets forth values of peerhood for society. For example, from *Children and Their Friends* (Hartup, in press):

(*a*) *What is a peer?*

All in all the existing data show that social behavior in same and mixed age conditions is not identical, and that social adaptation is facilitated by both the same age and mixed age interaction. (p. 7)

(*b*) *What is the importance of peer relations?*

The evidence suggests that whenever give and take (i.e., reciprocity) is an essential element in a social skill, peer relations contribute to social competence. Reciprocal elements in peer interaction would seem to underlie both aggressive and sexual socialization, as well as the socialization of moral values. (p. 15)

(*c*) What is the developmental course of these (benign) groups?

The current literature suggests that the development of peer relations proceeds from simple organizations to complex hierarchies, from loosely differentiated interchanges to differentiated interaction, and from primitive awareness of the needs of others to reciprocal relations based on complex attributions. (p. 27)

(*d*) *What are friends?*

Considerable agreement exists in the literature on children's descriptions of their friends: with age, increases occur in the number of interpersonal constructs used, the flexibility and precision with which they are used, the complexity and organization of information and the ideas about one's friends, the level of analysis used in interpreting the behavior of other individuals and the recognition of certain attributes as characteristic of friends. (p. 37).

(*e*) *Conclusion*

Social competence derives from children's interactions with other children. Both social skills and emotional effectance are acquired within these contexts.

While Hartup is appropriately modest about the surety provided by research, the major focus of this field, as he represents it, is on the way in which the peers make their own distinctive contribution to the social regulation of the body politic.

The *implicit epistemology* of this area of research then is structural-functional; that is, the virtues and contributions of the research focus (peer interactions) to the social order. This is not irrelevant or worthless, but it is limited.

WHAT ALTERNATIVES DO WE HAVE?

The Child's View

The big shift in anthropology, of course, has been to consider the epistemology of the natives. How do they see the matter? In the present case this would mean an attempt to penetrate the life view of the peers. Unfortunately the life views of peers under the age of 7 years are not very explicit even to themselves. Asking questions is simply not enough. Even Piagetian "clinical" questions founder on the strangeness of the investigators to the children who are the subjects (Gelman, 1978). And in psychology in general, subjective reports, while critically important in clinical work, do not seem to have been very powerful research predictors when compared with performance indicators.

With children and their peer interactions, however, we are vouchsafed another method. Since children give the greater part of their own free time together to play and games, it would seem that focusing on those might give us a new and privileged access to what their world means to themselves. We all acknowledge the virtue of the contributions of the folklorists Newall, Gomme, Douglas, Howard and the Opies to our sense of the child's world, but then having commented on the anecdotal character of their methods we usually pass on to higher things. Perhaps we should rather try to do it better. Perhaps we should take it seriously that children spend most of their time in those activities. We might reasonably infer that the most important thing to know about peer culture is what is going on there. That is, that we might learn more of structure and more of function if we first studied *what the action is*. And perhaps if we began with the performances that are central to children, our ideas of structure and function might also change considerably. We might even be less adultcentric and conservative in the way we are going about this matter.

Still, we also know there is no privileged access to anything. The desire to study how children perform together in their play is merely a preliminary aspiration. We always approach them from some perspective or other. To imagine we can merely document their world is, as Bateson (1979), has said recently, an epistemological funk hole.

Our Own View

The choice that will be made here is to use a variety of theories of children's play as if they are each partial models of child behavior. In this way we pay heed to those who have been most concerned to discuss children's playful performances, as well as bring our leading assumptions into the foreground.

In our view there are four major kinds of play theory of current importance. There are those theories which discuss play largely:

(*a*) in terms of COMMUNICATION;
(*b*) in terms of STRUCTURE (cognitive);
(*c*) in terms of MODULATION (affective);
(*d*) in terms of CONTROLS (conative)
(*e*) and there is discussion of the FUNCTIONS of these processes.

A. Play as Communication   Here play is viewed as a kind of message or communication, and the assumption is made that by so doing we are learning most centrally about peer interactions. There are various levels of discussion.

In its larger sense this is the view that play is a kind of interpretation or "reading" that a society provides to itself. The "messages" that are given, of course, vary with the society, but the implication is that in play "deeper" or "antithetical" or "supportive" clarity and connotations about cultural norms are conveyed. It seems probable that only in play can some of the ambiguities of human relationships be communicated. When my young daughter urges me to play with her while I am reading the newspaper, I convert quickly to a caricatural Frankenstein, pursuing her while she eludes me with shrieking delight. My irritation at being disturbed, and my affection for her are both transmogrified and synthesized in the hyperbolic Mr. Frankenstein. The hyperbole for its own part says to my daughter that the matters of ambiguity are under control and that this representation is in no way to be confused with the original (Sutton-Smith, 1978b). The line of development of this interpretation of play includes Bateson (1972), Geertz (1976), Turner (1974) and Goffman (1974), and in children's play, Kirshenblatt-Gimblett (1976), Garvey (1977) and Schwartzman (1979). Some modern interpretations of sports are almost entirely in these terms (Loy, McPherson, & Kenyon, 1978).

In this kind of thinking, play is not distinct from reality, but as a communication about ordinary life, in combination with that ordinary life, it constitutes reality. Play then is a kind of work of communication. As Garvey (1977) says, "playing is saying," or as Schwartzman (1979) puts it, "play is an orientation or framing and defining context that players adopt towards something (an object, a person, a role, an activity, an event, etc.) which produces a text characterized by allusion . . . transformation . . . and purported imitation" (p. 330). We look at children's play in these terms to see what they are saying about the society in which they live and to see how they are reconstituting it as their own kind of generative grammar of cultural happenings.

Because of the special character of these framed worlds, much of the early childhood years will be given over to distinctions between the literal and the pretend. In her interesting analysis of this problem, Garvey illustrates the way in which 3-year-old children develop these differentiations through various negations of identity ("I am not a dragon anymore"), imaginary objects ("I don't see any cookies"), object transformations ("I stole your cake." "I don't care. It's not a cake anymore.''), and so on. If one pursues a social definitionist vein of thought (as in Goffman, 1974), it is possible to argue that the only difference between these earlier kinds of play framing and later adult kinds of a more "serious" character is the scale and scope of the construction. The children's micro constructions are seen as only pretense by adults. The macro constructions of games and sports are taken somewhat more portentously. And the cosmic constructions of ideology and religion are seen as ultimate meanings without which none of the rest make any sense. Other people's religions or ideologies are, of course, often denigrated as mere "fairy tales," mere "child's play" (Sutton-Smith, 1979a).

2. Investigators who consider play as an interpretation of society are usually also much involved in the nature of the communications, especially the *negotiations* that take place prior to and within play. It appears that negotiating is relatively more important the younger the group and the less well known they are to each other. The longer children have played together the less time must be given to negotiating roles, territories, etc. Garvey's work, which is especially good in this connection, perhaps overemphasizes these kinds of communications because of the relative strangeness of the experimental situation and the other experimental subject to the children. Corsaro (1978) has shown that the children he studied from 2 to 4 years were able to enter their well established play groups at the nursery school nonverbally or simply by producing a variant of ongoing behavior about two-thirds of the time. Negotiation was not obvious, though of course communication or signals were involved.

3. Still, when play is underway, *communications about play procedure* continue to be important, and Schwartzman (1979) has attempted to formulate these as formation statements ("Let's play house"), connection statements ("Can I play with you?"), acceptance statements ("OK, I am eating it"), counterdefinition statements ("I am not a baby"), maintenance statements (pretending that hurt is part of the play), reformulations ("Let's play babies"). At the earliest age, 1 to 2 years, the communications that permit progress are more implicit and involve such actions as mutual involvement with objects (Mueller & Vandell, 1979), turn-alternatives, successive repetitions (Hays & Ross, 1979), etc.

4. Sometimes negotiations and communications are *foregrounded* as the substance of the play, rather than its context. The struggle to present an interpretation of reality in order to get the action going can itself become the performance. So there are verbal contests, insult matches, etc. The work of Schlomo Ariel (1979) shows there are both cultural and individual differences in the use of this negotiational play with negotiators being better at make-believe and cognitive performances (as contrasted with block builders, who are more figurative and evaluative in style). Claire Farrer (1981), under the title of "Contesting," gives a vivid example of this kind of foregrounded power play.

5. There is evidence that boys and girls develop distinctive *patterns of negotiation*. Perhaps we can call these sex role negotiational structures. Savasta

and I (1979) discovered that 2- and 3-year-old girls more often used inclusion-exclusion techniques to get their way in play, and that boys more often used strategy, physical power and arbitrary command, and that in addition boys spend more of their voluntary time in such tactical battles. Reading the work of Freedman (1974), etc., makes it appear probable that this sex difference reflects a traditional distinction between a primary and intimate group orientation as compared with a secondary and impersonal group orientation. Putting it anecdotally, we might say that it is difficult to get into a girls' group but nice once you are in, and that it is easy to get into a boys' group (they always need an outfielder), but that it doesn't do you much good unless you are also skillful. You still have to make out at bat. Lever (1976) has made the case that the difference between girls' and boys' play underlies the differences between men and women in political education. She contrasts boys' endless arguing but not giving up the game, with girls who quickly withdraw when challenged. Some current analyses of women at work make similar comparisons (Sutton-Smith, 1979b). However, we should not move too quickly to such easy distinctions. A recent intensive analysis of the game of "Redlight" by Christine A. von Glascoe (1978) leads to the following analysis:

> When disputes arise between director and other players, the game of "redlight" . . . stops. A second game, which concerns dispute settlement, is substituted in its place. This interior game I refer to as "Redlight II." The substantive nature of these disputes addresses the question of whether or not the director observed some player to move during the "no-go" condition. A surprising order of philosophical inquiry emerges in the course of such debates. Arguments are grounded in terms of player-members' doctrines about intentional acts, unconscious acts, "accidental" acts, goal-directedness of acts, and fate-determined acts. A summary of directors' arguments is expressed in the following paradigm: I saw you move, and your move was intentional and goal-oriented, therefore you must return to the start line. A summary of the player's response would be: I didn't move, and if I did it wasn't goal-directed, and if it was goal-directed it wasn't intentional, and if it was goal-directed and intentional, you didn't see me. (p. 3)

This looks like good legal education at the very least. The point we are making is that there are networks of negotiation and patterns of communication which characterize children's peer groups. Furthermore, these societies seek to protect their fragile stability by various in-group and out-group practices such as jeering, insults, joking pranks, scapegoating, and so on, a series of folk kinds of behaviors currently being described in this new way as forms of impression management by Gary Fine (1978).

The communication theorists thus open up to us vistas of peer group communication networks of considerable intricacy. There is much formulating of social meaning afoot, and it is rather over simplified to discuss this kind of data as is often done currently simply as the socialization of aggression. More is lost than gained by this kind of reductionism. What we need to know are the range of negotiational structures and foregroundings. When do they function as "deep play" in Geertz's sense, and when as forms of normative conventional socialization. As play often exploits the boundaries of ordinary behavior and conformity, we need to understand its own peculiar dialectic between innovation and imitation. What are we to do, for example, about sex talk and fartlore? Are we to save the children from these, and if not, what is it about child socialization that we need to understand in order to understand these matters?

B. Play as Structure. Here we deal with the fact that as well as the metalanguage of play (that having to do with the relationships between the players) there is also an object language of play (Guilmette & Duthie, 1979). The players suggest to each other an interpretation of reality and society, and then proceed to play according to the dramas inherent in the text that has been suggested. Thus they attack, or chase, or escape, or kiss, or construct, or buy or sell. There seems at present some tendency in the literature to "reduce" these inherent dramas to the communicational structures that have been described above (Garvey, 1977; Schwartzman, 1979). But in establishing that social play cannot be thought about easily apart from communicational phenomena, it is not necessary therefore to reduce its "object" language upwards to the metalanguage. There seems no more sense in that than there is in going the other way and reducing play to kinds of arousal phenomena, which is another popular trend in the other direction (Ellis, 1974).

In looking at the play structures which children acquire from folk tradition or build through their own activity, there are two alternative kinds of interpretation. It is a current vogue to show just how flexible, facile, and paradoxical players can be in their structures, their joking and their confusions of metalanguage and object language levels ("I wouldn't want to be a member of any society that would have me"—Groucho). In 19th century anthropology it was the habit to see children's play constructions as strictly imitative. Whether this was due to the prevailing functionalist climate, the maleness of the anthropologists (Schwartzman, 1979), or to the character of tribal (as compared to urban) play, is uncertain. What we can say is that play theorists vary in their ideas about play structure along a continuum which emphasizes play's TEMPLATE characteristics at one end or its TRANSFORMATIONAL characteristics at the other.

The current vogue is seen in the Titles of recent books on play: *Playfulness* by Nina Lieberman (1977), *Transformations* by Helen Schwartzman (1979), and *The Childs World of Make Believe* by Jerome Singer (1973). But just as there are realistic novels (Dickens, Hugo), so there are novels of a transformational character (Nabokov, Barth, etc), which warns us that both kinds of structure probably exist. What we do here is suggest that children interact as peers in order to share and participate in certain templates or transformations (or combinations of both) of society.

1. Templates. The ways in which children copy their society are multiple. In the first place they borrow the social forms of play from interactions with nurtur- and persons. Play involves actor and counter-actor, and often also a director and an audience. We have presented the position elsewhere that there may be sex differences in the ready acquisition of these roles, with girls being earlier at acquiring the director and audience roles than boys because of their more easy imitation of the mother (Sutton-Smith, 1979b). Bruner and Sherwood (1976) have traced some of the steps in the acquisition of these roles for the game of peek-a-boo. Schwartzman (1979) has suggested that one can see in the forms of preschool children's play their taking over basic kinds of interactional structure such as symmetrical dyads, assymetrical dyads, symmetrical groups, assymmetrical groups, etc. At the childhood level we have in turn sought to trace group play structures in terms of primary, secondary and tertiary communications, in terms of role reversals, role and action reversals, internal and external group coordinations, etc. (Sutton-Smith, 1976). Or if one focuses on kinds of ludic action rather than on social structure, the argument can be made that play and games incorporate basic dialectics of order and disorder, approach and avoidance, acceptance-rejection, accumulation-deprivation, achievement-failure (Sutton-Smith, 1978a). Again one can focus on spatial or temporal aspects and trace similar lines of development (Herron & Sutton-Smith, 1971).

2. Transformations. There are times and places, however, where we are more impressed with the transformations wrought in play that with their generative mimesis. There are many kinds of transformations and their full study would include at least the following reversals: (a) from ordinary to make believe reality; (b) of social control; (c) of power tactics, (d) of identity; (e) of fate, (f) of rules; (g) of expectancies, etc., along with various other kinds of transformations of boundaries, time and space, action and identity (see Redl, Gump, & Sutton-Smith, 1971, for the listing of possibilities). Nowhere in the literature do we get a sense of the individual or group profiles for this template-transformational array of performances that are available and used in peer interaction, either at different age levels or across the same age level.

C. Play as Arousal Modulation. Here we come into more conventional psychological territory. By and large the implicit (if here conjoined) play paradigm for most psychologists has been that it is an activity of a solitary individual responding to the stimulus characteristics of objects and suffering an arousal in response level with outcomes variously defined as pleasurable, masterful, or creative. Whether we attend to the arousal school (Berlyne, 1960; Ellis, 1974; Schultz, 1979; Hutt, 1979), the ego psychological group (Singer, 1973) or the phenomenology of Csikszentmihalyi (1979a), we are in all cases talking about some kind of affect whether on neurological or experiential levels. There is the basic notion that the players in their performance are concerned with the modulation of excitement, and that this is the heart of why the peers interact together. Here they can gain a "flow" or vivification of experience that is not available elsewhere.

The problem here is that the play performances seem to have a duality that has not been clearly sorted out. Solitary play appears mostly to have an idling, peripheral attending, variable heart rate character (Hutt, 1979). Perhaps much parallel play does also. But contests and games on the other hand have the constant problem-solving kind of heart rate characteristic of "flow" (Csikszentmihalyi 1979a). What are the kinds and varieties of such experience that peers seek across age levels, we might ask? How are their peer interactions geared to obtaining and maintaining these? How does the structural character change from arousal to anticipating to crescendo to climax in the different domains? Are there biphasic rhythms as Ellis asserts? Or patterns of euphoria and dysphoria, as suggested by Goffman?

Certainly a very strong case could be made that peers come together for these kinds of arousal. They come together to be where the action is, and this is the major reason for peer interactions in the first place. The commmunications that are necessary to keep the excitement alive, the structures that are necessary to make it live, could all be regarded as subsidiary to these climactic ends. Though wisdom would suggest that individuals probably vary in the emphasis they place and the satisfaction they derive from the different kinds of play dimensions. From this point of view socialization is not the end of play, but pleasure is.

D. Play as Autonomy and Control. In many play theories the dialectic between control and freedom is the critical one emphasized to express this meaning. We are familiar with the concepts: from passive to active (Freud,), autotelia (O. K. Morre) and leeway (Erikson), while Mihaly Csikszentimihalyi (1979b) has recently taken the position that play is the awareness of choices; it is a restructuring of reality (not simply an adaptation to it); it is an awareness of alternatives. Play hinges on the awareness of the difference between actual and possible rules, he says. We have ourselves talked of play as the envisagement of possibility and adaptive potentiation.

This perspective leads one to analyze play and therefore peer performances for the kinds of competences to which they give children access. The question is what controls do you get by playing which you do not get when not playing? Obviously there are controls over skill (physical and symbolic) to which motor learning theory is most relevant. But there are also controls over levels, of commitment to action (idling versus intensive), over one's own variability and flexibility, or the lack of it. There is control over time pressure, over the amount of novelty that one wishes to engage. There is even control over how much one wishes to risk (whether a deep or shallow play). And controls, too, over space, secret, private or public. All the major modes of human motivation, with respect to action, interaction, agencies, time and space can be here explored as expressive of control and autonomy.

CONCLUSION

We have suggested that to look at peer interaction in terms of socialization into adult ways, while it has historical roots, perhaps misses a full understanding of what peer interaction is really about. It is suggested instead that peers get together mainly to play, and that, therefore, the analysis of play may tell us more of their motivation and the meaning of peer interaction than other kinds of approaches. To this end we have examined four major kinds of play theory: play theory which emphasizes the role of communication in play (after Bateson); play theory which emphasizes the role of cognition (after Piaget); play theory which emphasizes the role of affect (after Berlyne); and play theory emphasizing the role of conation (after Erikson).

We would now conclude that what this analysis suggests is that a peer group strives to be a kind of club or community pursuing whatever excitements are available, and that in so doing it does not differ from what adults do in their own recreative circumstances. Adults do not in general go to their clubs to be made more moral, sophisticated or angelic. Nor, therefore, do children. We go to our clubs for friendship, for meaningful and exciting actions and because in these places we can control what we do. Children do the same. An approach to peer groups only in terms of their "socialization" value is in these terms mistaking an occasional consequence (sometimes an important consequence, sometimes a trivial one) for the central meaning of the activity. Peer interaction is not a preparation for life. It is life itself. It is life's interpretation in action, a making of life a meaningful event often in a largely symbolic manner. Play with peers allows for a buffered orientation to experience within which it can be restructured to afford more flexible control and excitement with others. This is what peer interaction seeks to be about and when successful makes its members enjoy their lives on this planet.

So we end with the question of why it has been so difficult for researchers on peer interaction to focus in on the things with which peers are most concerned. Part of the answer must lie in the historical change in the relationships between children and adults that we have mentioned. But part must lie also in the typical Western adult amnesis for childhood experience which is itself a puzzling phenomenon. Why do we find it more easy to think of children as "primitives" in need of socialization, than of ourselves as no less primitive in our needs for enjoyment? That our misdirection continues is illustrated by Diana Baumrind in her 1979 paper to the Society for Research in Child Development, in which she says: "children by virtue of their immaturity and dependent status are not the originators of their own actions in the same sense that their parents are or should be.''

When we do regard children as the originators of their own actions, as we have already in linguistics, perhaps the study of peer interaction will take a new leap forward.

REFERENCES

Ariel, S. *What makes the activities of children dynamic and colorful*. Paper presented to the Annual Meeting of The Association for the Anthropological Study of Play, Henniker, N.H., March, 1979.

Bateson, G. *Steps to an ecology of mind*. New York: Ballantine, 1972.

Bateson, G. Communication. In B. Sutton-Smith (Ed.), *The Newsletter of the Association for the Anthropological Study of Play*, 1979, 5 (4), 3.

Baumrind, D. *New directions in socialization research*. Paper presented to the Annual Meeting of the Society for Research in Child Development, San Francisco, CA., March 1979.

Berlyne, D. E. *Conflict, arousal and curiosity*. New York: McGraw-Hill, 1960.

Bruner, J. S., & Sherwood, V. Early rule structure: The case of "peekaboo." In R. Harré (Ed.), *Life sentences*. New York: Wiley, 1976.

Campbell, J. D. Peer relations in childhood. In M. L. Hoffman & L. W. Hoffman (Eds.), *Review of child development research*. New York: Russell Sage, 1964.

Cavallo, P. *Muscles, morals and team sports: Americans organize children's play*. Philadelphia, PA: University of Pennsylvania Press, 1981.

Corsaro, W. A., & Tomlinson, G. *Spontaneous play and social learning in nursery school*. Unpublished Report, Indiana University, 1978.

Csikszentmihalyi, M. The concept of flow. in B. Sutton-Smith (Ed.), *Play and learning*. New York: Gardner Press, 1979. (a)

Csikszentmihalyi, M. *Some paradoxes in the definition of play*. Paper presented to the Annual Meeting of The Association for the Anthropological Study of Play, Henniker, N.H., March, 1979. (b)

Ellis, M. J. *Why people play*. Englewood Cliffs, N.J.: Prentice-Hall, 1974.

Farrer, C. *Contesting*. In Alyce T. Cheska (Ed.), *Play as context*. New York: Leisure Press, 1981. pp. 195–209.

Fine, G. *Impression management and preadolescent behavior: Friends as socializers*. Paper presented at a Society for Research in Child Development Study Group on the Development of Friendship, University of Illinois, October, 1978.

Freedman, D. G. *Human infancy: An evolutionary perspective*. New York: Wiley, 1974.

Garvey, C. *Play*. Cambridge, MA: Harvard University Press, 1977.

Geertz, C. Deep play: A description of the Balinese cockfight. In J. S. Bruner, A. Jolly, & K. Sylva (Eds.), *Play: Its role in development and evolution*. Harmondsworth: Penguin, 1976, 656–674.

Gelman, R. Cognitive development. In M. R. Rosenzweig & L. W. Porter (Eds.), *Annual review of psychology*. Palo Alto, CA: Annual Reviews, 1978.

Goffman, E. *Frame analysis*. Cambridge, MA: Harvard University Press, 1974.

Guilmette, A. M., & Duthie, J. H. *Play: A multiparadoxical phenomenon*. Paper presented at the Annual Meeting of The Association for the Anthropological Study of Play, Henniker, N.H., March 1979.

Hartup, W. W. Children and their friends. In H. McGurk (Ed.), *Child social development*. London: Methuen, in press.

Hays, D., & Ross, H. First social games. In B. Sutton-Smith (Ed.), *Play and learning*. New York: Gardner Press, 1979.

Herron, R. E. & Sutton-Smith, B. (Eds.), *Child's play*. New York: Wiley, 1971.

Hutt, C. Exploration and play. In B. Sutton-Smith (Ed.), *Play and learning*. New York: Gardner Press, 1979.

Katz, M. *Class, bureaucracy, and schools*. New York: Praeger, 1975.

Kirshenblatt-Gimblett, B. (Ed.). *Speech play*. Philadelphia, PA: University of Pennsylvania Press, 1976.

Kirshenblatt-Gimblett, B. Speech play and verbal art. In B. Sutton-Smith (Ed.),*Play and learning*. New York: Gardner Press, 1979.

Lever, J. Sex differences in the games children play. *Social Problems*, 1976, *23*, 478–487.

Lieberman, J. N. *Playfulness*. New York: Academic Press, 1977.

Loy, J. W., McPherson, B. D., & Kenyon, G. *Sport and social system*. Boston, M.A.: Addison-Curley, 1978.

Mueller, E., & Vandell, D. Infant-infant interaction. In J. D. Osofsun (Ed.), *The handbook of infant development*. New York: Wiley, 1979.

Murphy, R. E. *The dialectics of social life*. New York: Basic Books, 1971.

Piaget, J. *Play, dreams and imitation in childhood*. New York: W. W. Norton, 1962.

Redl, F., Gump, P., & Sutton-Smith, B. The dimensions of games. In E. Avedon & B. Sutton-Smith (Eds.), *The study of games*. New York: Wiley, 1971.

Savasta, M. L., & Sutton-Smith, B., Sex differences in play and power. In B. Sutton-Smith (Ed.), *Die Dialektk des Spiels*. Schorndoff: Holtman, 1979, 143–150.

Schwartzman, H. *Transformations: The anthropology of children's play*. New York: Plenum, 1979.

Singer, J. L. *The child's world of make believe*. New York: Academic Press, 1973.

Sutton-Smith, B. A structural grammar of games and sports. *International Review of Sport Sociology*, 1976, *2*, 117–137.

Sutton-Smith, B. *Die dialektik des Spiele*. Schorndorf: Verlag Karl Hoffman, 1978a.

Sutton-Smith, B. Initial education as caricature. *Keystone Folklore*, 1978b, *22*, 37–52.

Sutton-Smith, B. Play as metaperformance. In B. Sutton-Smith (Ed.), *Play and learning*. New York: Gardner Press, 1979. (a)

Sutton-Smith, B. The play of girls. In C. B. Kopp & M. Kirkpatrick (Eds.), *Women in context*. New York: Plenum, 1979, 229–257. (b)

Sutton-Smith, B. *A history of children's play: The New Zealand playground*, 1840–1950. Philadelphia: University of Pennsylvania Press, 1981.

Turner, V. Liminal to liminoid, in play, flow and ritual: An essay in comparative symbology. *Rice University Studies*, 1974, *60*, 53–92.

von Glascoe, C. A. *The work of playing "Redlight."* In H. Schwartzman (Ed.), *Play and culture*. New York: Leisine Press, 1980, 228–230.

III LANGUAGE AS A PRIMARY SOCIALIZER: NORMALLY DEVELOPING CHILDREN

4 Are Parents Language Teachers?

Catherine E. Snow
Harvard University

Linguists in general consider the answer to the question posed in the title of this paper to be an unqualified no. Children acquire language naturally, without any need to be taught it as we are taught geography or arithmetic. Educators, on the other hand, especially elementary school teachers, are in general, equally unanimous in declaring that parents do teach their children to talk. Parents' responses are probably more diverse—some feel very strongly that their own role is a didactic one, whereas others feel that children don't need much direct help from adults, that development "just happens." Which of these answers is correct, and what explains the diversity of feeling on this topic?

In some sense, of course, all three answers are correct, and each is understandable in terms of the experiences of the person who gives it. Teachers who experience the wide range of language skill in any kindergarten or first-grade classroom have data which strongly support the position that parents—at least some parents—provide extensive amounts of the teaching which prepares children to answer questions, to tell stories, to be interested in reading, to count, to name the letters of the alphabet, to use words like *reason, result, longer, wider, solid, fluid*—all skills which contribute to early school success. It is not surprising, then, that these teachers are convinced that the parents of the linguistically more advanced children have provided their children with their special skills, have "taught them language." Parents, on the other hand, reflecting on the realities of child care, recognize that relatively little of their time is spent in instruction. Much child-parent interaction in the first 18 months or so of the child's life centers around caretaking—feeding, giving baths, changing diapers, dressing—and most of the rest is an attempt to keep the child amused, not to train or teach him.

Of course, incidental training does go on in many areas—how to eat with a spoon, how to use the potty, how to say *please* and *thank you*—but when this is directed toward language, it is usually with reference to the social niceties of language, not to its basic structure or nature. In fact, linguists point out that it is really impossible to teach the basic structure of language. Language is a system of rules which are not known explicitly to most speakers, and which operate by referring to abstract structures, i.e., structures not identified at all in the sentences we hear. Thus, they say, it is not only unlikely, but actually impossible, that parents teach most aspects of language, though parents do, of course, provide the linguistic input on the basis of which the child can, using his innate ability, discover language for himself. Furthermore, they point out, all children do acquire language, even though they might not have acquired precisely those skills valued by first-grade teachers.

My purpose in this chapter is to reach a synthesis of these three points of view on the didactic role of parents in first language acquisition. I agree with the teachers' point of view, that parents function as instructors in crucial linguistic skills, and that children whose parents do not so function are linguistically retarded or disadvantaged. I agree with the parents that they don't intend to function as language teachers. Effectiveness in teaching one's child to talk must not be confused with intentional instruction in language. Nonetheless, an analysis of many of the activities routinely engaged in by adults with small children, for purposes of caretaking, having fun with them, keeping them busy, trying to figure out what they want, and even restricting their activities, can, I think, be demonstrated to function as language training. An assessment, then, of the extent to which parents do function as language teachers must rest upon a consideration of what constitutes language teaching. What activities that occur in the life of the infant or preschool child contribute to the child's acquisition of language? After this question is answered, one can go on to collect data on the frequncy with which these activities occur in the life of the average child, and the amount of time devoted to them.

Deciding which of the activities engaged in with preschool children contributes to their acquisition of language requires, of course, a notion of how language acquisition occurs. What would the ideal language curriculum consist of? It has been suggested (Newport, Gleitman, & Gleitman, 1977) that one could look to second language teaching curricula as a basis for judging whether the activities engaged in by parents with children are truly pedagogical. There are many reasons, however, for not accepting second language teaching programs as a good model for the ideal language-teaching curriculum. Firstly, second-language teaching is not notoriously effective, unless it accompanies a real need to communicate in the language being learned and is supplemented by opportunities to use that language communicatively. Secondly, the nature of what is to be learned is very different for the second language learner, even a 5 or 6-year-old second language learner, and the first language learner. A second language learner has acquired the basic principles of communication, and a sense of the options available for coding meaning linguistically. He will have to acquire some new semantic distinctions, some new articulatory patterns, many new rules of morphology and syntax, and thousands of new lexical items; all of this is a formidable task, but one which is considerably simpler than that facing the first language learner. The first language learner must acquire the notion that communication with another human being is possible, the articulatory skills requisite to vocal communication, the idea that there are rules limiting the structure of communicative interchanges, the principle of naming, as well as all of the specific rules governing word order and inflections in his native language. The second language learner's curriculum need emphasize only vocabulary and form; the first language learner's curriculum must provide opportunities for learning much more than this. Designing the ideal first language curriculum requires taking into account the needs of the child at many points during the course of the four, five or more years needed to acquire a language fully. A few years ago, it was generally asserted by developmental psycholinguists that language acquisition was a very fast process, accomplished in the few months between the child's first word (12–15 months of age) and his having displayed all the syntactic patterns of his first language (36–40 months of age). It was thought that children had acquired all the patterns and the rules, and that only irregular forms and exceptions to rules still needed to be learned. More recent analyses of children's complex utterance, however, suggest that many of those utterances might be produced using fairly simple heuristics, which enable the child to circumvent the full scale transformational generation of the sentences in question. Coming to understand how such sentences are rule-generated, and the transformational relationships among sets of sentences, may require several years of talking, listening, and thinking about language beyond the age of four or five (Clark, 1978; Ingram, 1975).

The curriculum for the first language learner, then, must be much more extensive than that for the second language learner. In infancy, the first language learner must be provided with experiences of contingent reponse, in order to learn about the nature of communication (Snow, 1979, 1981). Later, between 6 and 12 months of age, experiences with hearing the names of objects being attended to (Bruner, 1975a,b; Collis & Schaffer, 1975), playing games like peek-a-boo, give and take, and patty cake (Bruner, 1975a, 1975b; Ratner & Bruner, 1978; Snow, deBlauw, & Dubber, in press), and looking at books (Ninio & Bruner, 1978) constitute important language lessons. Evidence is available that the language teaching function of contingent responding in early infancy and of games and social routines in later infancy is available to infants in different social classes (e.g., deBlauw, Dubber, van Roosmalen, & Snow, 1978; Snow et al., in press) and different cultures (Snow, 1979, 1981) in significant quantities.

Somewhere between 10 and 16 months of age, most children have started to use single words to express their intentions. After having acquired, often quite slowly, a vocabulary of 20 to 50 words, children typically show an explosion of language activity, learning many new words very quickly, and starting to produce two-word utterances. By their third birthdays, most children have the ability to produce sentences of 15 or 20 words in length, to express very complex ideas with their sentences, and to express relations between sentences using words like *first, because, (in order) to,* and *afterwards.* By far the greatest amount of research on the didactic functions of parental speech to children has focused on this period of rapid language acquisition. The most directly relevant research papers, those by Newport, Gleitman, and Gleitman (1977), Cross (1978), and Furrow, Nelson, and Benedict (1979) produced opposite conclusions. Newport et al. (1977) correlated different syntactic variables in mothers' speech to their daughters with the daughters' improvement on various indices of syntactic development during the subsequent 6 months. They found a very small number of significant correlations which could be hypothesized to reflect a direct effect of the mothers' speech on the children's development. The few correlations they did find made good sense. Mothers who used many expressions of the type "That's a red ball" or "There are three elephants" had daughters with relatively fast growth in the length of their noun phrases. In other words, the mothers' frequent use of noun phrases in standard sentence frames contributed to the daughters' learning how to use adjectives and qualifiers attributively. The other significant correlation was between the mothers' use of complete yes-no questions like "Do you want to go to the playground?" and "Have you had enough to eat?" and the increase in the daughters' use of verbal auxiliaries. This correlation, too, makes sense, since the mothers' questions highlight auxiliary verbs by putting them in the first position, thus making it more likely that the children would notice and start to use these otherwise unstressed elements. Aside from these two interesting but rather minor effects of maternal speech on children's language acquisition, Newport, Gleitman, and Gleitman found no significant correlations, and concluded that parents do not function as language teachers, but that children "would rather do it" themselves.

Furrow et al. (1979) replicated the Newport et al. study; instead, however, of using statistical manipulations to deal with the problem that the children tested were at different points in their language development, they selected children who were all at the same age and language level. Their subjects were 18-months old and at the end of the one-word stage at the first test session. Furrow et al. repeated the Newport et al. observation and analysis procedures, adding some measures of maternal speech to those used by Newport et al. They found that greater maternal use of words, verbs, pronouns, contractions, and copulas per utterance at 18 months correlated negatively with the child's language ability at 27 months. Maternal use of yes-no questions and of nouns correlated positively with children's language growth. Furrow et al. concluded that maternal speech does have significant and wide-ranging effects on children's language acquisition, but that different didactic effects must be expected at different stages in children's development.

Cross' (1978) study took a somewhat different approach to the analysis of maternal speech, and also found a large number of maternal speech variables which correlated significantly with various indices of children's speech production and with their comprehension ability. The maternal speech variables which produced the most significant correlations were not, however, syntactic; they were variables having to do with the extent to which the mother's utterances were contingent on or semantically related to their children's immediately preceding utterances. Cross concluded, then, that parents do function as language teachers, and that their teaching consists not of talking a certain way but of talking about certain things.

For her study, Cross selected children who were learning language very fast, because she wanted to describe the crucial characteristics of interaction which resulted in extremely efficient language acquisition. The fact that her subjects were limited to very fast language learners makes the conclusions from her correlational analysis much stronger, since it is more difficult to find correlations with any variable that is tested over an artifically truncated range. The use of these subjects, all of whom were from middle-class homes and had a single primary caretaker, casts some doubt however, on attempts to generalize Cross' description of the nature of mother-child interaction. What happens to children from less privileged and language-conscious homes? Children who spend time regularly in play groups or with baby-sitters? Second children whose older siblings are still young enough to demand considerable maternal attention and time? Children whose parents have not attended a university, and do not highly value cognitive and linguistic achievement on their children's part? Can the adults in these children's environments also be described as functioning like language teachers? Another problem is that Cross analyzed language from intensive play sessions between mother and child. How can we extrapolate from such play sessions to the normal experience of the child in the course of a day or a week?

Before I describe two small studies undertaken to answer these questions, perhaps it is useful to define in more detail what the "language curriculum" used by the mothers in Cross's study looked like. As mentioned above, the basic principle of this curriculum was semantic relatedness; the "good language teachers" let their children determine the conversational topics to be discussed, and continued the conversations by adding related information, expanding upon or extending the child's initiative, not by introducing new conversational topics. The following conversation between a mother and her 30-month-old son, taken from my own data, can be used to illustrate both the "Cross curriculum" and deviation from that curriculum. A characterization of the utterances in Cross's terms is given in the right hand column:

| Child: | This a this? Who's this? Da this? | (introduces new conversational topic) |
| Mother: | This is a special tape recorder, Nathaniel. | (response to child's question: *semantically related.*) |

Child: Special tape recorder
         Mummy's tape recorder

Mother: Mummy's special tape recorder   (repetition of child's utterances;
                                            semantically related)

         It's a . . . like a television   (adding new information to child's
                                            utterance and to own previous
Child: Television tape recorder.   utterance; *semantic extension
                                            and self repetition*)

Mother: It takes pictures too.   (continues same topic, adds new
                                            information; *semantic extension*)
Child: Makes tapes too
         Makes tapes too

Mother: Makes tapes too?   (repetition of child utterance to
                                            demand clarification: *semantically
                                            related*)

         Yeah.
         Why don't you wind up   (introduces new topic: *not
         monkey?   semantically related*)

Cross's findings, translated into concrete terms, was that mothers who produced many of the kinds of utterance illustrated in the discussion of the videorecorder, utterances dependent on what the child had just been saying and limited to conversational topics introduced by the child, were good language teachers, whereas mothers who produced many utterances like the one above about the monkey, diverting the child's attention to a new, mother-selected topic, were relatively bad language teachers.

The theory of language acquisition related to this language teaching curriculum is the "correspondence theory"—that children learn language most effectively by experiencing many occasions of correspondence between their own semantic intentions and what they are hearing. The child's perceptual encoding of an event in the outside world creates a "space" in his head which can be filled in with language if someone at that precise moment provides the corresponding linguistic encoding. In the previous example, noticing the presence of an unfamiliar object created a cognitive space for which Nathaniel specifically demanded a linguistic plug by asking the name of the object. (He did not, in fact, succeed in eliciting the correct name of the object in question, a video tape deck, but he had no way of knowing that!) His continued interest in the object, evidenced by his repetitions of the adult utterances about it, elicited two additional bits of information about the function of the tape deck as well as linguistic information about such problems as the order of prenominals. (At the time of this conversation, Nathaniel was having lots of trouble with the order of adjectives and possessives, producing utterances like "two mummy's shoes" and "big

Nathaniel's hot chocolate milk''; the information about the order of such elements offered in his mother's utterance ''mummy's special tape recorder'' might, thus, have been directly useful to him.)

There are two questions, then, which arise concerning the generalizability of Cross's results:

1. Do all kinds of children have access to the same kind of semantically-related adult speech Cross's mothers used, or is this phenomenon largely limited to middle class children whose language-conscious and child-centered mothers are their primary caretakers?

2. Do children have access to such speech regularly and frequently in the course of a normal day or week, or is it typical only of short ''play sessions'' and periods when mothers know they are being observed by psycholinguists?

In order to answer these questions, we have carried out two observational studies of adult-child interaction. In the first, 10 mothers were observed at home for one hour with their 17-month-old children. The families were selected to represent a range of social classes. All the children observed were second children. The observations were carried out to determine to what extent variables like social class and the presence of the older sibling affected the mother's ability to function as a language teacher, using Cross's type of analysis on the mothers' speech. In the second study much longer (5–8 hour) observations were carried out on two children who spent part of the day in a group day-care setting and part of the day at home with their mothers. These observations focused much less on the quality of the adult-child interaction, and more on the availability of the adult to the child over a long period of time. The length of the observation sessions made it impossible for the mothers or baby-sitters to engage continuously in intensive play sessions with the child, such as often happens in half-hour or one-hour observations, so a much more ecologically valid assessment of the child's access to language teaching would be made.

INTERACTION WITH 17-MONTH OLDS

Subjects. The subjects in this study were 10 17-month-old children, four girls and six boys, living in Amsterdam, The Netherlands. All were second children whose older siblings were 2 to 3 years older. Five of the families could be identified as middle class, using father's profession and both parents' educational level as criteria, and five as lower middle or working class. All the subjects had participated in earlier observations at 3, 4½, and 6 months of age, carried out by one of the two observers at the 17 month session.

Observations. One hour observations were carried out, within a week of the day when the child became 17-months-old. Aside from the two observers, the only adult present at the session was the mother. The older sibling was also present in six of the 10 cases. The observations sessions were tape-recorded and running notes were made of gestures, nonverbal context, and other information that would be needed to supplement the transcripts of the tapes.

Scoring.   An attempt was made to use the scoring utilized by Cross (1977, 1978) as faithfully as possible. It soon became apparent, however, that the children in our study were linguistically considerably behind the children studied by Cross, and this made direct use of her scoring scheme impossible. The major categorization in the Cross scoring had to do with the semantic-relatedness of the maternal utterances to the child's preceding utterance. The 17-month-olds in our study produced so little interpretable speech that it would have been impossible for their mothers to produce semantically related utterances in Cross's sense. However, it was clear that many of the maternal utterances were related to the child's activities or nonspeech vocalizations. In order, then, to replicate the spirit if not the practice of Cross's scheme, we devised a coding that included the following categories:

1. Maternal utterance related to the child's activity.
   1. To what he is looking at. Example: child turns to look at observer, mother says "That's Clara."
   b. To what he is pointing to. Example: child points to picture in book, mother says "Dingo just had another accident."
   c. To an action he is carrying out. Example: child bumps tower, mother says "You knocked it over."
2. Maternal utterance related to the child's nonverbal vocalization.
   a. Imitation of the child's previous vocalization. Example: Child says "bababa," mother says "Bababa yourself."
   b. Interpretation of the child's vocalization, using cues from the situation, Example: Child says "aaah" while knocking tower over, mother says "Fall down," imitating the child's vowel in *fall*.
   c. Interpretation of the child's vocalization using only its sound as a cue. Example: Child says "aaah" with a whiny tone, mother says, "Don't you feel good?"
   d. Elicitation of more vocalizations on the basis of previous ones. Example: Child babbles, mother says "Come on, tell us the rest of the story."
3. Maternal utterance related to the child's utterance.
   a. Imitation, partial or complete, of preceding child utterance. Example: Child says "da da baby," mother says "Baby."
   b. Expansion of the child's utterance, adding no new information but filling in omitted function words and grammatical markers. Example: Child says "clock," mother says "That's the clock, yes."

    c. Semantic extension of the child utterance, in which both new informa-
tion and grammatical markers and function words are added. Example:
Child says "down," mother says "Tower fell down, boom."

    d. Elicitation of words related to child's previous utterance. Example:
Child says "duck," mother says "Yes, what's his name? What do you
call him? Is that Donald? Say Donald!"

4. Maternal utterance not related to child's activity, vocalization, or utterance.

In addition to being scored on semantic relatedness, the maternal utterances
were scored as self-repetitions, using the following categorization.

1. Exact self-repetitions, e.g., "That's the clock. That's the clock."
2. Partial self-repetitions, e.g., "That is the clock. The clock."
3. Expanded self repetitions, e.g., "That's a clock. That's a clock, like in
your book."

If-repetitions were scored because of suggestions (Snow, 1972; Cross, 1977;
1978) that they also contribute to the child's ability to learn language.

Results. The most striking result is that a mean of 68% of the maternal
utterances could be classified as semantically-related. The range for semantic
relatedness was 48% to 85%. Clearly, even the least well-off child in the group
studied heard a high porportion of utterances which corresponded to his own
activities or gave information about the appropriateness of his own utterances.
Neither social class, sex, nor presence of an older sibling made any difference in
proportion of semantically related adult utterances (see Table 4.1).

Table 4.1.

Effect of sex, social class, and presence of an older sibling on proportion of
maternal utterances which were semantically related to the child's activities

Factor	Mean	Significance[1]
Class		n.s.
Lower	73.1	
Middle	63.3	
Sex		n.s.
Boys	66.7	
Girls	70.5	
Sibling present		n.s.
no	68.5	
yes	68.1	

[1]These and all other means tests reported t-tests.

The similarities across mothers in percentages of utterances which were semantically related to the child's activities do not imply, however, that all the children heard equal numbers of semantically related utterances. The mothers observed differed greatly in the number of child-directed utterances produced during the one-hour observation session, with the lowest number being 73 and the highest 605. The mean number of maternal utterances directed to the child was 299.6 and the mean number of semantically related utterances was 205.6. Nonetheless, one child heard only 55 semantically related maternal utterances, and another heard only 83. Neither sex of child nor social class had any significant effect on frequency of maternal utterances, but the presence of an older sibling had a dramatic and significant effect (see Table 4.2). Seventeen-month-olds alone with their mothers heard an average of 464 maternal utterances in an hour, whereas those whose older siblings were present heard only 190. In view of this enormous effect, it is not surprising that second children are generally considered to be slower language learners than first children.

The availability of the mother to the 17-month-old, as reflected in the number of maternal utterances addressed to him, had a strong effect on the number of child vocalizations. There was a correlation of .78 ($p < .004$) between frequency of child vocalizations and frequency of maternal vocalizations directed to the child. Once again, the effect of the older sibling's presence was very strong; 17-month-olds alone with their mothers produced a mean of 264.3 vocalizations (including interpretable utterances), whereas those whose older siblings were present produced a mean of 110.5 ($p < .03$).

The mean percentage maternal self-repetitions was 14.8. There were no significant effects of social class, sex, or presence of the sibling on percentage self-repetitions, though the children whose older siblings were not present did, of course, hear more maternal self-repetitions, since they heard more maternal utterances.

Table 4.2.
Effect of sex, social class, and presence of an older sibling
on frequency of maternal utterances to the child

Factor	Mean	Significance
Class		n.s.
Lower	368.6	
Middle	230.6	
Sex		n.s.
Boys	268.3	
Girls	346.5	
Sibling present		$p < .002$
no	464.5	
yes	189.7	

Discussion. The children in our study showed a fair degree of variation in the extent to which they were experiencing the ideal language curriculum described by Cross (1977; 1978). Nonetheless, even the "least privileged" among them did hear some maternal speech which was directly related to their own activities, and we must conclude, then, that all these children were being taught about correspondences between cognitive and linguistic encodings of events. Furthermore, all the children were receiving linguistic information that was simple and repetitive enough to be decodable, and thus useful as a model for their own utterances.

As mentioned earlier, none of the children in our study were fast language learners. None were using multiword utterances, and five of the 10 were using fewer than 10 different words spontaneously at 17 months. (We had not asked the mothers to maintain a cumulative diary, so cannot present any data on total number of words the children had acquired, only on those which we observed and/or the mother reported to be in use at the time of the observation.) The most linguistically advanced child used 21 different words. (For comparison, in Nelson, (1973) the mean age of acquisition of 10 words was 15 months.) It is tempting to relate their nonprecocious acquisition to their being second-born, and their resultant need to share maternal teaching time with older siblings. Since our study did not incorporate a matched control group of first borns who turned out to learn language faster, such a conclusion is at present unjustified. However, within this group a significant correlation (.70) was found between the number of different words the child knew and the number of semantically related utterances in his mother's speech to him, as well as with the total number of maternal utterances to him (.74). As pointed out in the results section, the major variable determining whether a child heard much or little maternal speech was the presence of the sibling. These results suggest, than, that the children who have more sole access to their mothers because their older siblings attended preschools or playgroups (and thus could not be present at the observation) were more advanced linguistically—just what one would predict if mothers do indeed function as language teachers!

INTERACTION THROUGHOUT THE DAY

The most striking finding of the study with the 17-month-olds was the relative paucity of parent-child interaction, even during a scheduled observation by two psycholinguists obviously interested in the child's language, if another child was present. It is likely that even only children have rather little access to interaction with adults, and thus to language teaching, when their mothers are busy with household chores, and during formal or informal group play sessions or multiple babysitting. To determine, then just how much access children have to adults at different periods during a normal day, two children were observed over much of one day. The measures taken included the frequency of interaction with adults, the length of periods of interaction with adults, and the initiator of interaction periods, in order to obtain a clearer impression of the density of social contact for a typical child. It should be emphasized that the data to be presented here are preliminary in the extreme. Only two children were looked at; they were not selected in such a way that these data are generalizable to larger groups, and no special measures were taken to ensure that the day of the observation was absolutely typical. The purpose of this study is not to draw conclusions about access to social interaction of a group of children, but to illustrate the factors that can increase or decrease a child's access to language teaching and to suggest how language teaching might fit into a child's daily experience.

Subjects.   Two first-born children of academic middle-class families, M and L, were observed. Both were girls and only children. L was 22 months and M 28 months old. Both the children were cared for part of the day outside the home, because their mothers were studying. L attended a play-group with six children and two–three adults for about 3 hours every morning. M spent 4 hours a day at the home of a baby-sitter who had a 3-year-old daughter of her own.

Observations.   Both children were observed from 8:30 AM to mid afternoon. The observations started at the child's home, continued at the playgroup/babysitter's and then were terminated in M's case at the beginning of and in L's case about an hour after the end of the child's afternoon nap.

The observer tape-recorded much of the observation sessions, but the data to be presented here come from notes made on the spot, of time of onset and offset of interactions between the target child and any adult. In addition, it was noted who initiated such interactions. Furthermore, note was taken of periods during which an adult was attending to the child and prepared to interact with her, though not necessarily talking or listening continuously. Furthermore, note was made of periods during which the child was watching an adult interact with another child, as these were considered to be potential language-teaching situations as well.

Results.   The results for the two children are presented in Table 4.3. It can be seen that the home and the group-care settings differ enormously in the percentage of awake time spent in interaction with adults, and in the length of the interactions. Both girls experienced much more extended periods of interaction with their mothers at home than with any adult (even the mother, if present) in the group care setting. The extended interactions at home were often goal oriented—during dressing, or preparing and eating lunch—but could also be purely for fun, e.g., reading a book or playing with the child's toys. In the group care situations, adult-child interactions were much more likely to involve caretaking—wiping the child's nose, or using the potty. The children played in

Table 4.3.
Density of social interaction available to two children

| | Group Care | | At Home | |
	L	M	L	M
Total obs. time	155 min	252 min 40 sec	284 min 20 sec	39 min 26 sec
Total time in interaction	27 min 50 sec	52 min 15 sec	88 min 15 sec	23 min 20 sec
# of interactions	110	62	7	6
mean length of int.	15 sec	51 sec	12 min 36 sec	3 min 53 sec
"watching" time	4 min 24 sec	19 min 10 sec	–	–
adult available, not interacting	11 min 20 sec	66 min 20 sec	–	–
child asleep	–	–	180 min 30 sec	–

these situations either alone, in parallel with the other children, or interactively with them, not with the adults. L initiated 24% of the interaction she had with adults during play group with some communicative behavior (i.e., not just by falling down or spilling juice, but by pointing, whining, or saying something), and M initiated 50% of those she engaged in. Thus, the child is to a large extent in control of the number of interactions experienced with adults in group care situations.

The interactions both girls experienced at home were much longer and more elaborate than those in the group care situation (note that the home observation periods did not happen to include times when the mothers were engaged in major, attention-consuming tasks like house-cleaning, fixing dinner, or typing term papers). Although no formal qualitative analysis of these interactions was undertaken, they clearly did display the characteristics of semantic relatedness between adult speech and child activities previously discussed. In addition, there were examples of specific teaching, and of routines (e.g., naming body parts, counting, naming colors) directed to language practice.

Discussion. Even on the basis of this ecologically more valid assessment of the availability of social interaction than is normally presented, it is clear that many children do experience significant amounts of social interaction of a type which could contribute directly to language learning. The "highest quality" periods of interaction occurred during caretaking and play sessions alone with the mother but large numbers of short interactions with adults occurred even in the very chaotic environment of a playgroup consisting of six children under the age of two (one of whom was celebrating a birthday on the day of the observation!). In these more chaotic situations, the child's personality and ability to initiate contact was a very important factor in regulating the amount of adult interaction available, whereas in a one-to-one situation the adult's willingness to interact was of greater importance.

The fact that the periods of interaction were much longer in the home than the group-care situation recalls earlier findings with children aged three to six months, suggesting that such factors as social class of the family, the mother's interpretation of the observer's purpose, the presence of other adults who were potential interactors with the mother, and the presence of other children could greatly affect the length of periods of social interaction, but not their frequency (Snow, de Blauw, & van Roosmalen, 1979). In other words, a mother whose attention is divided between her infant and many other potential interactors and activities will spend less time on each interaction with the infant, but will respond to him as frequently as if she were alone with him. When alone, she will be able to extend each interaction, but will not necessarily respond more frequently to the infant or initiate interactions with him more often. In the present study, the children experienced many more instances of social interaction in the group care than in the home situation, but these were almost all very short compared to the interactions they experienced with their mothers.

CONCLUSIONS

The conclusions to be drawn from the studies previously described are:

1. Adults provide a significant proportion of semantically related speech to children in the course of everyday caretaking and play activities.
2. The amount of semantically related speech available from caretakers is most strongly influenced by the number of other children competing for the adult's time and attention.
3. In multiple-child caretaking situations, children are themselves largely responsible for initiating interactions with the available adults. Retiring, introverted children may well have significantly less access to adult speech in these situations than more extroverted, demanding children.
4. Even in multiple-child caretaking situations, most children do have access to a significant amount of interaction with adults, and thus to speech which is related to the child's activities.

Adults probably intend to function as language teachers only very rarely in their interactions with children. In fact, though, by virtue simply of talking about what the children are doing, answering their questions, responding to their conversational initiatives, and directing their behavior, adults provide exposure to precisely the kind of language that is best fitted to teach their children to talk.

REFERENCES

Bruner, J. From communication to language: A psychological perspective. *Cognition,* 1975, *3,* 255-285. (a)

Bruner, J. The ontogenesis of speech acts. *Journal of Child Language* 1975, *2,* 1-20. (b)

Clark, R. Some even simpler ways to learn to talk. In N. Waterson & C. Snow (Eds.), *The development of communication.* London: Wiley, 1978.

Collis, G., & Schaffer, H. Synchronisation of visual attention in mother-infant pairs. *Journal of Child Psychology,* 1975, *16,* 315-320.

Cross, T. Mothers' speech adjustments: The contribution of selected child listener variables. In C. Snow & C. Ferguson (Eds.), *Talking to children.* Cambridge University Press, Cambridge. 1977.

Cross, T. Motherese: Its association with the rate of syntactic acquisition in young children. In N. Waterson & C. Snow (Eds.), *The development of communication.* London: Wiley, 1978.

deBlauw, A., Dubber, C., van Roosmalen, G., & Snow, C. Sex and social class differences in mother-infant interaction. In O. Garnica & M. Ritchie (Eds.), *Children, language and society.* New York: Pergamom Press, 1978.

Furrow, D., Nelson, K., & Benedict, H. Mothers' speech to children and syntactic development: Some simple relationships. *Journal of Child Language,* 1979, *6,* 423-442.

Ingram, D. 1975. If and when transformations are acquired by children. In D. Dato (Ed.), *Georgetown University Roundtable on Languages and Linguistics, 1975.* Washington, D.C.: Georgetown University Press.

Nelson, K. Structure and strategy in learning to talk. *Monographs of The Society for Research in Child Development,* No. 149, 38, Nos. 1 and 2., 1973.

Newport, E., Gleitman, H., & Gleitman, L. Mother, I'd rather do it myself: Some effects and noneffects of maternal speech style. In C. Snow & C. Ferguson (Eds.), *Talking to children.* Cambridge, Eng.: Cambridge University Press, 1977.

Ninio, A., & Bruner, J. The achievement and antecedents of labelling. *Journal of Child Language,* 1978, *5,* 1-16.

Ratner, N., & Bruner, J. Games, social exchange, and the acquisition of languge. *Journal of Child Language,* 1978, *5,* 391-402.

Snow, C. E. Mothers' speech to children learning language. *Child Development,* 1972, *43,* 549-565.

Snow, C. E. The role of social interaction in language acquisition. In A. Collins (Ed.), *Children's language and communication.* Hillsdale, N.J.: Lawrence Erlbaum Associates, 1979.

Snow, C. E. Social interaction and language acquisition. In P. Dale & D. Ingram (Eds.), *Child language: An international perspective.* Baltimore: University Park Press, 1981.

Snow, C. E., deBlauw, A., & van Roosmalen, G. Talking and playing with babies. In M. Bullowa (Ed.), *Before speech.* Cambridge, Eng.: Cambridge University Press, 1979.

Snow, C. E., deBlauw, A., & Dubber, C. Routines in parent-child interaction. In L. Feagans & D. Farran (Eds.), *The language of children reared in poverty: Implications for evaluation and intervention.* New York: Academic Press, in press.

5 Construction of Social Norms by Teacher & Children: The First Year of School

Cynthia Wallat
National Institute of Education, Washington, D.C.

Judith Green
University of Delaware

ABSTRACT

If children are to become successfully rated members of the classroom society, they need to be able to identify the contexts of the classrooms and to know what behaviors are appropriate in each context. This paper describes the theoretical rationale and microethnographic methodology used in the analysis of contexts that were captured in videotapes from a kindergarten classroom during one school year.

In recent years, educational researchers have come to recognize the importance of both nonverbal and verbal messages in the classroom. The work described in this paper is viewed as a step towards clarifying our understanding of: the relationship between sociolinguistic and pedagogical communication variables; the development of social and instructional contexts of the classroom; and the conventions that develop in small group situations.

INTRODUCTION

Until recently, researchers had not considered the possibility that the classroom should logically be approached as both content and context. This conceptualization is based on the premise that students learn contextually appropriate and inappropriate behavior whether or not they actually learn the academic content (Young & Beardsley, 1968). Also, it suggests that the task facing researchers concerned with socialization in educational settings is to describe "how the child learns to demonstrate his membership of the classroom society, to recognize and

97

practice the making of social events in common with others'' (Cook-Gumperz, 1973, p. 7). As Cook-Gumperz states, ''The key to this process which makes it *visible* for everyday members, and for members as researchers is language'' (p. 7).

Construction of Social Norms: Framing the Task

The need to capture social processes of childhood through the study of language in use centers around recognition of the child both as an interpreter of the world and as a source of influence on adults (Cook-Gumperz, 1973; Denzin, 1977). Skolnick (1976) suggests that the recent re-emergence of interest in developing a social psychology of childhood is due to our belated recognition that today's child must learn a complex set of symbolic social language skills. These skills are necessary if the child is to be prepared for the fact that modern society is not held in check by an inflexible set of rules, norms, and expectations of behavior. Today's child is faced with negotiating a complex system of arbitrary norms and rules within social institutions. In order to make oneself heard in a diverse society in which arbitrary norms and rules operate, an individual must become sensitive to the nuances of interpersonal situations. The descriptive system reviewed in this paper is a beginning step in capturing those nuances by mapping the nonverbal, verbal, and paralinguistic cues of social contexts.

As a result of past orientations to global descriptions of adult and child personality characteristics, we are still in the stage of rethinking past idealized views of adult socialization effectiveness and communicative competence. We still have not decided the continuing issues of: (1) whether we can realistically continue to assume that an ideal instructional situation and ideal speech situation exists (McCarthy, 1973; Mitzel, 1977), and (2) whether we can bring individuals together from many fields in order to make decisions about what a descriptive theory of classroom social life might look like (Ervin-Tripp, 1972; Erickson, 1979).

The existence of multiple beliefs regarding the nature of language and the nature of classroom social norm development can be seen in the discrepancies between recent research findings in social development and current public knowledge regarding an adult's enactment of a socializing role. The popular press phrase ''be consistent'' is still promoted as an essential adult strategy of upbringing and classroom discipline. Parents and teachers are accused of blanket indictments such as ''permissive parenting,'' ''lack of interest in consistent rule enforcement,'' and ''conflicting notions of appropriate and inappropriate behavior'' (Duke, 1978, pp. 425, 431). Although ''stability'' is still promoted as an essential adult strategy of upbringing and classroom discipline, current directions in social development have pointed out: (1) that the development of rules is far more complex than modeling and/or reinforcing particular behavioral norms valued by a child's parents and teachers (Parke, 1976; Damon, 1977); (2) that social development approaches which concentrate attention solely on the semantic content of rules advocated by parents and teachers in the child's world are inadequate (Gumperz, 1976; Takanishi, 1978); and (3) that research which continues to search for a unidirectional causal relation between the socializing agent's verbal instructions and direct changes in the child will remain "an area barren of confirmation" (Bell & Hertz, 1976, p. 7).

One of the reasons for continued inconsistent findings in socialization research is that we have not tested on a wide scale those theoretical models which posit that the child actively works to structure, create and/or resist socializing influences as he constructs his social knowledge out of interactions with others (Damon, 1977). The usefulness of theoretical paradigms which begin with viewing the child "as a constructor of reality—as one who puts together all sorts of things in a variety of ways—" (Almy, 1975, p. 125) and the adult as more of a clarifier of knowledge than an agent of change have generally remained untested. Damon (1977) suggests that the reason for this state of the research is that in recent years the predominant interest has been in the area of "social cognition" with particular emphasis on "person perception" or "understanding other persons." He states that:

> [the] assumption behind this approach is that the child learns about his or her social world merely by discovering the important chracteristics of other persons . . . The dynamic and subjective aspects of interpersonal relations are virtually ignored in this approach. The social world is operationalized as a collection of noninteracting objects about which one learns to make objective inferences and predictions. Such a view is inadequate for explaining the child's greatest difficulties and accomplishments in understanding the social world; for it is the child's knowledge of relations and transactions between persons that determines the characteristics of the child's social functioning. (pp. 6–7)

Although statements of rules can provide a clue to a child's knowledge of the purposes of social interaction, or a child's point of view about a particular social situation, these statements will not inform us about the development course of *how* individuals learn to recognize when to speak and when to remain silent during different instructional contexts.

The following example from Wallat's, *Field Notes,* will illustrate these issues:

> Two and one-half weeks before school ended in June, 1977, we had an opportunity to ask 24 kindergarten children during their group meeting time the following question: "How could you *show* someone that you are ready for first grade?" The first five classroom social behaviors we recorded were: "Hands up," "Be a good listener, but I don't do it all the time," "Don't move in circle," "*Try* to be quiet," and "Remember, one at a time." (1977, p. 1).

These five statements of interpretative procedures indicate that the children who answered have become aware of the social behaviors to be followed when a classroom group meets. However, this knowledge tells us little about how these children came to know these rules. The problem is even more complex given that socialization practices are not generally considered a distinct area in which prospective classroom teachers are trained. Therefore, the question that must be asked is how did these children come to know the norms of behavior that the classroom teacher was attempting to use to structure their school behavior? Once the theoretical question of how children come to know what they do is raised, the methodological question of how to capture the interrelatedness of cognitive-social-cultural expectations of adults who live or work with children becomes paramount. In this chapter, both of these questions are addressed.

Language and Socialization: Interrelated Processes

The discussion of the construction of classroom social norms presented in this chapter builds on the authors' current work in the reconceptualization of teaching as a communicative process (Green & Wallat, 1979; Wallat & Green, 1979). The approach we have taken to studying language as a primary socializer is based on recognition that the relationship between sociolinguistic and pedagogical variables and the development of social and instructional contexts of the classroom is still not clear. Although there is widespread recognition of the importance of studying the relationship between process-process variables such as adult/child interaction and social skill development, the fact remains that methods for capturing, describing, and analyzing socialization strategies found in classroom conversations are still in the pioneering stage (Gumperz, 1981).

Calls for a clearer understanding of social, communicative, and/or interaction competence, as it develops over time, in a variety of social and instructional contexts (e.g., Bellack & Davitz, 1972; Cazden, 1979; Cook-Gumperz, 1979; Corsaro, 1981; Ervin-Tripp, 1972; Fillmore, 1976; Green & Wallat, 1981; Gumperz & Herasimchik, 1973; Haberman & Stinnett, 1973; Hymes, 1967; McCarthy, 1973; Schaeffer, 1977; Young & Beardsky, 1968) center around recognition of the need to "find ways to understand, in a general and theoretical sense, the social functions of particular forms of language in specific contexts" (Mishler, 1972, p. 268).

One immediate problem in discussing the social functions of language and the construction of social norms in instructional situations is that it is somewhat artificial to separate sociolinguistic strategies from pedagogical strategies "since the former represent one type of instance of the latter" (Mishler, 1972, p. 284). In the classroom, instructional behaviors are not isolated strategies, such as—Present Content—, nor are social behaviors simply an outcome of—Group Time—. Instructional strategies and outcomes, and nonverbal and verbal social behavior strategies and outcomes, are part and parcel of complex interpersonal and ecological transactions.

While interpersonal transactions have been the focus of many studies, the argument has been made by Doyle (1977) that environmental demands, or ecological roles and relationships "which accompany teaching in classrooms interact with performance both to shape observed behavior and to establish limits on the range of response options" (p. 180). He suggests that attention to ecological roles and relationship demands appear "to have considerable heuristic potential for understanding the causes and consequences of behavior in classrooms" (p. 180).

Support for this view can be found in the work of researchers interested in language in use. For example, Labov and Fanshel (1977) have offered support for this direction in their discussion of cognitive and social components of adult/child conversations:

As we go deeper into the interactional events of reported conversations, there begin to appear other propositions based upon the underlying web of rights and obligations . . . It is evident that (both social and cognitive) propositions may be part of the direct content of conversation, or may be referred to with varying degrees of indirectness. (pp. 52-53)

A similar observation was made by Cazden (1972). In her explorations of children's use of language in educational settings, Cazden observed that:

In being socialized to school, children have to learn three relationships in increasing degree of specificity: that form and function do not always correspond; that, in school, nonimperative forms frequently express a directive intent; and that particular teachers use particular form-function equivalencies and expect appropriate responses to them. (p. 15)

These languages studies not only illustrate the interrelatedness of communicative, socialization and pedagogical strategies, they also suggest that the study of socialization can be approached through the study of the development of norms for interaction.

The approach to this problem that Cazden and others interested in language in use have called for includes descriptive accounts of classroom conversations which allow others "to *see* data as the interaction of language and social setting" (Hymes, 1967, p. 13). To date, analyses based on this conceptualization have indicated that norms of interaction are related to sociolinguistic rules for communicating which develop over time. These rules help inform individuals about when to speak, how to speak (i.e., what gestures, movements, intonation, stress, and pitch features should be used), how to get a turn, how to digress from a topic appropriately, how much to speak, and to whom messages should be addressed (Cicourel, 1968; Fillmore, 1976; Hammersley, 1976; Hymes, 1972; Speier, 1976).

The socialization issue in educational settings, therefore, can be restated in sociolinguistic terms. From this perspective, the study of socialization in educational settings is the study of how children and teachers arrive at an interpretation of the instructional content of a message that matches the social or ecological situation at that moment (Gumperz & Herasimchuk, 1973).

This view of ongoing socialization emphasizes the point that we cannot assume that because teachers and children speak the same words they also have a shared awareness of norms of interaction which are signalled through sociolinguistic cues such as gestures, movements, pitch, stress, and timing. Phrases such as "You may go to the discussion area," or "Who was working with the blocks?" can be delivered in different ways in different settings and situations. Depending on ecological characteristics of message delivery, units of interaction[1] carry cues to differentiated social behavior responsibilities. The nonverbal and paralinguistic language modes that co-occur with the verbal language mode require that the listener be able to evaluate how something is said as well as what was said in order to interpret the procedure that is expected.

Recent work, in the field generally called sociolinguistic ethnography of communication (cf. Labov, 1972; Gumperz & Hymes, 1972), has shown that a number of linguistic devices, referred to as contextualization cues, serve to communicate social meaning in situations (Gumperz & Herasimchuk, 1973). Cues such as phonemic, semantic, and syntactic elements; gestural and proxemic features, prosodic/paralinguistic features (pitch, stress, and intonation); and the manipulation of physical objects in the ecological setting contribute to social meaning in situations (Corsaro, 1981).

These contextualization cues, in addition to signaling message meaning, also help to define context. Erickson and Schultz (1981), pointing to the functional role of contextualization cues in the establishment of context, state that contexts are "not simply given in the physical setting . . . nor in combinations of persons . . . Rather, contexts are constituted by what people are doing and where and when they are doing it" (p. 148). Social contexts defined in this manner, "consist of mutually shared and ratified definitions of situations and in the social actions persons take on the basis of those definitions" (p. 148). Contexts, therefore, are products of conversations, and contextualization cues are the bits of information in this process used to establish and interpret meaning. This work indicates that the ability to use and interpret contextualization cues is an important skill for social participation. This ability, however, like other language skills, is developed over time.

Cook-Gumperz and Gumperz's (1976) and Cook-Gumperz and Corsaro's (1976) studies have shown that recognition and reliance on contextualization

---

[1]Units of interaction refer to a conversational structure identified in the first level of analysis. This unit, an Interaction Unit, consists of conversationally tied message units. For example, a question followed by a response is an Interaction Unit. On Figure 5.1, the sequence that begins with AH (line 030) and ends with OK (line 034) is an Interaction Unit. Consideration of contextualization cues permits the identification of this conversational unit. For a more explicit definition see Green and Wallat, 1979 or Green and Wallat, 1981.

cues for constructing conversational contexts varies with age and language ex-periences. In addition, their work suggests: (a) that contextualization cues may be an important cause of miscommunication or an important cause of conversa-tional cohesion between children and adults, and (b) that appropriate and/or acceptable use of contextualization cues is acquired as part of socialization pro-cesses. Given the interrelatedness of the socialization and communication pro-cesses, the task for the researcher concerned with childhood socialization is the description of how the social processes are constructed as a part of the ongoing communications of the everyday events in the classroom. In other words, we must capture how classroom members establish, maintain, check, and suspend social events in the classroom (Blumer, 1969).

Studying Group Coordination Norms: Purpose and Underlying Constructs

In this chapter we provide the reader with an understanding of the sociolinguistic ethnographic perspective that we employ to study the evolution of group coordi-nation norms. The focus for describing, analyzing, and theorizing about so-cialization processes is the natural classroom communications of an everyday event which took place over the 1977–78 school year in a kindergarten classroom in Northeastern Ohio. The overall teacher goal of that event was described as "establishment of a feeling of group" (Teacher M goals, 1977). Timewise, the event under scrutiny began the moment the teacher played a chord on the piano and continued until the time the teacher, on viewing videotapes from the school year, confirmed that group focus was established.

Our long-range goal in studying classroom societies is to try to symbolize how teachers and children construct "a system of standards for perceiving, believing, evaluating, and acting" (Goodenough, 1971, p. 41) in differentiated instruc-tional contexts. The descriptive system that we have created for the study of face-to-face interaction in social settings permits the researcher to map out the situationally specific strategies that are used by adults and children. The struc-tural maps of ongoing classroom conversations serve to symbolize the contextual data needed for examining how social processes are being constructed, modified, selected, checked, suspended, terminated and recommended (Blumer, 1969).

Our approach is based on the belief that one socialization question that must be addressed whether one thinks of society as a whole country or society as a community, family, or classroom, is: How does a child become a member of a group? On this point, Denzin (1977) has observed that socialization "represents a fluid, shifting relationship between persons attempting to fit their lines of action together into some workable, interactive relationship . . . It is therefore a process that cannot be separated from the demands of social situations" (p. 3).

Taking this process view of socialization means that the question: How does a child become a member of the classroom society? can be approached by observing and describing the pedagogical and sociolinguistic strategies that develop for producing social situations. This approach to observing naturally occurring social situations in classrooms rests on the argument that a theory of socialization must address the relationship between a child's developing view of his world and the symbolic, interactional, and linguistic experiences in which he participates both at home and at school.

Based on this conceptualization and in light of recent research, we argue that socialization processes must move beyond the stage of representing socialization as an overall pattern of norms of social interaction which are the result of predetermined motives and goals of specific adults who work and live with children. Our view of socialization as process rather than discrete sets of norms and rules inculcated into passive participants is based on increasing cumulative evidence that points out that children and adults act in ways that reflect an unfolding, or evolving definition of social situations (Cook-Gumperz, 1973; Cook-Gumperz, 1981; Corsaro, 1981; Erickson, 1975a; Erickson & Schultz, 1981; Gumperz & Herasimchuk, 1973; McDermott, 1977; Parke, 1976; Slama-Cazacu, 1976).

Before proceeding to the discussion of the design and methodology we have used to generate hypotheses regarding a theory of social action,[2] we believe it is necessary to address the issue of why the type of sociolinguistic ethnography represented in this chapter was adopted.

A Sociolinguistic Ethnography: The Underlying Constructs

The decision to represent socialization in these sociolinguistic and ethnographic terms seems justified for a number of reasons. Sociolinguistics is concerned with working out empirical methods and validation procedures to account for contextualization cues that are available to participants for interpreting the social implications of messages. This means that sociolinguistic ethnography is concerned with becoming aware of possible interpretations of the meanings of messages by attending to participants' reactions to and uses of:

1. semantic content of the immediate message
2. syntax features of the message
3. nonverbal delivery
4. paralinguistic delivery (intonation, stress, speech, rhythm)
5. behavioral norms associated with the lesson goals

---

[2]The theory of social action guiding the project which is reported in part in this presentation is based on a theoretical application of Etzioni's (1968) conceptualization of contextuating orientation (Cf., Etzioni, A. *The Active Society*. New York: Free Press, 1968). For a more explicit discussion of the theoretical aspects of this project use Green and Wallat 1979.

6. behavioral norms associated with the ecological context, and
7. ordering of messages, (i.e., what all the above variables are tied to) (Gumperz & Herasimchuk, 1973).

These features are not separate cues to meaning; rather, they occur in varying combinations and provide a degree of redundancy for message interpretation. Features such as paralinguistic signals of voice, pitch, stress, intonation, along with the nonverbal signals of gaze direction, proxemic distance, body motion and gestures co-occur with the syntactic and lexical features of the conversation and effect the interpretation of the communication (Gumperz, 1976). In addition to these features, there are other aspects of conversations which influence the interpretation of communication. Features, such as status, social identities, and social relationships effect the nature and structure of conversations. These features, Gumperz (1972) suggests, "are signalled in the act of speaking and have a function in the communication process which is akin to that of syntax in the communication of referential meaning" (p. 99). Analysis of conversations, therefore, requires consideration of a broad range of complex sociolinguistic features that contribute to message interpretation and conversational structure.

In addition to these features, sociolinguistic studies have pointed out that the nature of the unit of analysis is important. Analysis procedures which focus on the duration of a behavior or the frequency of any given behavior provide little information about how and when a behavior is used. Sociolinguistic analysis of conversations is directly concerned with this question. Such analysis is based on the premise that meaning is context-bound and that relationships or ties exist among various behaviors in a dialogue (Green & Wallat, 1979; Gumperz & Herasimchuk, 1973).

Identification of these ties is possible when the context-bound or situated nature of meaning is considered. As Gumperz and Herasimchuk (1973) have shown:

A major important analytic principle to emerge from recent work in this area is that it is impossible to interpret situated meanings apart from the total context of what has been said before and what is said afterwards. The interpretation of a message is not a constant; it depends on what it is in response to and how it has been received. What is said at one point in a conversation may change the interpretation of everything that has gone before. (p. 103)

These two factors, the situated nature of meaning and the existence of ties among units, suggest that mapping the flow of classroom conversations into units with common content and/or conversational intent can provide the basis for analysis of nature of interaction. Analysis of these conversational units or segments then provides the data about the distribution of interaction patterns and the effect of these patterns on not only the conversational structure but the outcome of the conversation in terms of both teacher and child strategies.

   The following brief segment from the teacher-child dialogue during transition time will illustrate this point:

   This sample map (Fig. 5.1) from our data analysis contains a great deal of pertinent information concerning the use of sociolinguistic strategies by children and teachers. This information is reduced into a descriptive coding method which serves as a tool for later analyses of social actions (cf. Green & Wallat, 1981). For example, on this map segment the teacher concludes an interaction with a group of children (line 029). The message, YES I WORKED ON THEM, is a restatement (19) of a student's question about who worked with the math activity kits. The teacher focuses (8) on her own behavior (23) in the previous lesson (25). In addition, the message serves as confirmation (10) of the student's indirect statement of a classroom social norm: individuals' are responsible for cleaning up the materials they work with. Consideration of the paralinguistic and nonverbal contextualization cues indicated that the teacher began a new interaction unit with the message AH. (line 030). This message, AH, acts as a framing strategy ([8]) and a turn place-holder strategy (16). The teacher, with this message, tells listeners that she still has the floor and that they need to attend. In line 031, AH ROGAN, she signals paralinguistically that the message is a focusing message (8) addressed to Rogan R_r. This message is tied to both an object (i.e. what the teacher refers to as "a structure") that Rogan had made with blocks prior to the transition time (24), and the general lesson, clean-up and transition (25).

Line	IU	Message Unit Transcript Text	Potentially Divergent Units	Thematically Tied Units
029		YES I WORKED ON THEM		[2] $\begin{smallmatrix}8\\10\\19\end{smallmatrix}$ [R] $\begin{smallmatrix}23\\25\end{smallmatrix}$
030		AH		[3] $\begin{smallmatrix}[8]\\16\end{smallmatrix}$ [R] 23
031		AH ROGAN		$\begin{smallmatrix}8\\16\end{smallmatrix}$ [R_R] 24
032		ROGAN DID YOU WANT TO SAVE YOUR STRUCTURE?		$\begin{smallmatrix}8\\10\\15\end{smallmatrix}$ [Q_R] $\begin{smallmatrix}24\\25\end{smallmatrix}$
033		Rogan: (shakes head affirmatively off camera)		10 [r_R] $\begin{smallmatrix}23\\25\end{smallmatrix}$ 10 [R_R] 24
034		OK		
035		James: Put it over here.	8 (r_j) $\begin{smallmatrix}23\\24\\25\end{smallmatrix}$	

FIG. 5.1.   Sample Map

In line 032, the teacher asks Rogan a question Q_r, ROGAN, DID YOU WANT TO SAVE YOUR STRUCTURE? This question served a variety of functions. It focused Rogan on the structure (8), asked him for confirmation (10) and asked him to clarify his desires (15). This question is tied both to the student's goal (24) and to the general lesson, clean-up and transition (25). Rogan responds r_R to this request for confirmation affirmatively (10), thus tying to the teacher's comment (23) and to the goal of the lesson (25). The teacher then confirms the appropriateness of this action (10) and the student's actions (24).

These descriptive coding and mapping procedures serve as micro-ethnographic tools for capturing the evolving conversation and social action norms. Analysis of conversation, therefore, provides knowledge about the development of both the teacher's and children's use of communicative strategies in instructional situations. In addition, the coding of the teacher's strategies over the year permits the research team to capture what types of strategies have been effective in accomplishing goals with a particular group of children. In other words, the maps permit exploration of process-process relationships. They permit identification of process-process relationships that show how changes are made between different stages of instructional activities within and between lessons, as well as exploration of how a set of verbal and nonverbal social "actions serve to attain certain results and to guard against others" (Smith, 1967, p. 49).

One of the assumptions behind this perspective is that group contexts are not simply given but are constructed by participants during social interaction processes of contextualization. Another assumption of this research is that in order to arrive at a description of social competence requirements in a particular classroom, it is necessary to look in detail at how the adult works with both her own and the children's message in order to affect what functions of language can occur in an instructional context.

In addition to the sociolinguistic features discussed earlier, our work also builds on insights concerning what is available in the environment for children to act upon and insights about the relationships between socialization processes, group participation structures, and the characteristics of learning contexts that have developed from ethnographic descriptions. These factors have been reported elsewhere (Green & Wallat, 1979; 1981); three are of particular importance to this discussion. The first factor relates to the question of units of focus, or, in other words, what is "holistic" in terms of ethnographic research. Erickson (1977) has tied to influence our rethinking the research implications behind the word "holistic" in terms of ethnographic research. He argues that because the study of interactions in social settings involves consideration of relations between parts and the whole, such work is "holistic not because of the size of the social unit, but because the units of analysis are considered analytically as wholes, whether that whole be a community, a school system . . . or the beginning of one lesson in a single classroom" (p. 59). From this perspective, the various conversational contexts that occur in classrooms can be the analytic wholes. Analysis of demands for social actions within and across context thus forms a basis for the identification of social norms for behavior.

Furthermore, Erickson points out the need for considering what has functional relevance for teachers and students when doing ethnography. By the term "functional relevance," Erickson (1979) is referring to the need for researchers to insure that their descriptions of what is going on "at least make contact" (p. 5) with the points of view of the participants about what is going on. This question of functional relevance has also been voiced by Tikunoff and Ward (1978). They suggest that studies of teaching can be judged as reliable and valid by describing and analyzing the appropriateness of the teaching-learning act in terms of the context in which it occurs. Tikunoff and Ward suggest that in studies of the context-bound nature of teaching:

> Reliability becomes a measure of the extent to which . . . teaching/learning conditions . . . results in appropriate interactions . . . acts and strategies. In other words, is the teaching consistently appropriate given the context in which it appears?
> Validity becomes a multidimensional judgment of the teacher and the students, as well as the researcher, observer and trainer . . . ; assessment of teaching must build from an inside/outside perspective. (p. 35)

The latter issue of validity when viewed from this perspective, moves the study of teaching towards the optimistic anthropological view that, "There is no ultimate truth; all we can do is try to arrive at several legitimate interpretations of the truth and look at the processes by which they were derived. By using a form of triangulation[3], we may possibly come closer to some kind of neutrality or a more inclusive truth" (Gumperz, 1981b, p. 275).

Consideration of these issues underlies the sociolinguistic approach being described. In our work, the teacher is an active member of the research team (Wallat, Green, Conlin, Haramis, 1981). She not only records her goals daily, but also helps clarify the analysis and validates the findings. Given that the children are young (5–6-year-olds), their role in validation is more limited; however, as reported elsewhere (Wallat & Green, 1979), the children's perspective is used to clarify and validate findings on the social norms.

This question of focus is also related to the second factor, the approach to identification of patterns from the evolving patterns.

Gumperz (1981a) has pointed out that we are at the beginning point of recognizing that children's and adults' use of intonation and stress in creating contexts and adult differences in use of intonation and stress are related to establishing contexts and keeping conversations going. To learn this we have had to learn to

---

[3]Triangulation is a general term that refers to multiple methods of observation and collection of multiple views of a situation (Cf., Denzin, N. K., *The Research Act,* 2nd ed., New York: McGraw Hill, 1978).

attend to the strategies children and teachers decide to use in creating, maintaining, and completing interaction sequences. This means that researchers concerned with capturing the contextualization cues and, as such, the creation of differentiated contexts of classroom structures, have had to think of observation systems as heuristic systems that can be used by both the researcher and the teacher for capturing differences in classrooms (Stenhouse, 1975). Gumperz also suggests that we can view the stream of behavior in classrooms in terms of what kinds of nonverbal and verbal contextualization cues are associated with goals that are realized and what types of contextualization cues lead to divergent behaviors. In addition, Cicourel (1974) suggests that in viewing language uses in schools, we must treat "errors and misunderstandings as natural aspects of educational encounters" (p. 6). Consideration of divergent behaviors and misunderstandings has been shown to highlight what the behavioral expectations for communicative participation are (Mehan, Cazden, Coles, Fisher, & Maroules, 1976; Green & Wallat, 1981). For example, if all children are singing and a child tries to get the teacher's attention, the teacher may indicate that "WE'RE SINGING NOW" (Green & Wallat, 1981). The teacher's action indicates simultaneously that the child's behavior was inappropriate and that singing or rather group participation is the appropriate behavior. In other words, by focusing on patterns of how children and teachers build on and work with each others' suggestions and behaviors, we can begin to identify social norms and patterns of interaction within and across contexts.

The concept of divergence also relates to the third factor.

We now know that not every teacher will use the pedagogical strategies identified to date in the same patterns (Haberman & Stinnett, 1973). Nor will every teacher use the same nonverbal, verbal and paralinguistic cohesion patterns in the same way (Green & Wallat, 1979). Gumperz (1981a) has succinctly captured how previous work in observations of processes and strategies has moved us closer to realizing this aspect of the context-bound nature of teaching. He believes that what is significant about past research in the study of teaching is that we are able to adapt observation systems in order to get closer to testing the premise that classroom language is content *and* information about context. While recognizing that an adequate description of activities and their contexts must correct past oversights in validity by including gaining access to the view of the participants under study, Gumperz has acknowledged the positive contribution of past research. One of the "good insights" he has outlined is that we can no longer assume that the classroom is an undifferentiated environment. Equally important, educational research has pointed out that as classroom participant structures change the demands on children for recognizing unstated access boundaries may change. In attempting to get closer to how behavior expectations for working in differentiated classroom structures may be signaled through unstated cues and paralinguistic cues, researchers have had to move towards micro descriptions of classroom discourse. The work of researchers such as Bellack,

Kliebard, Hyman, and Smith (1966) and Sinclair and Coulthard (1974) has shown the value of pragmatic linguistic studies. The combined positive directions in the study of teaching and ethnography can help focus the positive directions from past research on construct differences in teaching strategies and gross differences in classroom structures. This means that we can build on the strengths of observation systems and linguistic ethnography to permit researchers to ask questions such as: How do certain kinds of social convention meanings develop over time if not all rules and behavior expectations are always explicitly stated?

SUMMARY

In this chapter we presented arguments for using micro-analysis in the form of sociolinguistic ethnography of communication to identify and describe the socialization processes that are being selected, terminated, modified, suspended, and recommended by the teachers and students during the everyday interactions of the classroom (cf. Blumer, 1969). We have argued that such a methodology permits exploration of process-process outcomes that lead to an understanding of the relationship between teaching strategies and social behavior expectations and to an understanding of what is involved in becoming a member of a classroom society.

As part of this argument, we briefly overviewed our sociolinguistic ethnographic approach to the study of the construction of social norms. As indicated, this approach consists of a multistep process that includes (1) construction of structural maps of evolving conversations by attending to verbal and nonverbal contextualization cues; (2) identification of social norms through analysis of patterns of interaction; and (3) validation of findings with participants. Because the methodology for the description of conversational structure and the construction of structural maps has been described in detail elsewhere (Green & Wallat, 1979; Green & Wallat, 1981), this aspect of the methodology is not reviewed here. Rather, in the remainder of this chapter, we discuss issues in identifying and validating the process of the construction of social rules using the structural maps as a heuristic tool.

CONSTRUCTION OF SOCIAL NORMS: A STRATEGY OF SEARCH

In this section, we present the approach we use to describe the identification of social norms. The vehicle for the discussion is teacher/child interactions that occurred during the transition time between individual work at arrival time and group meeting time in a kindergarten classroom.

The question that we explore is: How do certain kinds of social convention meanings develop over time if not all rules and behavior expectations are always explicitly stated? To facilitate the discussion, the following table of the entire repertoire of *verbal* socialization signals used by the teacher in the transition period from individual work time to group meeting time is used.

Table 5.1 includes a frequency count of statements relating to six general areas of group coordination norms identified from an analysis of teacher/child interaction during transition times throughout the first year of school. These six areas are subdivided into specific social behavior expectations that were referred to by the teacher during the transition time to group meeting on the days listed on the chart. The major point regarding socialization techniques as represented in the charts is not the frequency distribution of how many times a particular expectation was stated. If the reader focused on the spread of the frequency count, she/he could make a wrong judgment about consistency versus inconsistency of this teacher's socialization repertoire. What is represented on the charts is the fact that the children throughout the year were continually focused on six Group Coordination Norms which represented the requirements of the social structure of this classroom.

The repertoire of the teacher's socialization processes is reflected in the wide differences in the occurrence of the norms both within and across days. These differences suggest that in order to examine socialization strategies, we cannot concentrate solely on an additive procedure for determining norms. Rather, we need to analyze each context over time in order to determine overall social requirements that must be monitored by participants. What Table 5.1 shows, therefore, is the six norms of participation for identifying when is group transition and the actions that are consistent throughout the year.

Table 5.1 was determined partially by consideration of verbal statements of norms. These statements are reflected in the frequency counts. However, consideration of nonverbal behaviors helped to verify the existence of these norms. Since norms help guide behavior, consideration of nonverbal contextualization behaviors that indicate adherence to rules provides the bases for further definition of social norms.

Table 5.2 provides an example of this process.

In this segment, the teacher uses nonverbal cues such as eye gaze, body position, gesture and pause (silence) to indicate and reinforce the meaning of the norm represented by the signal. Analysis over time of the teacher's actions related to the signal showed that the teacher used the nonverbal behaviors each day in a similar manner to indicate what was expected. In fact, over time the nonverbal behavior served to symbolize and signal her social norm.

In addition, observation of children's nonverbal behavior—body movement, cessation of talk, eye gaze, etc., showed adherence to the meaning of the signal—stop, look, and listen. While the teacher provided a verbal cue to the

Table 5.1

STEPS TO STRUCTURING AND RESTRUCTURING GROUP
DURING TRANSITION TIMES

Group Coordination Norms	Social Behaviors	September 15	September 16	September 19	September 21	October 5	February 8	May 23[a]
TRANSITION LENGTH IN MINUTES		2:53	2:52	4:34	4:32	2:37	4:57	---
1. Responsibility for signaling involvement	a. Piano chords (non-negotiable)	1	1	1	1	1	1	--
	b. Teacher identifies *individuals* who have interpreted meaning of signal (stop work, look to teacher, listen for directions) (non-negotiable)	2	3	5	2	1	0	--
	c. Elicits meaning of signal (rule non-negotiable)	0	0	0	1	1	1	--
2. Responsibility for Work Space	a. Finish work and clean space (context dependent)	2	1	1	1	1	1	--
	b. Clean up work space previously occupied (non-negotiable)	3	0	0	0	0	0	--

112

c. Leave work at space to finish later (negotiable)	0	3	2	0	0	5	—
d. Plan ahead for choice of work (choice of activities negotiable)	0	0	4	0	0	0	—
3. Responsibility for Work Objects							
a. Work object has own general space in room (e.g., arrival shelf materials) (non-negotiable)	1	1	0	0	0	0	—
b. Student's personal objects and/or projects are to be placed in a "safe" place by student and student responsible for its care (e.g. locker, Teacher's office) (responsibility for it non-negotiable)	1	0	1	0	0	0	—
c. If individual has produced a product and wishes to share product a holding space is available (placement is negotiable)	1	0	0	0	0	0	—

(Continued)

Table 5.1 (Continued)

Group Coordination Norms	Social Behaviors	September 15	September 16	September 19	September 21	October 5	February 8	May 23[a]
TRANSITION LENGTH IN MINUTES		2:53	2:52	4:34	4:32	2:37	4:57	—
4. Responsibility for Signaling Change of Group Structure	a. Directions addressed to group	2	4	2	1	1	0	—
	b. Directions addressed to individuals (e.g. meet in new area) (non-negotiable)	5	0	0	1	0	3	—
5. Responsibility for Physical Orientation	a. The group has a specific physical structure (e.g. Circle) (non-negotiable)	0	2	6	1	2	0	—
	b. Find and stay in individual space within the physical structure (negotiable)	9	9	10	7	4	1	5(circle time)

114

c. There is a specific way to sit so that others can see (non-negotiable)	0	2	0	0	0	0	2(circle time)
6. Responsibility for Cooperative Effort							
a. During songs, everybody sings and works together (e.g. children sing with Teacher and are not directly/overtly taught song) (non-negotiable)	2	4	3	1	0	1	1(circle time)
b. During discussion, we speak one at a time (non-negotiable)	3	2	0	1	0	0	0(circle time)
c. When someone is speaking, we listen to the speaker (non-negotiable)	5	1	6	9	0	0	2(circle time)

[a]The structure for this day was different due to a Math Program. A circle time was held at a later time than usual, and the transition from Math to Group Meeting Time merely included moving from the tables to the work area (i.e., The children did not need time to replace individual work). Selected findings are presented from this group meeting that illustrate the existence of the norms established for behavior within group.

Table 5.2
Cue Record/Transcript Segment

Transcript Lines	Message Units	Contextualization Cues to Message Units	Interaction Unit Length	Contextualization Cues to Interaction Units
002	AH LET'S SEE	1. Said as T raises body from piano 2. T turns to face Sts 3. T's hands down at her sides 4. Message said evenly-no stress but volume loud enough for Sts to hear	1 MU (Message Unit)	Change of body position. Hand gestures. Intonation patterns. Gaze direction.
003	OH	1. Pitch changes-higher 2. Tone held 3. Hand raises from side with finger extended pointing upward 4. Noise level (children talking) stops 5. T gazes around group 6. Pause (.0193 secs)		
004	PETER REMEMBERED THE SIGNAL	1. T's body moves toward Peter and away from center 2. Head moves and eye gaze moves to Peter 3. T points to Peter 4. Hand brought back to T's body 5. Sts who are talking cease as she says "Peter" 6. Hand held at shoulder level 7. Pitch and volume remain the same		
005	STEPHANIE REMEMBERED THE SIGNAL	1. T's head turns to Stephanie 2. T's body returns to center 3. Pitch remains the same during 4 words 4. Volume remains the same during 4 words	3 MU	Pause after AH LET'S SEE. Change in intonation from line 002 is held from 003 to 005.

(Continued)

Table 5.2 (Continued)
Cue Record/Transcript Segment

Transcript Lines	Message Units	Contextualization Cues to Message Units	Interaction Unit Length	Contextualization Cues to Interaction Units
		5. Pitch and volume same as line 004		
		6. Silence on Sts' part maintained		
		7. Hand drops slightly		
		8. Head drops slightly at end of message		
006	IT IS NOW TIME	1. Hand drops @ 2'' returns to original position and then moves forward @ 4''		
		2. Hand slides forward matching rhythm of message (words)		
		3. No pause		

expected normative behaviors, (lines 004 and 005) she did so indirectly. She used nonverbal pointing simultaneously with the verbal message to signal to Stephanie and Peter that they were to stop, look, and listen. Over time analysis of children's verbal and nonverbal behaviors showed that not only do children adhere to the signal, but that later in the year children could state the meaning of the signal.

What this brief discussion shows is that the nonverbal as well as the verbal signaling system appears to be an essential element in the construction of social norms. In other words, these findings indicate that in order to determine the communicative and social demands of the classroom contexts, the students had to process more than simple direct statements of rules. The students had to learn that the teacher's use of phrases such as "PETER REMEMBERED THE SIGNAL," or "WE'RE SINGING NOW," or "WE'RE LISTENING TO _____ NOW," reaches far beyond the universal factual dictionary meaning of these phrases. Analysis of the ecological setting in which these phrases were produced as well as the analysis of contextualization features indicate that these phrases serve to inform participants of multiple norms that should be occurring. In our study, a phrase such as "WE'RE SINGING NOW" served to signal contextualization expectations regarding how the individual should signal their involvement and coordinate their actions with the rest of the group. Analysis of group meeting time has shown this phrase can mean: begin singing; move back into the circle; stop talking to your neighbor; stop moving; or even use your hands and body to illustrate song phrases and group context norms. If we had presented the latter message as merely a factual statement in a discussion of the construction of social norms, we would not be able to answer sociolinguistic questions such as what contextual factors affect the emergence of behaviors, how does nonverbal and verbal language enter into socialization processes in different classrooms, and how do teachers and children organize themselves to maintain the contexts in different classrooms?

This discussion shows that the presentation of data in tabular form limits examination of socialization processes in as much as social norms are more than mechanistic rules.

What we have found in our study of social norms over the course of a school year is that every instructional context is essentially a question of solving a coordination problem. Every context identified to date included time spent on establishing the meaning of coordination signals. We have found that an adequate account of socialization processes must include the meaning of both verbal and nonverbal symbols to this coordination process. As Lewis (1969) has pointed out, rules or norms are not merely continuously verbally stated regularities in behavior. "Some rules must be formulated in advance; others need not be. But in either case, the rule itself is distinct from a formulation or statement of that rule" (p. 108). A coordination rule or norm exists if the members of a community regulate their affairs according to agreed upon communication signals. In addition, Lewis suggests that "Communication by conventional signals is a commonplace phenomenon, so much so that we must make an effort not to take it for granted" (p. 122).

This view is consonant with a sociolinguistic view because in order to establish and maintain social interaction, the participants must have agreed upon signals for beginning and ending a single social occasion. These signals are the contextualization cues discussed previously that help participants in a conversation to interpret the context-bound meaning of the message. In other words, the same signaling system for coordinating the participants' actions, the contextualization cues, occurs repeatedly without need for verbal restatement every time (Lewis, 1969). Therefore, the problem facing those concerned with the construction of social norms or sociolinguistic rules for knowing when to speak is to capture the elements of a system of signalling coordination conventions including not only verbal statements but the participant's gestures in relation to objects in the environment.

CONCLUSION

With this description of group coordination, we end this chapter as we began— with a statement of the interrelatedness of language and socialization. Throughout our discussion we have argued for a reconceptualization of socialization from a process perspective, defined language as a communicative process through which socialization occurs, described briefly a system for sociolinguistic ethnography for symbolizing the communicative and socialization processes and built a rationale for viewing social norm development as a coordination process. With this chapter, then, we have pointed toward new directions for those concerned with the questions—how does a child become a member of a classroom society and how does a teacher organize group contexts in classrooms.

REFERENCES

Almy, M. *The early childhood educator at work.* New York: McGraw-Hill, 1975.

Bell, R. Q., & Hertz, T. W. Toward more comparability and generalizability of developmental research. *Child Development,* 1976, *47,* 6–13.

Bellack, A. A., Kliebard, H. M., Hyman, R. T. & Smith, F. L. *The language of the classroom.* New York: Teachers College Press, 1966.

Bellack, A. A., & Davitz, J. R. The language of the classroom. In A. Morrison & D. McIntyre (Eds.), *The social psychology of teaching.* Baltimore: Penguin Books, 1972.

Blumer, H. *Symbolic interactionism: perspective and method.* Englewood Cliffs, New Jersey: Prentice-Hall, 1969.

Cazden, C. B. *Child language and education.* New York: Holt, Rinehart & Winston, 1972.

Cazden, C. Language in education: variation in the teacher-talk register. In *Language in public life,* 30th Annual Georgetown University Roundtable on Language and Linguistics, 1979.

Cicourel, A. V. The acquisition of social structure: towards a developmental sociology of language and meaning. In J. Douglas (Ed.), *Understanding everyday life.* Boston: Routledge & Kegan Paul, 1968.

Cicourel, A. V. *Language use and school performance.* New York: Academic Press, 1974.

Cook-Gumperz, J. *Social control and socialization: a study of class differences in the language of maternal control.* Boston: Routledge & Kegan Paul, 1973.

Cook-Gumperz, J. *Language at home and at school: focusing on discourse.* Paper presented at the Annual Meeting of the National Council of Teachers of English, San Francisco, November, 1979.

Cook-Gumperz, J. Persuasive talk: the social organization of children's talk. In J. Green & C. Wallat (Eds.), *Ethnography and language in educational settings.* Norwood, New Jersey: Ablex, 1981.

Cook-Gumperz, J., & Corsaro, W. A. Social-ecological constraints on children's communicative strategies. In J. Cook-Gumperz & J. Gumperz (Eds.), *Papers on language and context.* University of California, Berkeley: Language Behavior Research Laboratory, Working Paper #46, 1976.

Cook-Gumperz, J., & Gumperz, J. J. Context in children's speech. In J. Cook-Gumperz & J. Gumperz (Eds.), *Papers on language and context.* University of California, Berkeley: Language Behavior Laboratory, Working Paper #46, 1976.

Corsaro, W. A. Entering the child's world: research strategies for field entry and data collection in a preschool setting. In J. Green & C. Wallat (Eds.), *Ethnography and language in educational settings.* Norwood, N.J.: Ablex, 1981.

Damon, W. *The social world of the child.* San Francisco: Jossey-Bass Pub., 1977.

Denzin, N. K. *Childhood socialization: studies in the development of language, social behavior, and identity.* San Francisco: Jossey-Bass, 1977.

Doyle, W. The uses of nonverbal behaviors: toward an ecological model of classrooms. *Merrill-Palmer Quarterly,* 1977, *23,* 179–192.

Duke, D. L. The etiology of student misbehavior and the depersonalization of blame. *Review of Educational Research,* 1978, *48,* 415-437.

Erickson, F. Afterthoughts. In A. Kendon, R. M. Harris, & M. R. Key (Eds.), *Organization of behavior in face-to-face interaction.* Chicago: Aldine, 1975. (a)

Erickson, F. Gatekeeping and the melting pot: interaction in counseling encounters. *Harvard Educational Review,* 1975, *45,* 44-70, (b).

Erickson, F. Some approaches to inquiry in school-community ethnography. *Anthropology and Education Quarterly,* 1977, *8,* 58-69.

Erickson, F. On *standards of descriptive validity in studies in classroom activity.* Occasional Paper No. 16. The Institute for Research on Teaching. East Lansing: Michigan State University, 1979.

Erickson, F., & Schultz, J. When is a context? Some issues and methods in the analysis of social competence, In J. Green & C. Wallat (Eds.) *Ethnography and language in educational settings.* Norwood, New Jersey: Ablex, 1981.

Ervin-Tripp, S. On sociolinguistic rules: alternation and co-occurrence. In J. Gumperz & D. Hymes (Eds.), *Directions in sociolinguistics: the ethnography of communication.* New York: Holt, Rinehart & Winston, 1972.

Fillmore, C. Frame semantics and the nature of language. In S. R. Harnard et al. (Ed.) *Origins and evolution of language and speech.* New York: Annals of the New York Academy of Sciences, Vol. 280, 1976.

Goodenough, W. *Culture, language, and society.* Reading, Mass.: Addison-Wesley Modular Publications, 1971.

Green, J. L., & Wallat, C. Mapping instructional conversations. In J. Green & C. Wallat (Eds.) *Ethnography and Language in educational settings.* Norwood, New Jersey: Ablex Publishing Co., 1981.

Green, J., & Wallat, C. What is an instruction context? An exploratory analysis of conversational shifts across time. In O. Garnica & M. King (Eds.), *Language, Children and Society.* New York: Pergamon Press, 1979.

Gumperz, J. Conversational inference and classroom learning. In J. Green & C. Wallat (Eds.) *Ethnography and Language, in Educational settings.* Norwood, New Jersey: Ablex, 1981. (a)

Gumperz, J. Language, Communication & Public Negotiation. In P. R. Sanday (Ed.), *Anthropology and the public interest,* N.Y.: Academic, 1976.

Gumperz, J. Roundtable comments. In B. Hudson (Ed.) Discussion—Needed directions in face-to-face interaction in educational settings. In J. Green & C. Wallat (Eds.), *Ethnography and language in educational settings.* Norwood, New Jersey: Ablex, 1981. (b)

Gumperz, J. J. Sociolinguistics and communication in small groups. In J. B. Pride & J. Holmes (Eds.), *Sociolinguistics.* Baltimore: Penguin, 1972.

Gumperz, J., & Herasimchuk, E. The conversational analysis of social meaning: a study of classroom interaction. In R. Shuy (Ed.), *Monograph Series on Language and Linguistics, 25, 23rd Annual Roundtable. Sociolinguistics: Current Trends and Prospects.* Georgetown University Press, 1973.

Gumperz, J., & Hymes, D. *Directions in sociolinguistics: the ethnography of communication.* New York: Holt, Rinehart & Winston, Inc. 1972.

Haberman, M., & Stinnett, T. M. *Teacher education and the new profession of teaching.* Berkeley, Ca.: McCutchan Pub., 1973.

Hammersley, M. The mobilization of pupil attention. In M. Hammersley & P. Woods (Eds.) *The Process of Schooling.* London: Routledge & Kegan Paul, 1976.

Hymes, D. H. Models of the interaction of language and social settings. *Journal of Social Issues,* 1967, *23,* 8-28.

Hymes, D. H. On communicative competence. In J. B. Pride & J. Holmes. *Sociolinguistics.* Baltimore, Md.: Penguin Books, 1972. (a)

Hymes, D. H. Models of the interaction of language and social life. In J. Gumperz & D. Hymes (Eds.), *Directions in sociolinguistics: the ethnography of communication.* New York: Holt, Rinehart & Winston, 1972. (b)

Labov. W. *Sociolinguistic patterns.* Philadelphia: University of Pennsylvania Press, 1972.

Labov, W. & Fanshel, D. *Therapeutic discourse.* New York: Academic, 1977.

Lewis, D. K. *Convention.* Cambridge: Harvard University Press, 1969.

McCarthy, T. A. A theory of communicative competence. *Philosophy of the Social Sciences,* 1973, *3,* 135-156.

McDermott, R. Social relations as contexts for learning in school. *Harvard Educational Review,* 1977, *47,* 198-213.

Mehan, H., Cazden, C., Coles, L., Fisher, S., & Maroules, N. *The social organization of classroom lessons.* Center for Human Information Processing University of San Diego, La Jolla, California, December, 1976.

Mishler, E. G. Implications of teacher strategies for language and cognition: observations in first-grade classrooms. In C. B. Cazden, V. P. John, D. Hymes (Eds.), *Functions of language in the classroom.* New York: Teachers College Press, 1972.

Mitzel, H. E. Increasing the impact of theory and research on programs of instruction. *Journal of Teacher Education,* 1977, *28,* 15-20.

Parke, R. D. Social cues, social control, and ecological validity. *Merrill-Palmer Quarterly,* 1976, *22,* 111-123.

Schaeffer, R. *Mothering.* Cambridge: Harvard University Press, 1977.

Sinclair, J. M., & Coulthard, R. M. *Towards an analysis of discourse: the English used by teachers and pupils,* London: Oxford University Press, 1974.

Skolnick, A. (Ed.) *Rethinking childhood.* Boston: Little, Brown & Co., 1976.

Slama-Cazacu, T. The role of social context in language acquisition. In W. C. McCormack & S. A. Wurm (Eds.) *Language and man: anthropological issues.* Chicago: Aldine (Mouton), 1976.

Smith, B. O., Meux, M. O., Coombs, J., Nuthall, G., & Precians, R. *A study of the strategies of teaching.* Urbana, Illinois: University of Illinois College of Ed., Bureau of Ed. Research, 1967.

Speier, M. The child as conversationalist. In M. Hammersley & P. Woods (Eds.), *The processes of schooling.* London: Routledge & Kegan Paul, 1976.

Stenhouse, L. *An introduction to curriculum research and development.* London: Heinemann, 1975.

Takanishi, R. Reviewers comments. *American Educational Research Journal,* 1978, *15,* 3.

Tikunoff, W. J., & Ward, B. J. Insuring reliability and validity in competency assessment. *Journal of Teacher Education,* 1978, *29,* 33-37.

Wallat, C. *Field notes,* Unpublished, 1977.

Wallat, C. & Green, J. Social rules and communicative contexts in kindergarten. *Theory into Practice,* 1978, *18,* 275-284.

Wallat, C., Green, J., Conlin, S. & Haramis, M. Issues related to action research in the classroom: the teacher and researcher as a team. In J. Green & C. Wallat (Eds.) *Ethnography and language in educational settings.* Norwood, New Jersey: Ablex Publishing Co., 1981.

Young, T. R., & Beardsley, P. The sociology of classroom teaching: a microfunctional analysis. *Journal of Educational Thought,* 1968, *2,* 175-186.

6

Cognition and Culture: Two Perpectives on "Free Play"

Kathryn M. Borman
University of Cincinnati

Nancy T. Lippincott
Miami University

Adults are rarely involved in the organization and supervision of children's playground games unless it is to announce their end (Polgar, 1976). Easily overlooked are the manifestation in play of children's underlying cognitive skills and the importance of games as social contexts for cultural learning. It is the primary purpose of this chapter to look at playground games in order to describe the rule-governed nature of a group of first-grade children's spontaneously organized playground games. Specifically, the analysis focuses upon hopscotch, kissers and chasers, and tag to examine the set of turn-taking and game maintenance skills which underlie these activities. In addition, as milieu for socialization, games provide settings for cultural learning. Therefore, a secondary purpose is to examine the contents of this cultural learning. A literature review of selected research on children's play follows immediately. This review explores two dimensions of children's games: the cognitive competence that supports children's ability to engage in playground games and the nature of the sociocultural environment that surrounds game-playing activity.

Though games may be dismissed by some as frivolous or trivial childish activity, the subject of children's games has by no means been neglected in social science research. We are hardly the first investigators to take children's games seriously. Approaches to the study of children's games are varied, ranging from the folklorist's interest in the historical origins of rhymes and chants which accompany such playground games as London Bridge or farmer in the dell, to the cognitive psychologist's concern with the role of play in stimulating the development of social cognitive abilities. Recent collections of research and scholarship on the subject of children's play illustrate this multidisciplinary range of research.[1]

SOCIAL COMPETENCE IN GAMES: THE PSYCHOGENIC PERSPECTIVE

The psychogenic perspective has recently focused on cognitive skills developed in spontaneous play. Whereas earlier work dealt with descriptions of the effects of emotional states and personality traits on play, many current studies describe cognitive ensembles which develop progressively in a hierarchical fashion throughout life (Avedon & Sutton-Smith, 1971). Consequently, from the psychological perspective, play emerges as a natural vehicle for the evolution of thought; so natural, Bruner has argued, that its bases are biological as well as psychological. Phylogenetically, play is associated with more complex species. As cognitive complexity increases, so too does the observable play among the juvenile members of the species (Bruner, 1972).

Definitions of games and play are considerably varied. Catherine Garvey's (1977) conceptualization is congruent with our particular interest in games as manifestations of social cognitive abilities. Garvey's research on play and games has examined aspects of children's language and its association with play (Garvey, 1974, 1977). According to Garvey, language both regulates the child's own motor movements and also serves important rehearsal functions for the preschooler who is developing skills in social interaction with his or her associates in play. In delineating the distinction between play and games, Garvey describes play as a subjective orientation, a nonliteral attitude towards objects, activities and others. In contrast, according to Garvey (1977):

> Games have the quality of "social objects"—that is, a game has a clear beginning and end, and its structure can be specified in terms of moves in a fixed sequence with a limited set of procedures for certain contingencies. Thus performances of the same game will be very similar. A particular situated performance can be recalled, talked about, evaluated, or planned in advance. Games, then, are more formal, conventionalized events than are incidents of spontaneous play. And rules are the essence of games. (p. 104)

The structure of games is arranged by participants to include the turns of each player, the round of turns comprising a sequence or episode of play, and the format or overall pattern of play characterized by a particular round of turns.

---

[1]The disciplines of anthropology, especially cultural and cognitive anthropology, and developmental psychology are foremost in these integrated studies. Examples of this trend are contained in *Play and Learning,* Brian Sutton-Smith (ed.), New York: Gardner Press, 1979.

Garvey's model provides for two types of overriding rules in games. The first are general procedural rules and serve as the unique components of games, making hopscotch hopscotch rather than tag. The second set, described above as the format of a particular round, is situationally specific and tempered by the idiosyncratic abilities and characteristics of the individual players in the particular game in question. Some fifth-grade girls, as an example, play hopscotch with rule provisions for "walking the line" to gain an advantage when throwing their markers. This modification of the rules may or may not be invoked in a particular game played by fifth-grade girls; however, it is not observed in games played by first-grade girls. The use of strategy in play is highly dependent upon age-related cognitive abilities of players and other factors including peer influences in developing and modifying rules which predispose fifth-grade girls to include strategic arrangements in their execution of a particular hopscotch game.

Using Garvey's conceptual framework, Jerome Bruner and V. Sherwood (1975) analyzed the interaction of mother-infant dyads playing peekaboo. Their research reveals that though peekaboo is not a set of game-like behaviors at the outset of its appearance in the interactional repertoire of the mother and her infant, its enactment becomes progressively more constrained by a set of rules which govern play. A set of turns including establishing initial contact; disappearance, reappearance; and reestablished contact characterize all recorded episodes of play across all observed experienced mother-infant pairs. In other words, parents and their children during the course of their social interaction in the game, develop a sequence of play which, by the time the infant is 18-months old, is constrained by a set of rules or turns which regulate all episodes of play. Social cognitive abilities of an infant underlying his or her ability to play peekaboo include the ability to coordinate actions with another around a common set of game-like routines, a coordination which appears to be a simple forerunner of the elaborate coordination of perspectives necessary for competitive game playing in middle childhood (Rubin & Pepler, 1980).

How do children make the transition from imitative play to highly constrained and organized competitive play at games? A developmental sequence of game playing skills, commensurate with more general cognitive development, characterizes children's passage from imitative play, as in peekaboo during early infancy, imaginative play in the preschool years, sociodramatic play in early childhood, to participation in the rule-governed social games of middle childhood.[2] Enhancing this development is the interaction experienced by the developing individual from infancy onwards in the company of parents and later of peers.

Piaget (1965) has described the stages through which both children's play and their theories about play evolve. When children first begin coordinated, rule-

---

[2]Although the Piagetian perspective emphasizes interaction between psychological processes and experience, some developmentalists, notably Vygotsky (1978), have argued that experience in the context of play and games serves as the engine driving social cognitive development.

bound game playing, they may actually fail to agree upon the exact definitions of their rules, while at the same time professing that these rules are necessarily invariant. Governed by a morality of constraint, fledgling game players believe rules to be the inflexible dictates of authority and their gamesmanship, the faithful execution of authority's will. Only later, at ten or so, do game players realize the democratic origin of rules and feel free to use the rules flexibly. At this point, players, governed by common consent, begin actively searching for rule variations which nevertheless maintain a fair balance among all participants.

Social cognitive abilities appear to evolve in progressive elaborations qualitatively different from one another and hence referred to as stages. Rudimentary forms are supplanted by more sophisticated ones. In early middle childhood, children still evaluate interconnected roles sequentially rather than simultaneously. The child can "put himself in another person's shoes" but finds it hard to do so while keeping track of his own. By late middle childhood, boys and girls have the capacity to understand role reversibility and reciprocal relationships. By ten, simultaneous perspective taking skills begin to emerge in the context of children's competitive game playing. Children of this age are well along in acquiring the developmental skills necessary for orchestrating perspective differing from their own and evaluating them from a third, universal perspective, one that self-consciously mediates game playing with the criteria of fairness and objectivity in mind.

CULTURAL LEARNING IN GAMES: THE SOCIOGENIC PERSPECTIVE

The sociogenic approach underscores the social utility of games. According to sociological theory, participants are judged to be rehearsing strategies which will have importance immediately in informal peer interaction, as with classmates and neighborhood friends, and which will later assume importance in adult life, as sets of learned competitive behaviors and the knowledge of complex bureaucratic arrangements (Lever, 1978; Polgar, 1976; Roberts, Arth, & Bush, 1959; Roberts, Sutton-Smith, & Kendon, 1963). In other words, the sociological approach assumes childhood games have a functional fit with behaviors required of adults in the same culture. Thus, the sociogenic approach, focusing on the social meaning of the game, complements the psychogenic approach in its concentration on the development of individual mental skill.

Some sociologists have taken a broad look at games, examining structural properties in addition to social functions. Avedon (1971) attempted one such synthesis, by combining mathematical, social interactional, and recreational models of games. He identified four components which are "necessary and invariant" in structuring games, at least as viewed by mathematical models. These elements are purpose, number of players, rules of the game, and "pay off.'' To the mathematicians' set of structural elements, Avedon adds two additional components derived from the social interactionist perspective of Mead (1934), Goffman (1967), and Szasz (1961). These are roles of the participants and participant interaction patterns. Finally, Avedon completes his analysis by analyzing the material constituents of games: environmental requirements, physical settings, and equipment. The effect of Avedon's structural model is to give a framework for understanding the functional links between games and the larger society.

If rules are the hallmark of games according to the psychogenic perspective, then from the sociogenic point of view, competition is the most important factor. By definition, games have winners and losers; and this unequal outcome for participants plays a central role in several different analyses. Games, unlike amusements pastimes, or stunts, are ''recreational activities characterized by organized play, competition, two or more sides, criteria for determining the winner, and agreed upon rules.'' (Roberts, Arth, & Bush, 1959, p. 597, quoted in Roberts & Sutton-Smith, 1971, p. 465.)

Though playful behavior has been uniformly observed across all human cultures, game play is more limited. There are extant cultures in which game playing has not been observed at all. Nongame playing cultures, when compared to cultures where games are regularly played, ''tend to be tropical groups with simple subsistence patterns, simple technology, low political organization, no class stratification, pan-homogeneous communities, and to have low stress in child socialization.'' (Avedon & Sutton-Smith, 1971, p. 4). Avedon and Sutton-Smith conclude that such cultures are ''relatively non-complex in a variety of ways, not just in failing to have games.'' Games, therefore, provide a context for distinctive forms of cultural learning, specifically, those associated with complexly ordered societies. Moreover, specific types of games are associated with specific cultural groups.

In game playing cultures whose technological base is highly industrialized, games of strategy are likely to be present. If, in addition, individual accomplishment is prized by most members of the society, games of physical skill will also predominate. Games are related to the technological characteristics of the society's system of production, or so it is argued by Roberts, Arth, and Bush (1959), who also enumerate specific skills which follow from the frequent engagement of individuals in games of strategy and physical skill: ''games of strategy may be related to mastery of the social system, games of chance may be linked with mastery of the supernatural, and games of physical skill are possibly associated with the mastery of self and of environment'' (p. 604).

American children appear to challenge themselves with games of physical skill and strategy. The mixture of one to the other depends on the game being played, which, in turn, may be related to the age of the players. During the early years of elementary school, when perspective-taking skills are building, physical skill seems to outweigh strategy. For example, hopscotch demands that players be agile and alert to the position of players' markers. Executing a successful turn at play depends more on accuracy in throwing one's marker and negotiating the form than in outwitting one's fellow players. Similarly, tag and kisser and chasers, though influenced by strategic matters such as choosing whom to chase or by pretending not to be 'It' when one is, remain predominantly games of running and dodging. If American children really do choose games of physical skill and strategy, then we would conclude that their society is more concerned with mastery of self, environment, and social systems than with mastery of the supernatural and that their training has already begun by the time they chase each other around the playground in organized games of tag.

Not only culture at large but also child rearing practices are said to influence play. In a review of ethnographic literature, Roberts and Sutton-Smith (1971) describe the relationship between parents' rearing practices and children's game choices. In their analysis, games are classified according to the major determinant of successful performance, as we have already noted: games of physical skill, in which motor activities of the players determine the outcome; games of strategy, in which plans of action largely determine outcomes; and games of chance, in which luck defines the game's resolution. This typology also includes games whose outcomes are determined by some combination of attributes, as those demanding both luck and skill.

Parental rewards for achievement are associated with games of physical skill and also with games combining physical skill and strategy. Severity of weaning, toilet training, and also use of love-oriented socializing techniques are associated with games of strategy. All these child-rearing practices are said to be more common of middle-class families, suggesting that middle class families especially encourage their children to master social systems. In such a manner, sociologists picture an interrelated social network where the technological arrangements of the society are reflected in its child-rearing practices and emerge on its playgrounds as the "free play" of the society's youth.

Cognition and Culture: A Summary

What, then, would we expect to find on the playground of an urban Appalachian neighborhood school, where we monitored and recorded daily playground activities during a 2-month period?

Despite the fact that these children came from predominantly working class homes, an earlier study had shown that their parents' self-reports of their child-rearing practices more closely resembled middle class than working class parents (Borman, Lippincott, & Matey, 1978). Though we did not study weaning or toilet training specifically, our compiled data still suggest we might expect to see games requiring physical and strategic excellence.

On the other hand, no matter what the child's cultural experience, games of strategy should not be expected to appear until the child is capable of *simultane-*

ously ordering his own perspective with that of others, a skill which does not generally emerge until late childhood, though it probably emerges as a consequence of participating in less strenuously strategic yet vigorously competitive games. We should expect to see, among the first and second graders, just such transitional games, games in which, while physical skill is paramount, lessons in strategy can be learned. If "legal experts" of codified games emerge at ten, then legal education should have begun by six. We should expect to see roles of victim and aggressor, loser and winner occupied in turn, sequentially analyzed, and experiments undertaken to minimize the former while enjoying the latter.

The Playground Games of Urban Appalachian First Grade Children

The data for the study consist of 19 audio taped records of the naturally occurring play of 7-year-old urban Appalachian children taken during a 2-month observation period at an inner-city elementary school playground. The observations include eight different games. Games most often observed during the 8-week period were the games of hopscotch, kissers and chasers and tag. Though subsequently reported analyses of turn taking include all observations of all games, discussion will make most use of the data collected for these three games: A description of the structural features of the games follows.

Hopscotch (N = 7 transcripts).

The purpose of hopscotch is to execute a succession of moves through a numbered framework of geometric shapes painted or drawn in a pattern on the pavement. Hopscotch can be played by any number of players; however, in our observations, usually two and occasionally three played at the game. The rules of the game include at least these basic provisions: Play is started by a toss of a marker into the first square. After a successful throw, the player hops across the sequence of numbred squares and semi-circles from one to ten and back again. Turns are taken in this manner with the marker being tossed successively into each numbered square or semicircle. The winner is the first one to complete the circuit. Care must be taken not to step on a line bounding one of the numbered units or in a unit containing one's or an opponent's marker. Besides the requirement of a numbered framework, participants need a stone as a marker for tossing during the course of successive turns at play, though we observed enterprising players making do with a scrap of orange peel or piece of broken glass.

Kissers and Chasers (N = 4 transcripts).

The purpose of kissers and chasers ostensibly is to embrace or kiss the person or persons whose capture is the object of the chase. However, since sequences of play more often involved rounds of chasing and resting rather than rounds of chasing and kissing, it is likely that kissers and chasers has other purposes, purposes that may not be consciously understood by participants since they serve to guide motor skill development, role rehearsal, practice in strategizing, etc.

Generally a group of children ranging in number from three to ten form a fluid collectivity of chasers, one or two occasionally dropping in and out of the game as it proceeds. If the game is played to its logical conclusion, the pay off is a measure of the successful conquests made during the course of the game. Participants in the chase interact with one another in brief strategizing sessions or at rest stops which serve to allow participants to catch their breath and reflect on the progress of the chase. A large expanse of playground space in which to conduct the chase is the only physical requirement.

Tag (N = 3 transcripts).

The purpose of tag is to elude the reach of "it" when a player is "not it" and as "it to tag a "not it" who will then assume the "it" role. Tag can be played with a large number of participants as "not its." There usually is a single "it" who functions to entice the others from "safety" or "base" or "home", usually a fence or other designated territory that functions as a preserve or safety zone for players in the game. As in kissers and chasers, in tag a large open space is required for running and chasing. Also necessary is some physical prop such as a fence which may serve as a safety zone.

Also observed were a set of chanting or rhyming games which lack the clearly structured character of the three competitive social games just described:

Farmer in the Dell (N = 2 observations)
London Bridge (N = 1 observation)
Duck, Duck, Goose (N = 1 observation)
Follow the Leader (N = 1 observation)

These ritualized games have in common the selection of major roles in an arbitrary manner. For example, the farmer's wife is selected by the farmer in a whimsical fashion and not on the basis of a player's successful performance at a turn at play in the game. The recorded episodes of these games, it should be noted, were also the only observations made of these games on the school playground. Finally, spontaneously organized racing games were observed on two occasions. These sequences differed from chase sequences as in tag or kissers and chasers in that participants raced against each other to determine who could cover a predetermined distance in the shortest time.

Method

With the exception of three records which were begun by the observer after the child had entered the playground and initiated play, observations were made at the same time and under the same conditions every morning. All children included in the study were enrolled as students in first-grade classrooms in the school. Children attending the school came from working class homes in which one or both parents were employed as laborers, factory, or service workers. (See Borman, Lippincott, & Matey, 1978).

Observations were made every morning from approximately 8:00 a.m., when most children entered the playground, to 8:30 a.m. when the school bell rang and children formed lines to be led into the school by their teachers. In all cases the child being taped wore a lightweight backpack which contained a portable tape recorder. In addition to the taped record of activity, the observer took detailed field notes chronicling the process of play, the identity of individual speakers whose play was recorded in the session, etc. All children whose play was recorded were willing participants in the research. They were also fully informed of our intentions to obtain a record of children's play. In this manner audio tapes were collected and later transcribed. Transcriptions provided scripts of the playground games in which individual children had been observed and recorded. These records contain documentation of the length of turn, the conversation throughout the game the identity of speakers/players, and gestures and movement related to the progress of the game.

Data Analysis

Turns at Play. Following Garvey, the format of social games is seen as determined by the patterned set of turns that characterizes all episodes of play for a particular game. In order to understand the sequence of turns within each activity, careful readings of the transcripts were made and attention given to the pattern of moves made by participants. Turns at play in all three games are dependent upon the progress of one's opponents in the game.

In hopscotch, participants alternate turns at play following the initial contact that constitutes the invitation or challenge to play. Players surrender their turns at play after acknowledging a misstep or error: for example, stepping on a line, executing a poor throw of the marker, or stepping in a square containing the opponent's marker. In this manner, turns are exchanged back and forth between participants until one or the other player successfully executes play up one length of the squares from one to ten and back again or until the bell rings.

Turns at play in the chase games of kissers and chasers and tag consist of chase and rest sequences which successively follow each other during the course of the game. Rest periods in tag revolve around the safety zone of a tar patch on the ground. Participants in kissers and chasers as either pursuers or pursued seek refuge in any convenient place: school building steps, the open playground in a huddle with "team" members, and, at least upon one observed occasion, across the street from the school on a neighborhood sidewalk.

The turn served as the basic unit of analysis in both sets of procedures carried out in this study. The number of turns available to participants and the length of time allotted to players during individual turns constitute an important structural component of social games. Yet, turn taking is engineered by children themselves who are players in the game. The number and placing of turns determine who will participate in play and how equitably turns will be distributed during the sequence of play of a particular game. The range in number of turns varied from one to 17 across all observed games. The average number of turns per game ranged from 12 in tag to four in London Bridge and duck, duck, goose. The average number of turns in games of hopscotch was eight and in kissers and chasers, six.

Likewise, the range in length of turns was great. The shortest turns were associated with hopscotch. Average length of turn in this game was 20 seconds, with a range of 7 to 82 seconds. Turns of greatest duration were recorded in games of tag with the average turn lasting 50 seconds. Falling between these two games in length of turn was kissers and chasers with an average turn taking 25 seconds.

The Analyses.   Two sets of analyses were carried out on all observed games. The objective of both analyses was to examine the turn taking structure of playground games and to judge children's success at turn taking and game maintenance. The first analysis was a descriptive account of the round of turns. In the case of each observed game, the following set of questions was asked:

1. Does each player gain a turn according to a specific pattern of turn rotation?
2. Do a large number of players have to compete for a turn?
3. Are players in the game constantly active or must they accept enforced waits until their turns reappear?

These questions highlight the turn taking nature of children's social games but also allow the examination of more strictly sociological features, such as number of participants, as in question two, and patterns of interaction, as in questions one and three.

In the second analysis all turns were examined to judge the relationship between the length of turns in seconds and the engagement of the child(ren) awaiting a turn. Of particular interest with regard to engagement is the nature of any possible distraction which functions to disengage the child(ren) from the activity of the game. Distractions were judged a priori to be of importance since they made a particular turn at play problematic. That is, distractions could lead to the cessation of play or to its renegotiation. As a break with the continuity of the game, distractions threatened maintenance of the game. How successfully the children could negotiate distractions, inevitable on a crowded playground, and still maintain the ongoing game was considered to be evidence of underlying social competencies which are basic to both the cognitive and cultural purposes of play since they involve understanding reciprocal relationships and role reversibility, a social competency that is inherent in the process of taking a turn and in awaiting a turn at play.

Distractions took the following forms: (1) interference by other children not participating in the game; (2) verbalization of impatience by a player; for example, complaining or taunting; (3) abandoning the game; and (4) changing the rules or changing the game. In changing or altering rules in tag, for example, a child might offer him or herself to "it" to be tagged or negotiate the role of "it." To change the game, a participant might demand that another game be substituted for the one being played.

Distractions did not include remarks made by the waiting player monitoring the active player or by breaks in action associated with game-related functions. Children's commentary in these cases served to further the continuity of the game. For example, in the following instance, Angela is taking a turn and notes that she is out, having stepped on a line. The rest of the exchange is marked by a cooperative search for Angela's marker.

Angela: Oh, look. I'm out. (( )) I don't even know where my marker is (See footnote 3).
Barbara: In fivers.
Angela: I don't see it.
Barbara: ((Right there)) (pointing)
Angela: Oh. # Can you step in five?
Barbara: (doesn't respond, but watches as Angela moves her marker)

We see that children learn as much about cooperation in games as they do about competition. Breaks to discuss equipment and procedure are easily tolerated and do not threaten the continuity of games, even though Garvey (1977) has suggested junctures, such as changes of turns, can be problematical situations. While these incidents may not qualify as distractions as such, they nevertheless demonstrate game maintenance skills. Nor is the game always so easily maintained as in the preceding example. Among the most volatile confrontations were those in which players disagreed about a rule infraction.

Sonya: You're out. # On eighters. (to bystander) She's out.
Angela: Uh-uh (no)
Sonya: (loudly while demonstrating) You got out on eighters. Right here. You gotta put your foot like this and it's too big. You keep steppin' on that line.
Angela: Uh-uh. (demonstrating) I went like this ((And stepped in seveners)) I picked up my marker.

In this instance, Angela retains her disputed turn. Children as a rule did not accept an opponent's judgment about a misstep, etc., unless it was quite clear to the child herself that she had committed a fault. Still, even quarrels not resolved to all players' satisfaction did not threaten continuity. Indeed the quarrels quickly subsided and often appeared to be contests of power rather than of principle. The act of victory ended any dispute.

Results and Discussion

Analysis One. All games were analyzed with regard to patterns of turn rotation. It was convenient in the same analysis to consider the activity of players involved in the game during the course of the progress of the game. The results of this descriptive analysis was reported in Table 6.1. The only game assuring a turn to all players in a fixed sequence or pattern of rotation was hopscotch. Thus, players were forced to wait for a turn but assured of having one. Kissers and chasers, tag, and duck, duck, goose were also structured in such a way that players were encumbered by rules requiring waiting. In other words, players were *not* constantly busy, physically participating in play. The difference between these games and hopscotch was that, while rules determined the exchange of turns, players who had tolerantly waited had no assurance that they would necessarily win an active turn. The attentions of the roving "It" might never be focused in a given player's direction.

As illustrated in Table 6.1, all other playground games are contrived in a manner that assures participants keep constantly busy, actively contributing to the ongoing game in the roles of circlers and chanters of the accompanying rhyme, as in farmer in the dell and London Bridge, or by otherwise being constant physical participators, as in follow the leader and foot races. The physical participation of players in these games is key to the maintenance of play itself. Game activity ceases if players halt these motions. For example, if all those running a race simply gave up their efforts to beat their competitors by

Table 6.1.
Games classified by their turn-taking procedures

	Games assured turns in a fixed rotation	Games without fixed rotations but with procedures governing exchange of turns	Games with neither fixed rotations nor exchange procedures	Games without turns
Players not constantly active	Hopscotch (N = 1)	Kissers & chasers, tag, duck, duck, goose (N = 3)	(N = 0)	(N = 0)
All players constantly active	(N = 0)	farmer in the dell (N = 1)	follow the leader, London bridge (N = 2)	running races (N = 1)

coming to a stop before reaching the predetermined finish line, the race would, in fact, be over. In these games players do not receive a turn according to a pattern of turn rotation. Rather, as in follow the leader or farmer in the dell, role switching is completely dependent upon the decision of another player with the consequence that a given child might never gain a turn to lead or occupy any special role, as the farmer's wife.

The analysis of games along the dimensions of taking turns and the activity of players leads to several conclusions about the evolution of playground games in the repertoires of schoolaged children. First, the sequence of children's play at games proceeds from engagement in games that have simple procedural rules, nominal division of roles, no competition, and hence, no real turns, as London Bridge. Motor activity predominates; interest is maintained by constant activity. Since such games are generally played before role-taking thought has progressed too far, players are not burdened with competition. Subsequently, games appear that divide roles into competitive or agonistic roles, rudimentary competition in games which have an "It" and a "not It."

Second, the structure and frequency of first graders' play, at least in the case of this particular sample, indicate that children of this age are in transition, progressing *toward* games which fix strategic interrelationships in roles through codes of rules, while at the same time moving *from* engagement in games not marked by such division of roles. This conclusion seems warranted for the following reasons. The simplest games, as London Bridge (those games without any strategic interrelationships) were all played in a single play session and partly chosen to impress the observer. While running races occurred in other sessions, they were not only used as games but also as the simplest way of crossing the playground. Therefore, these games appeared more as relics of the past than the passion of the present.

The spontaneous, ever-recurring games were kissers and chasers, tag, and hopscotch. Thus, the characteristics of these games seem to portray the current developmental level of the first graders.

Assuming that children's freely chosen games reflect role taking skills, then it follows that younger children, without the ability to differentiate and order several roles at a time, and caught up with mastery of bodily movement as a preeminent developmental task, find enough challenge in games such as races or farmer in the dell. As social role taking skill develops, however, games which do not allow for strategic interrelationships may become less compelling because they do not test and extend increasing ability to engage in reciprocal relationships, order events sequentially, etc. Therefore, the choice of these more strategic games seems to show an increasing desire to learn and express rules about interrelationships and coordination of roles.

With regard to these children specifically, though games of tag and kissers and chasers are characterized by rule-governed exchanges of turns, such a structure did not insure a turn. It is the likely case that role taking has proceeded far enough to allow the child to differentiate roles and to order turns sequentially but not so far as to allow the child consistently to keep in mind whether all players have been incorporated into the network of play to allow turns for all players.

Analysis Two.   The second analysis was conducted to determine how length of a turn at play was associated with the distractibility of a child who, while a participant in the game, was not actively involved in taking a turn. Length of turn was an important predictor of distractibility, as can be seen from the following data. Participants in any game who are not actively involved in taking a turn are likely to become distracted if their opponent's turn at play last longer than 50 seconds as illustrated in Table 6.2. Conversely, shorter turns, those less than 50 seconds, are associated with comparatively fewer distractions (chi square = 43.9, df = 3, p < .01). Furthermore, a Pearson product moment correlation indicates that the longer the turn, the greater the number of distractions (r = .64, df = 92, p < .005). For short turns, those less than 50 seconds, players waiting to take a turn were distracted about once in every five turns at waiting. During turns lasting over 50 seconds, all players became distracted. Indeed, under such conditions, children average about two distractions per turn.

Since all observed games occurred on a crowded playground filled with children of all ages who were generally unsupervised by adults, it is not surprising that distractions plagued participants in all games. As reported in Table 6.3, turns in tag were the most likely to be associated with a distraction in comparison with turns in kissers and chasers or in hopscotch. In a total of 20 turns taken in tag, 12 or 60% were associated with a distraction regardless of length of turn. The comparable percentages for kissers and chasers and hopscotch are 11% and 15%. Accordingly, the greatest number of distractions involved tag, then hopscotch, and finally kissers and chasers.

As supported by the statistics, distractions were important because they represented a threat to the continuity of the game and consequently challenged bur-

Table 6.3.
Number of turns with distractions by length of turn and game

	Length of turn					
	0-50 seconds			51-200 seconds		
	Tag	K & C*	Hop	Tag	K & C	Hop
no distractions	8	12	39	0	0	0
one or more distractions	4	4	5	8	2	2
	12	16	44	8	2	2

*Kissers and chasers

Table 6.2.
Number of turns with distractions by length of turn

Number of distractions	Length of turn	
	0-50 seconds	51-200 seconds
0	63	1
1 or more	12	18
total number of turns	75	19

chi-square = 43.9, df = 3

geoning game-strategy skills. Nominal role divisions give way to competitive ones. The price of this advance is time spent waiting for one's turn. Negotiating this wait and handling its attendant distractions emerge as the characteristic problems of first grade games. In the extreme, distracted children simply abandoned the game. Generally, however, lengthy waits were borne as a trial. How was participation maintained despite the lures of other attractions? How did the patient waiter signal his need of attention?

The most frequently appearing distraction in all games was the diversion of attention caused by interference from the sidelines. If a waiting child witnessed another child on the playground being pushed or accidentally falling, usually the onlooker tried to take a hand in assisting the injured child. A far more common disruption, however, was the interruption of the game by other children who, intent upon their own play, unintentionally disturbed players in an ongoing game. Hopscotch, because of its location along a well traveled route, was frequently interrupted either by a group of running children, as in the example that follows immediately, or by kibbitzers, as in the second example.

Note: Toni is taking her turn at play when a group of children dash across her path. Shelley is her partner in play and two children, one a boy, are onlookers.
Billy: (to Toni) You touched the li-on.
Toni: I am 'cuz they made me.
  (Toni continues to take her turn)
Shelley: Uh un (no). Still counts.
Onlooker: (to Toni) your turn.
Toni: Heh heh. (laughs, continuing turn)

In this example, the onlookers support the two players in maintaining their game. Though not as inclined as participants awaiting a turn to monitor the progress of players, onlookers frequently speak among themselves and to participants. In this case it appears that onlookers' remarks are perceived to be more objective commentary on Toni's turn than her partner's observations and, in fact, decide the issue at hand. Shelley expresses her unwillingness to allow Toni's rationale to hold as justification for stepping on a line, a rule violation that in usual circumstances causes a player to lose a turn. The onlookers, though they do not articulate a justification, support Toni by urging her to continue her turn. Again, power—in this case the power of majority—wins the quarrel and settles the dispute. If principle is involved, it is not articulated as such. In addition, we note that kibbitzers seldom attempted to engage the attention of a player involved in taking a turn in hopscotch, except to perform the monitoring functions as in the forementioned example. By reinforcing concentration on the game, kibbitzers displayed game maintenance skills of their own.

One episode of hopscotch provided an exception. In the example that follows, Anne completes a turn at play in hopscotch and signals her partner to take a turn with the utterance: your turn? After 8 seconds of her opponent's turn pass, Anne is approached by two classmates, Susan and Tracy. Susan and Tracy approach Anne after her turn has been completed and offer to tell her a joke. Though Anne does not appear particularly eager to listen, she does cooperate with the jokesters. Stacy, taking her turn, remains invulnerable to the onlookers' bid to get in on the joke, perhaps wishing to avoid the unpleasant experience of having a loud "cluck" made in her ear, but in any event, maintaining her focus upon her turn at play.

Tracy: Anne, she wants to tell ya somethin'.
Anne: (doesn't respond, but moves close to Susan and assumes position to receive a whispered message.)
Susan: (bending close to Anne's ear) and making three loud clucks with her tongue) Ain't the phone ringin'?
Anne: She did it in my ear.
Tracy: I know. She (( ))
Stacy: (Taking her turn at hopscotch and calling out) I got trapped in eighters.
Tracy: Hey, Stacy, when you're done, let her tell ya somethin'.
Stacy: What?
Tracy: Come here.
Stacy: (Turning back and continuing turn) I know what it is.
Tracy: Well let her tell ya. See what it [does to] your ears.
Anne: [My ears.]
Tracy: Do ya hear? It's fun. (Three seconds pass)

Since Stacy's turn at play in this case was of average length, Anne's distractability was not necessarily induced by a prolonged wait, though another 6 seconds passed before Anne gained her turn at play. The kibbitzers remained on the sidelines with Anne until her turn was underway. Stacy's game maintenance skills are illustrated in the preceding example since she resists leaving her turn at play to take part in the joke on the side-lines, probably aided in her persistence by the patent unattractiveness of the alternative. And, although Anne is distracted briefly from the game, she remains in sight of her opponent and resumes the game when it is her turn.

The greatest challenges to game stability, however, came during those lengthy waits in tag. In particular, Willie, a dedicated tag player, was frequently overlooked by the slightly older children with whom he habitually played. For awhile, he might catch upon the latest "news" with fellow denizens of blackpatch, the patch of tar that served as safety. Nevertheless, Willie eventually ran low on patience and was forced to take action. In the following example, Willie, a "not It" in this turn at tag, produces an initial utterance, a taunt after taking a step off the safety zone. The second utterance, made after he has begun to run, appears to be intended to rally the other players still standing on blackpatch.

Willie: (Stepping off the safety zone) Ain't nobody gets me!
 (He begins to run.)
 (To players in the safety zone) Hey, you guys, let's run. Come on.

Willie's cry to "It" is effective in gaining the player's attention. Willie is chased and caught directly after his last utterance.

Even after such provocation, however, "It" sometimes continued to ignore Willie. In that case, Willie would resort to wild screaming and running as if being chased. These two reactions to waiting—taunting or baiting "It" or acting as if chased—were Willie's favorite resolutions. Nevertheless, on at least one occasion, Willie gave up and joined friend Donny in the vigorous rounds of kissers and chasers.

In hopscotch, complaints generally followed a perceived infraction and were centered upon the disputation of a rule. Typically, the participant serving a turn as onlooker describes the mistake of her partner while the partner continues her turn, denying any wrongdoing. Often, in spite of such denials and justifications, the erring player completed her turn and without comment surrendered the turn at play to her opponent, signalling her apparent agreement with the judgment despite initial protestations.

The least number of turn disruptions were caused by a participant's abandonment of the game. The press to maintain the game is clear in this observation since by abandoning the game, a player signals a complete unwillingness to play under the current circumstances. In the three observed cases of game defection, the players resumed play in the same game after a renegotiation of play. For example, a defector from hopscotch later joined another game with the same participants. The overriding concern in playground play is to maintain the action in the game. This finding is consistent with recent interview data gathered from children of both sexes at three elementary schools in two different grade levels who independently stated that play on the playground ends when the bell rings and not when players grow tired of the game, switch to another activity, etc.

What can be concluded from this discussion of turn-taking disruptions? First of all, it is important to point out that fully 82% of all observed turns at play took place without disruption. Complaints, diversions of attention, etc. must, therefore, be placed in context. We believe they should be seen as bids to retain continuity of play, to negotiate rules that might provide more equitable division of roles and to develop conceptions of fairness and reciprocity. A second conclusion, following from the first, concerns the implications such verbal monitoring may have for the development of children's role taking skills. By alternating turns at being "it" and "not it"; by negotiating differences in perception of turn taking procedures first from the perspective of "it" and next from the perspective of "not it," children gain experience in understanding the simultaneous relationships of different roles in the same game and in formulating procedural roles which benefit all participants.

WHAT KIND OF GAMES? WHICH SORTS OF SKILLS?

Urban Appalachian first-grade children observed during the period of research engaged in frequent games of tag, kissers and chasers, and hopscotch. These games require sequential ordering of turn taking roles. They are games that demand both motor skills and the use of at least rudimentary strategies.

Of the three, hopscotch fits most closely with Garvey's conception of social games as coherently ordered by a patterned sequence of turns. Hopscotch is also most clearly formulated to provide specific standards for determining the winner, i.e., completing the circuit of turns one through ten and ten through one, and thus is the playground game congruent with the sociogenic conception of games as centrally defined by competition. In fact, three games are structured to provide players with practice at competitive play as members of an opposition or team and can be seen as precursors of games such as football and baseball. Kissers and chasers is least like a strictly defined social game, but it provides the most opportunity for rehearsal of competitive roles. Its structure resembles sociodramatic play to the extent that much of the time it seems to be unclear to participants which individual or individuals constitute the object of the chase. In that sense, chasers appear merely to simulate agonistic role relationships rather than to execute them by capturing victims and embracing or kissing them, an outcome which is ostensibly the focus of a turn at play but which was rarely realized. Within the context of the chase in kissers and chasers, there are explicit verbal references made by players to membership on a team. Verbal strategizing constitutes an important aspect of membership, and attendant rehearsal of agonistic roles and role relationships forms yet another as component of play. The following example illustrates the awareness on the part of chasers of team membership, role relationships and the importance of verbally articulated strategies.

Note: This episode of play has been underway for approximately 10 minutes. There are seven participants in play. The chase sequence is momentarily stopped in its circling around the school grounds. One of the children, Tanya shouts to the others who gather in a huddle with her. (See footnote 3.)

Tanya: Phillip, Skippie, and Chan will take that-a-way (indicating a route around the school).

Several of the children groan.

Tanya (continuing [and Willie/Billie, me and her take that-a-way][1]

Billie: [You take that (( )) way and we'll take that way.][1]

Toni: Where do Chan and Dawn go?

Chan: (correcting Billie): [No, us three go that way.][2]

Tanya: And . . . [these three][2] . . . These three goes/one goes with me, and goes with you and ((you got)) left, and the other one goes with me.

(( )): Okay.

Billie: No, I go with her.

(( )): Okay. (( )) with me.

Tanya: (shouting) Chan, go with them. Come on, you guys.

(Twenty seconds of chasing follow)

In this example, Tanya makes an equitable division of players, three are to take one route and four children are to follow another in the chase. However, though strategizing is explicit in this and other recorded sequences of all observed games, strategies are not always executed as planned. In the example above, Tanya dictates a strategy for encircling the school by dividing the pack of chasers in two groups. After some initial confusion, the others agree to the plan. Their agreement is verbally cued by two unidentifiable children who separately utter "okay" as an affirmation of Tanya's plan. However, instead of taking different routes around the school as Tanya's plan proposed, all seven of these children took the same path in the 20-second chase which follows this "strategy session". This particular chase sequence was completed not with the capture of a victim but rather when it appeared that the chasers were simply too tired to continue. Thus, it is likely that play in kissers and chasers and in all other observed playground games, though characterized by rudimentary forms of agonistic role relationships and strategies is in actual practice dominated by motor activity in execution. Games requiring mastery of *both* motor skills and strategic planning are played by these children but are played without the skill that an older child would display. Here we see transitional games, games in which ideas of strategy are being formed to the limit of cognitive skill but which yet fall short of mature

---

[3]Transcription symbols and their meanings are as follows:

" " indicates utterance is unintelligible or speaker is unknown

((Here)) indicates utterance is transcribed as a "best guess"

# indicates a pause of less than 2 seconds

(pointing) indicates nonverbal activity or provides clarification of an utterance

[ ][1] indicates utterances produced simultaneously

[ ][1]

counterposed defense and offense. Clearly, these younger children recognize that games require "sides" and strategies as structural components; they are unable, however, to integrate these aspects of game playing in their spontaneous performances in order to coordinate the separate but complementary maneuvers of two groups of players. In summary, the three games played by first graders which were observed most frequently on the playground at this elementary school are competitive games in which physical skill chiefly determines the outcome of play but in which the contributions of strategy are appreciated. Games preeminently characterized by the understanding and skillful use of complex strategies and the coordination of team effort will not dominate playground play until children's cognitive development allows fuller understanding of simultaneous role taking and the coordination of social interaction. Even at this early age, however, lessons in mastery of complex social systems have begun.

REFERENCES

Avedon, E. M. The structural elements of games. In Avedon, E. M. & Smith, B. (Eds.), *The study of games*. New York: Wiley, 1971.

Avedon, E. M., & Sutton-Smith, B. The function of games. In E. M. Avedon & B. Sutton-Smith. (Eds.), *The study of games*. New York: Wiley, 1971.

Borman, K. M., Lippincott, N. T., & Matey, C. M. Family and classroom control in an urban Appalachian neighborhood, *Education and Urban Society*, 1978, *11*, 61–86.

Bruner, J. S. Nature and uses of unmaturity. In J. S. Bruner, A. Jolly, K. Sylva (Eds.), *Play*. New York: Basic Books, 1972/1976.

Bruner, J., & Sherwood, V. Peekaboo and the learning of rule structures. In J. Bruner, A. Jolly, & K. Sylva (Eds.), *Play*. New York: Basic Books, 1975/1976.

Garvey, C. Some Properties of Social Play. *Merrill-Palmer Quarterly*, 1974, *20*, 163–180.

Garvey, C. *Play*. Cambridge: Harvard University Press, 1977.

Goffman, E. *Interaction Revival: Essays on face to face behavior*. New York: Anchor Books, 1967.

Lever, J. Sex differences in the complexity of Children's play. *American Sociological Review*, 1978 (43) 471–482.

Mead, G. H. Play, the game and the generalized other. In Morris, C. W. (Ed.), *Mine, Self and Society*. Chicago: University of Chicago Press, 1934.

Piaget, J. *The moral judgment of the child*. New York: Free Press, 1965.

Polgar, S. K. The social context of games or when is play not play. *Sociology of Education*, 1976 (49), 265–271.

Roberts, J. M., Sutton-Smith, B. Child training and game involvement. In E. M. Avedon & B. Sutton-Smith (Eds.), *The study of games*. New York: Wiley, 1971.

Roberts, J. M., Arth, M. J., & Bush, R. R. Games in culture. *American Anthropologist*, 1959, 61 (4), 597–605.

Roberts, J. M., Sutton-Smith, B., & Kendon, A. Strategy in folktales and games. *Journal of Social Psychology*, 1963, *61*, 185–199.

Rubin, K. H., & Pepler, D. J. The relationship of child's play to social-cognitive growth and development. In H. Foot, J. Chapman, & S. Smith (Eds.), *Friendship and childhood relationship*. Chichester, Eng.: Wiley, 1980.

Szasz, T. S. *The myth of mental illness*. New York: Holber Medical Dursean, Harper and Row, 1961.

IV LANGUAGE AS A PRIMARY SOCIALIZER: DEVELOPMENTALLY DELAYED CHILDREN

7 The Abecedarian[1] Approach to Social Competence: Cognitive and Linguistic Intervention for Disadvantaged Preschoolers

Craig T. Ramey
Gael D. McGinness
Lee Cross
Albert M. Collier
Sandie Barrie-Blackley
University of North Carolina at Chapel Hill

> "...*it is not easy for an education, with which love has mingled, to be entirely thrown away.*"
>
> —Rousseau

It is axiomatic in education that environments affect development. It is also generally accepted that children from poor and under-educated parents have more difficulty in school than children from affluent and well-educated parents (see, for a recent empirical example, Ramey, Stedman, Borders-Patterson, & Mengel, 1978). The causes of this school difficulty, and in the extreme, school failure, are undoubtedly multiple and interactive. Educators have been assigned the large task of carrying out social reform: of diminishing the likelihood of school difficulty or school failure for the disadvantaged, and thereby increasing their likelihood of socioeconomic success. That facilitating educational success can guarantee later socioeconomic success is an assumption society has rightly begun to question: education may be a necessary rather than sufficient condition for social or economic achievement. Given this large task, educators have been allotted relatively meager resources for accomplishing it. They are forced, then, to use the most powerful tools that limited knowledge and resources have to offer.

---

[1] Abecedarian (ā[1] bi si där ι ən): a pupil who is learning the letters of the alphabet; 2. a beginner; 3. primary: rudimentary.

Education always occurs in particular cultural contexts with presumptions being made about the backgrounds of the learners. Therefore, to be maximally effective in exerting educational leverage to the benefit of disadvantaged children, it is important that we know the disadvantaged child's typical ecologies. Knowledge of the typical ecological forces will allow more precise and carefully targeted use of the limited resources available to the educator. As a beginning step in the generation of that knowledge, this chapter will summarize the information which has been obtained from a longitudinal early intervention program that has collected extensive preschool ecological and child development data for the past 10 years. The chapter begins with a description of the child's physical, social, and attitudinal ecologies and proceeds to an extensive description of the educational settings and practices that were designed as part of the Carolina Abecedarian Project to assist young disadvantaged children attain educational competence. We present a sampling of results from this work on experimentally altering the educational ecology of children of poverty and conclude with the implications that we draw from these results concerning social policy for preschool programs.

ECOLOGY OF THE DISADVANTAGED PRESCHOOLER

The disadvantaged child lives in a very different world from his upper middleclass peer. His world looks different, smells different, tastes different, feels different and sounds different. To be sure, there are similarities. Both can know joy, love, fear, and want; but, at almost every turn the paths for the advantaged and the disadvantaged diverge. The more desirable of these two paths is almost always trod by the advantaged—and, both the advantaged and disadvantaged know this truth. It is these differences in ecologies that we assume to be of paramount importance for determining life satisfaction and contribution to society. We begin this chapter by describing some of the things that we have learned in the past 10 years of the Abecedarian Project about the physical, social, and attitudinal ecologies of advantaged and disadvantaged children. It is these predisposing ecologies that are the context for our educational efforts.

Physical Environment

Information about the physical setting of the home for advantaged and disadvantaged infants has been presented by Ramey, Mills, Campbell, and O'Brien (1975). Using Caldwell, Heider, and Kaplan's (1966) *The Inventory of Home Stimulation* we found that lower socioeconomic status homes were characterized by relatively disorganized environments and lacked age-appropriate toys and opportunity for variety in daily stimulation when infants were 6 months of age. The homes also tended to be poorly lighted, to have a high density of people, and to vary considerably from one another on many physical and other dimensions.

Table 7.1 is an attempt to provide a quick synopsis of some salient characteristics of these homes.

Several points are to be noted from Table 7.1. First, 45% of the families live in households containing five or more members. Thus, the households tend to be somewhat larger than is typical for today's nuclear family. Further, about 15–18% of the houses are rated as dilapidated and unfit for occupancy. The children tend to sleep in rooms containing not only other children but also one or more adults which in all probability indicates a serious crowding situation. Finally, these somewhat crowded households typically contain one or more members who smoke. The extent to which these conditions contribute to the child's development is at present unknown; however, it is abundantly clear that these physical arrangements are vastly different from those enjoyed by socioeconomically more advantaged children. Further, as the second column of figures in Table 7.1 indicate, there is remarkable stability in these characteristics over a 3-year period.

Attitudinal Environment

Attitudes represent a set of assumptions which bear some as yet only partially understood relationship to specific parenting practices. Nevertheless, the attitudes of advantaged and disadvantaged parents differ in ways that are parallel to the differences in their children's development. Whether these attitudinal dif-

Table 7.1
Information on the Physical Ecology of High-
Risk Children in the First and Third Years of Life

Characteristic	1st Year N = 56	3rd Year N = 40
Number in Household		
≤ 5	55%	48%
5-7	45%	37%
≥ 8	13%	5%
% houses with 1 or more other preschool children	98%	100%
% houses with 1 or more elementary school children	52%	47%
% houses with 1 or more junior or senior high school students	44%	27%
Type of Housing		
Single Family	53%	35%
Multiple Family	47%	65%
Dilapidated	18%	15%
Sleeping in Room with Child		
1 or more preschool children	7%	26%
1 or more older children	41%	33%
1 or more adults	73%	77%
Families with 1 or more members who smoke	80%	82%

ferences are causes or correlates of child change is at present unknown. However, they are part of the psychological environment of the child and probably are not trivial. We know that by the time their infants are 6 months of age lower socioeconomic status (SES) mothers score as more authoritarian and less democratic in their child-rearing attitudes but also as less hostile toward and rejecting of the homemaking role than their more advantaged peers. They also perceive themselves, probably realistically, as more controlled by external forces than as internally controlled (Ramey & Campbell, 1976). Such attitudes lead us to presume that there is less creative flexibility in child rearing and more pessimistic fatalism in the environment of the disadvantaged child compared to the advantaged one. Further, this somewhat glum maternal perception of life exists essentially from the child's birth and is relatively unchanged during, at least, the first 2 years of its life (Ramey, Farran, & Campbell, 1979).

Social Interactional Environment

Beginning as early as 6 months and continuing throughout the preschool years, the disadvantaged child is interacted with by adults somewhat differently than is the advantaged child. The differences appear to be smaller in early infancy and to become larger as the child grows older. For example, Ramey, Mills, Campbell, and O'Brien (1975) have reported that the mothers of disadvantaged infants tend to be less responsive verbally and emotionally, more punitive and less involved with their infants when observed within their own homes. These results have been replicated and extended in a recent report by Ramey, Farran, and Campbell (1979) who used both naturalistic mother-child observations in the child's home and constrained observations in a laboratory setting. We found that disadvantaged mothers talked less to their 6-month-old infants than advantaged mothers even though those two groups of infants did not differ in their rates of nonfussy vocalizations. At 20 months, advantaged mothers continue to talk more to their children and to interact with them more frequently in a laboratory setting. Farran and Ramey (1979) have recently reported a factor analysis from these interactional observations in which a first factor labeled as "Dyadic Involvement" was isolated at both 6 and 20 months. Disadvantaged and advantaged dyads did not differ significantly on this dimension at 6 months but were different at 20 months with the advantaged dyads scoring as more involved. Further, the factor scores on this dimension significantly predicted the child's IQ at 48 months.

Thus, some of the evidence available from the Abecedarian Project seems to suggest that infants and their mothers share different social, attitudinal, and physical ecologies from the child's early infancy depending on what social niche they occupy. The at-home and laboratory observations suggest that the early language environments of advantaged and disadvantaged children may be a major difference between the two groups. Further, these language environments are linked to the child's subsequent general intelligence and, presumably, to his subsequent school achievement. Therefore, to the extent that this relationship is causal and not just correlative, it becomes a particularly salient target for educational intervention.

After a brief description of the overall organization of the educational intervention component of the Abecedarian Project we present a conceptual framework and plan for daily action that guides our language-oriented intervention program during the latter part of the preschool years.

DESCRIPTION OF THE ABECEDARIAN INTERVENTION PROGRAM

Admission of Families

The Carolina Abecedarian Project began in 1972 to intervene with infants and children believed to be at high risk for school failure. Families were referred to the project through local hospitals, clinics, the Orange County Department of Social Services, and other referral sources. Once families had been identified as potentially eligible, a staff member visited them at home to explain the program and to determine whether they appeared to meet selection criteria. If so, mothers were invited to the Frank Porter Graham Center for an interview and psychological assessment.

During their visit to the Center, which typically occurred in the last trimester of pregnancy, demographic information about the family was obtained and mothers were assessed with the Wechsler Adult Intelligence Scale (WAIS; Wechsler, 1955). Final determination of eligibility was made following this visit. Criteria for selection included maternal IQ, family income, parent education, intactness of family, and seven other factors that were weighted and combined to yield a single score called the High Risk Index (see Ramey & Smith, 1977, for details). Only families at or above a predetermined cutoff score were considered eligible.

We admitted four cohorts or groups of families between 1972 and 1977. The oldest children are now over 10 years of age and are attending the local public schools; the youngest children are now approximately 5 years of age. Of 122 families judged to be eligible for participation, 121 families initially agreed to participate knowing that they would be assigned randomly to an educationally treated group or to a control group. When these 121 families were randomly assigned to the Day Care group or to the Control group, 116 or 95.9% accepted their group assignment. Of these 116, three children have died and 1 child has been diagnosed as retarded due to organic etiology. Not counting these four children we have, then, a base sample of 112 children. Of these 112 initially normal children, 8 have dropped from our sample as of September 1, 1978.

Table 7.2
Demographic Data by Experimental and Control Groups
Cohorts I-IV

Group	N	Female-headed Family	Mean Financial Income in Year of Birth	Mother's Education at Child's Birth	Mean Maternal IQ at Birth
Experimental	64	82.81%	$1,230	10.27	84.92
Control	57	77.19%	$1,080	10.00	84.19

Thus, not counting attrition by death or severe biological abnormality, 92.9% of our sample is intact. Some characteristics of families admitted to the Abecedarian Day Care and Control groups are summarized in Table 7.2.

General Characteristics of The Early Childhood Education Program

The early childhood program serves up to 50 children who participate in the Abecedarian project. Most of the children enter the program at 6 weeks and stay in the program until they enter public school kindergarten. When there are openings for additional children, they are recruited from the community to provide a racial and socioeconomic mix. The educational program occupies all of one floor and a portion of another floor of a four story research building. The educational program is open 5 days a week for 50 weeks of the year from 7:30 to 5:15 p.m.

Staff. Twelve teachers and assistants are responsible for providing the educational program for children. Following are the teacher/child ratios and group size for each age group:

1978–79 School Year

Age	Teacher/Child Ratio	Number of Staff	Group Size
6 wks.–12 mos.	1:4	3	12
12 mos.–24 mos.	1:4	2	7
24 mos.–36 mos.	1:4	2	7
36 mos.–48 mos.	1:6	2	12
48 mos.–60 mos.	1:6	2	12

In addition to the teaching staff there are three administrative staff: the program director, a secretary, and a transportation supervisor.

Teaching staff vary in their level of formal training. Some teachers have A.B. or M.A. degrees but some staff who are in head-teacher positions have demonstrated skill and competencies in working with young children in lieu of formal education and degrees. The average number of years experience of staff who work with young children is 7 years. Staff development is an on-going process. The language training program which has been one of our major staff training activities will be described later in this chapter. In addition to the individuals who staff the classrooms, a consultant in behavior management and social development is available to teachers on an on-going basis. Consultants conduct staff workshops and meet with staff on an individual basis to discuss problems of individual children and general classroom organization and management strategies. Other consultants are brought in to conduct workshops when the need arises.

Opportunities are provided for staff to attend local, state, and national workshops pertaining to the education of young children. In addition, staff are encouraged to pursue child-related courses through technical institutes and the state university system.

Medical Care.   The medical care component at the Frank Porter Graham Child Development Center provides complete medical care for the Abecedarian Project children who attend the Center. The health care team is also actively involved in research on respiratory tract infections and their complications—a common problem with preschool-aged children. The health care team is composed of three pediatricians, a family nurse practitioner and a licensed practical nurse.

Well Child Care.   Assessments are made at ages 2, 4, 6, 9, 12, 18, and 24 months, and yearly thereafter. The parents are present at the assessments for an exchange of information and counseling. A health history and a social history are obtained and a complete physical examination is performed. Parents are taught and counseled in the areas of feeding and nutrition, weaning, cleanliness, skin care, child growth and development, behavior, toilet training, accident prevention, and dental hygiene. Parents are encouraged to express their concerns and to discuss problems that they are facing.

Appropriate immunizations (diptheria, pertussis, tetanus, polio, measles, mumps, and rubella) as recommended by the American Academy of Pediatrics are given. A sickle cell preparation is obtained at age 9 and 12 months from all black children. A skin test for tuberculosis is given yearly. A hematocrit is done at age 9 and 18 months and yearly thereafter. Routine screening for vision and hearing is provided annually.

Ill Child Care.   There is daily surveillance of all children in the Center for illness. The children are allowed to continue to attend the Center when ill except in the case of chickenpox. The children are seen when ill by one of the health care staff. A history is obtained and a physical examination done. Appropriate laboratory tests and cultures are performed. Parents are informed of the nature of the child's ailment, and the prescribed treatment is discussed with the parents by note or phone. The child is followed through the illness until recovery.

The Educational Characteristics of the Program.   Because a description of the infant toddler program can be found in previous papers (e.g. Ramey, Collier, Sparling, Loda, Campbell, Ingram, & Finkelstein, 1976; Ramey, Holmberg, Sparling, & Collier, 1977; Ramey & Campbell, 1979; Ramey & Haskins, 1981) the primary focus of this section is a description of the program for 3 and 4-year-olds. The development of the program for threes and fours has been a cumulative process. When appropriate, outside consultants have provided assistance and input. However, the most vital people in the development of the program are the teachers who have taken ideas from a number of sources and integrated and applied them in their respective classroom situations on an hourly basis.

The program has stabilized over time, but there will always be changes as the staff continually strive to develop a program to meet the needs of individual children. In describing the educational program, four major areas will be discussed: the physical environment, the daily schedule, the curriculum, and the parent component.

Physical Environment.   One of the distinctive features of the program is the organization of the physical environment. Large areas of space are divided into classroom areas of approximately 1000 square feet by creating low walls with a series of 5 feet × 2 feet modular blocks. The physical space in each classroom is organized using the following principles discussed in greater detail by Harms and Cross (1977). Nuturant day care environments are:

Predictable and promote self-help.
Supportive and facilitate social-emotional adjustment.
Reflective of the child's age, ability, and interest.
Varied in activities.

In accordance with these principles, classrooms are organized to promote self-help and independence. Child-sized furniture is used and materials are stored on low open shelves to promote easy accessibility. Pictures of the toy material or symbols are used to designate the space the material occupies on the shelf or wherever the material is to be stored. For example, big trucks in the 4-year-old class are stored in a "garage" designated by masking tape. When children clean up or are finished with the trucks, they match the size of the truck with the marked off space. Blocks are stored on shelves in the space designated by the size and shape of the block. Through the use of pictorial labeling, children are able to function independently in that they are able to select materials and put them away without the assistance of the teachers.

Materials are organized in well defined interest areas; thus, children are able to function systematically in their environment. It is clear to children where in the classroom each activity is to take place. The following centers are within the classrooms of three and four-year-olds; blocks and construction materials, science, listening, book corner, manipulative games, housekeeping/dramatic play, and art. The value of having a space where a child can be alone is recognized and provided for in each classroom. In day care where children are frequently part of a group, children need to be able to have privacy once in a while. In each classroom, a private space is available for the child who wants to get away from the group and be alone. In addition, each classroom has a warm, cozy area with a rug and pillows which children can enjoy.

Children's work is displayed throughout the room and predominates over teacher-made bulletin boards. Conventional display space is at a minimum; therefore, one can see art work, picture stories as well as three-dimensional work (art dough, clay) on cabinets, walls, doors, and windows. We strive to have children feel that they are contributing to the appearance of the classroom and that their work is valued.

One of the greatest challenges we have faced in day care is to provide variety in the daily program and at the same time ensure program continuity. This is particularly true in the Abecedarian program because the children attend the day care program for the first 5 years of their lives. There is a danger that everyone will develop dulling routines. Therefore, variety is consciously provided in a number of ways. There is both indoor and outdoor space for the development of motor skills. The outdoor area is used frequently for activities that are traditionally indoor activities such as art, dramatic play, sand and water, and science.

Through field trips, the setting for learning is broadened. Particularly during nice weather, children explore and learn through trips to various community settings. There is a sequence of activities that teachers typically follow which includes planning and preparing children for the trip and a systematic follow-up on returning to the center. Unusual places are explored such as a turkey farm, the dog pound, the reservoir, or a grist mill in addition to more common places like the fire station and the library. In the summer, trips to swimming pools and to playgrounds are planned just for fun.

Variety is also provided by rotating, changing and adding materials to various learning centers. For example, the science center changes often depending upon the educational objectives to be accomplished. One week the center might include a water table with floating and sinking objects. The next week there might be a color mixing activity. The nature of the block center also changes. For example, farm animals might be added after a trip to the farm. The housekeeping area is easily converted into a grocery store by adding a cash register, boxes, cans and a check-out area. Frequently, a non-permanent center such as cooking or woodworking may be added for a few days each week. It takes a great deal of creative teacher planning and preparation to continually motivate young children day after day by providing variety in day care.

Daily Schedule. The Daily Schedule of three's and four's can be found in Table 7.3. As can be noted, there are a number of similarities between the two age groups. In planning daily activities, there is a mixture of teacher-planned structured activities, creative experiences, and opportunities for child-selected activities. Activities are planned for large groups, small groups, and one-to-one interactions. Small group activities focus on developing specific skills in language, reasoning, mathematical concepts, and writing. In addition, small group activities are valuable in developing attending behavior, task orientation, listening skills, and working towards task completion.

The objectives for the small groups are based on individual needs of children and a checklist is used to assess individual children's needs. Thus, activities of small groups are adapted to meet individual needs within each group.

Table 7.3

Daily Schedule

8:00	Arrival, free choice – outside play or table activities, and breakfast
9:45	Circle I – Calendar helpers and discussion. *Small groups – Language and Math Concepts*
	Circle II – Action games, music songs, etc. Planning
	Center time – Art, books, blocks, games, housekeeping, listening, science
	Circle II – Evaluation and discussion (Children tell what they like about products)
11:30	Clean up and outside play
12:00	Workshop, lunch
12:30	Preparation for rest
12:45	Storytime
1:00	Rest
2:30	Snack and clean up
3:00	Outside play
3:30	Departure of transported children
3:30 – 5:15	Departure of children picked up by parents

During circle time, concepts, units and themes are developed. For example, a unit on transportation may be discussed over a number of days. This unit might be coordinated with field trips to the airport, the bus station, or a garage. Action songs, finger plays, flannel board stories, story telling, and listening to rhymes take place. Young 3-year-olds spend a very short time in a large group, about 5 to 10 minutes at a time. As the time nears for children to enter public school, the length of time spent in a large group increases and the circle becomes more academically oriented.

Children's Planning.   A short circle time each day is devoted to children's planning before center time. At this time a child has to make a decision about which center he will go to and what he will do there. The purpose of this aspect of the program is to encourage each child to plan and make decisions about his immediate future. This avoids the aimless wandering that sometimes happens when children are given unplanned free choice. Teachers encourage children to follow through on their plans and to report their accomplishments.

Center Times.   For center time, teachers make special plans for two or three centers. One day there may be a special art activity in the art center as well as a special science activity in the science center. The remainder of the centers will be available to the children but will not be highly dependent on adult supervision. The role of teachers during this time in the special centers is to interact with children and to insure that children are following through on their plans and carrying out the activities of the special centers for the day. In the last few months before children go to public schools, the nature of the times in the centers changes.

The Cognitive Curriculum.   Curriculum is defined as the activities and interactions that children are involved in during the day. Most of these activities and interactions are planned. However, the informal interactions and unplanned experiences that are generated during the day are also an integral part of the curriculum. With respect to the formal curriculum, there is not just one set of packaged activities for teachers to draw from. Rather, teachers are able to choose from the best of what is available keeping in mind the specific needs of individual children. Some of the curriculum resources which are used are the GOAL math program (Karnes, 1973), Peabody Early Experiences Kit (Dunn, Chun, Crowell, Dunn, Avery, & Yachel, 1976), and Bridges to Reading (Greenberg & Epstein, 1973).

Social and Adaptive Behavior.   The daily program is to create an ecology in which adaptive and social behaviors can be manifested and reinforced. The program aim is designed to elicit social and adaptive behaviors through creating an environment in which these skills can be fostered and by using a specific social curriculum which makes children aware of appropriate behaviors and feelings. The area of social and adaptive behavior has been influenced more than any other area by opinions of public school teachers. There are three major priorities which are addressed by activities in this area:

1. Improving and strengthening task-oriented behavior
2. Improving peer relations and interactions
3. Improving teacher (adult)-child relationships

My Friends and Me (Davis, 1977) was selected as a packaged social curriculum for the purpose of making children aware of their own feelings and emotions, and of appropriate responses to these feelings. In addition, lessons are chosen from this program to help children understand cooperation, sharing, and being kind and helpful to others. Teachers realize that they must help children generalize from the specific activities to situations in the classrooms as they occur.

During the late spring and summer before children go to public school kindergarten, the environment is consciously engineered to prepare the children for the social and behavioral demands of the public schools. In order to increase the children's ability to function independently with high task-orientation, the following activities and procedures are carried out.

The daily schedule is posted on the wall. The schedule is discussed daily. Children are frequently asked, "What are you going to do next?" "What are we doing now?"

Center activities are reorganized. Specific tasks are set up in all centers. Children are expected to complete tasks and then move to another center. Each task has a definite beginning and end. The adult role is to plan the activities, explain the activities to the children, supervise the centers, take data, and interact with the children at the completion of the task in center. Children are asked frequently to work independently in centers without immediate adult supervision. An example of a sequence is as follows:

Housekeeping
In this center the children are to do the following:
1. Set the table with knife, fork, spoon, plate for four people.
2. Put pretend coffee on the stove.
3. Pretend to cook vegetables in a pot on the stove.
4. Pretend to serve the vegetables on the plates and serve the coffee in cups.
5. They are to sit down and call the teacher.
6. While they are pretend-eating, the teacher will engage them in conversation for about 5 minutes.

7. They are to take the dishes off the table and put them in the sink.
8. They are to pretend to wash the dishes and put them away.
9. When they are finished with this, they are to put their names on the table to indicate to the teacher that they have completed all of the activities in that center.

Instead of praising children's work, the teachers try to get the children to start reinforcing themselves and to be relatively independent of adult feedback. Instead of the teacher's saying, "That's a pretty picture," the child is asked "Why do you like your picture?" The teachers focus on giving feedback on the effort rather than the product. Teachers begin to use descriptors rather than praise. The reason behind this is to give the children feedback without qualifying the product as good or bad. For example: "You are building a red block road. I see that you used the small red blocks for the curves."

Parent Program. The focus of the parent program is to improve communication between parents and the teachers. We hope that by letting parents know what is taking place in the program, parents will, in turn, become more supportive and reinforcing of the program's goals for their child. Various strategies are employed to enhance communication. Group meetings are held to explain the goals of each classroom and the curriculum. Individual conferences are held between parents and teachers to discuss individual children. At least once a month children take home a special newsletter. The prime focus of the newsletter is a "Do Together Page" (see Table 7.4 for a sample page). The purpose of the

Table 7.4
Science Activity (Do Together Page)
Some Things To Talk About.

---

1. What did we do with water on the day it was real cold? (Put outside in pan to freeze).
2. Why did the water freeze?
3. What happened to the ice when we brought it inside? Why?
4. What would happen if all the water in Chapel Hill got frozen?
5. Where can we get water from other than the water faucet? (Fruit, veg.)

What we can use water for:
Ask your child to mark the picture that shows:

1. Water helping to put out a fire.
2. Water helping to wash vegetables.
3. An animal drinking water.
4. A garden being watered.
5. Water used for cooking.
6. Water helping us keep clean.
7. Water used to clean streets.
8. Water used to help us have fun. (2 pictures)

"Do Together Page" is to involve the parent in reinforcing an activity being done at the Center. Each "Do Together Page" is constructed so as to encourage verbal communication between the parent and child.

Parents are invited and encouraged to come to class and to share their skills and talents with the children in special activities such as weaving, making cookies, or knitting.

A parent advisory group meets periodically to plan social activities and share parent concerns about the program.

As part of the end-point evaluation of the preschool program, parents of the day-care-attending children are asked to complete a Parent Satisfaction Questionnaire. This scale is composed of questions that have forced-choice alternatives that vary on a scale from 3 to 1 in terms of their desirability. For the first 21 children who have graduated into the public schools we have tabulated results from six of the more general questions asked. Table 7.5 contains the means and standard deviations associated with each of those seven questions.

These figures seem to indicate that the parents are quite enthusiastic about the preschool program. This impression is buttressed by the spontaneous comments made by the mothers during the end of preschool interviews.

Table 7.5
General Evaluative Questions and Responses
from the Parent Satisfaction Questionnaire
(N = 21)

Questions	Mean	Standard Deviation
1. Do you feel your child benefited from day care at Frank Porter Graham?		
Very Much (3) Some (2) Not At All (1)	3.0	0.0
2. Did you notice positive changes in your child because of day care?		
A Lot of Changes (3) Some Changes (2) No Changes (1)	2.71	.56
3. Did the teachers contact you by phone, in person or by letter to let you know what was happening in day care?		
Frequently (3) Some (2) Never (1)	2.62	.50
4. Did you feel at ease in visiting the classroom?		
Very At Ease (3) A Little At Ease (2) Never At Ease (1)	2.84	.37
5. How satisfied were you with participating in the research at Frank Porter Graham?		
Extremely Satisfied (3) A Little Satisfied (2) Never Satisfied (1)	2.90	.30
6. How satisfied were you with the day care services at Frank Porter Graham?		
Extremely Satisfied (3) A Little Satisfied (2) Never Satisfied (1)	3.0	0.0

THE ABECEDARIAN APPROACH TO THE DEVELOPMENT OF COMMUNICATION SKILLS

What Linguistic Research Has to Say

Since it is the middle SES child who does well in expressive language, we turned to the literature on differential communicative environments provided in middle versus lower-class homes to find clues for organizing our day care environment. The following general teacher strategies that we use have been extrapolated from the research on adult-child verbal interaction.

1. *Talk to children often; even short, simple utterances help if they are frequent.* Mothers and caregivers who talk frequently to children, even in language characterized by relatively more imperative, directive statements, still manage to produce children with average receptive competence. Tizard, Cooperman, Joseph, and Tizard (1972) conducted observational studies in long-stay British residential nurseries that suggested even low-quality talk (short, simple utterances tied to the immediate situational context) can foster linguistic ability ranking at the mean on standardized tests (Minnesota Preschool Scale and Reynell Scales of Receptive/Expressive Language) if it occurs often enough (from 38–65% of observation blocks). Loban (1963), Streissguth and Bee (1972), and Tulkin and Kagan (1972) also found that preschool children who are talked to frequently, regardless of the quality of the talk, tend to do better in academic situations later on. However, in the Tizard et al. (1972) report, the institutionalized nursery children who were average in comprehension (receptive language) did less well in expressive language, and did not appear to initiate talk with adults nearly so often as do children with typical middle class home environments. The authors speculate that this may be owing to active discouragement of close caregiver-child relationships in the 13 British nurseries and to the attendants' perfunctory responses (e.g., ''That's nice'') when children did initiate. ''Very significant correlations'' were found between frequency of informative talk and frequency of answering the children, and children's comprehension scores. The implication is therefore strongly made in the Tizard et al. findings that *amount* of talk alone can be helpful, but specific qualitative levels of caregiver language are required for good receptive development. Thus, the second general strategy:

2. *Model high quality talk for optimal development—talk that is informative: reflective, problem-solving, creative, and abstract.* (see also Bernstein, 1961; Hess & Shipman, 1966; Levenstein, 1969).

3. *Respond to child-initiated conversation by active, reflective listening and by extending what the child has said in further comments.* (Cazden, 1972). Cazden (1967) studied three categories of contingent responses to toddler vocalizations: *repetitions* (repeating what the child has said word for word); *expansions* (repeating and correcting grammatically); and *extensions* (picking up on

the content of the child's talk and extending it by another question, comment, or exclamation logically related to it). Of the three, only *extensions* positively influenced development after children were 24 months old. To promote more and better expressive language, then, caregivers need to "keep the conversational ball in the air" (Rieke, 1975; Rieke, Lynch, & Soltman, 1977) by follow-up verbalizations that extend what the child has begun.

4. *Ask questions, and use pauses and repetitions of a child's previous comments, when appropriate, to promote active child responding and conversational mutuality* (multiple speaking turns for both partners in communication). Stein (1973) investigated mothers' versus fathers' speech and found that mothers' dialogues with their children were characterized by more speaker changes (turns). In mother-child talk, both parties in the interchange hold the floor, implying mutuality.

5. *Keep directive, behavior-managing talk down to a minimum.* A low incidence of imperatives in maternal speech appears positively related to language acquisition (Streissguth & Bee, 1972). Imperatives are concomitants of language that aim at managing behavior ("Sit down," "Keep quiet"), rather than initiating an interchange or stimulating thought. Nelson (1973) found that only 35% of middle class mothers' language to children under three was comprised of directive commands and requests; other researchers have also shown that mothers become even less directive and more informative, as well as linguistically complex, in their speech to older children (Snow, 1972; Phillips, 1973). Ward (1971) postulated that imperatives and directive forms of language in general are characteristic of environments in which children's linguistic mastery is devalued; Bernstein (1961) earlier produced evidence for this in his sociolinguistic research. Hess and Shipman (1966) found that the specificity of mothers' information was positively related to language acquisition, whereas the incidence of using imperatives was negatively related.

6. *Increase the probability that steps 1–5 will occur by arranging for frequent 1:1 tutorial-type sessions;* there, adult attention can be focused on a child and sustained dialogues involving several speaking turns can go on (Blank, 1973; Tough, 1976; Cazden, 1972; Bruner, 1971). Most of what the literature has shown to be facilitative of language growth is hardly surprising: we would expect that, in order to learn to communicate well, children need to hear a great deal of language; need opportunities to practice with a responsive audience; and need models who follow up child conversational leads, providing high quality demonstrations of "what more could be said." They also need speech input to be modified for their developmental levels (Snow, 1972; Phillips, 1973). All these facilitative elements presuppose frequent instances of continuous intimate interaction with a child. The evidence is that the more intimate the interaction, the better. One of the best-established empirical findings concerning sibling status is that eldest children achieve more intellectually and linguistically than later-borns

in the same family. Having the mother to herself or himself, the firstborn enjoys a degree of tutorial-intensity that promotes better learning.

7. *Read to a child daily in 1:1 or (very) small group sessions, cuddling the child, sharing his/her visual focus, and speaking in close auditory range.* So carried out, reading provides a positive experience of physical contact and shared pleasure; further, written language offers unique language stimulation, since the essence of written language is distance from the here and now. "It is important to remember," says Cazden, "that the child's linguistic environment is not limited to everyday speech interactions." Reading to children, especially (and their later reading to themselves), can be a "particularly potent form of language stimulation". Cazden further states:

> . . reading aloud is likely to stimulate meaningful conversation about the pictures to which both the adult and the child are attending.
> . . .Because language in books differs from speech in both structure and distance from nonverbal context, it may have qualitative as well as quantitative significance. . . (In a preschool book about a worm) one passage read "The worm's mouth is at the fat end, the worm's tail is at the thin end." Had the teachers been talking instead of reading, the children probably would have heard something like this: "His mouth is here (as she points), and his tail is here" (as she points again). Children's books also include idiomatic expressions. (Again, a book about a worm:) "He measured and measured, inch by inch, until he inched out of sight."
> (1972, p. 294)

In short, writing is "not just speech written down" (Kolers, 1970). The important point is that readers and listeners probably benefit from the difference. Stories also provide a child with opportunities to project into a character's experience, to share his viewpoint and feelings.

8. *Create activities for the classroom that stimulate discussion, and make discussion part of every suitable experience: particularly after the fact, when commentary and reflection will demand recall of a no-longer present stimulus* (Gahagan & Gahagan, 1972; Sigel, in press). Particularly useful is to support and extend children's imaginative play with comments, to enrich it *through language* (Tough, 1973, Levenstein, 1969).

9. *Structure situations that make certain language uses obligatory.* It can be very useful for teachers to stretch the child's abilities to alter communication referentially to suit a listener's needs (non-egocentric communication) by providing distance from a listener—as in telephone or walkie-talkie or blind screen games and tasks (Maratsos, 1973; Shantz, 1975) and imaginative role-playing exercises (Smilansky, 1968; Shaftel & Shaftel, 1967).

It is also useful to vary, on occasion, the intense, warm, responsive relationship that the child has with a "maternal" (not necessarily female) communicator by providing the exertion of a less intimate partner in conversation.

Mothers' speech contains more exclamations and questions, as well as "other indices of the close mother-child relationship" (Stein, 1973). This is contrasted with the fathers' tendency to involve the child less, to elicit child commentary less often, and to pay less attention to what the child says. Berko-Gleason (1975) also found evidence of this paternal tendency in the relatively less sensitive modifications in speech to children that fathers made: while fathers, like mothers and apparently all adults, shorten utterances and slow down their speech to children, fathers' mean length of utterance was less closely tied to the child's than was the mother's; and, where mothers used shorter, syntactically simpler utterances with the younger of two children, fathers tended to address longer utterances to *daughters* regardless of their age. Berko-Gleason notes that this difference is partly owing to fathers' tendency toward speech filled with imperatives, particularly in talk with sons: "Since imperatives have a zero preverb length, this contributes to the shorter average length of father-son utterances." (p. 291). Berko-Gleason offers one qualifier to the usual generalization about the type of adult language partner needed by the language-learning child. A warm, child-sensitive mother figure to interact with is important for development of expressive facility, but a distant, less sensitive father-like figure has a role as well:

> The children had to exert themselves for their fathers, and try harder to make themselves both heard and understood. . .The opportunity to try out new linguistic skills on someone not as intimate as your mother but closer than a stranger may be one of the hitherto unrecognized benefits of coming from an intact family. Perhaps the first step to the outside world, and the one in which linguistic skills get sharpened, is the one where you try to tell your father what happened while he was away. (pp. 293–294).

With the knowledge from linguistic research which we have just synthesized, we began to construct a language program to facilitate the communicative competence of our high-risk 3 and 4-year-old children.

Progress Toward Developing the Abecedarian Approach To Preschool Language/Communication

We have attempted to define an approach that gets beyond forms to the development of an elaborated code. In doing so, we have agreed with a position similar to that of the Duchess in Alice in Wonderland: "Take care of the sense and the sounds will take care of themselves."

The focus of our effort to date has been to promote a particular *kind* and *amount* of verbal interaction between teacher and day care pupil. The *kind* of verbal interaction is largely modeled on what a middle-class mother establishes with her child; the *amount* is rather higher, perhaps like what a tutorial hour might afford. Because our day care effort is competing with many hours of experience in another type of linguistic environment in the home, we have assumed that it cannot be as casual and diluted as normal family interaction. To raise certain types of linguistic functioning in the child's response hierarchy, then, we are trying to provide a large number of practice opportunities.

The Language Intervention Approach

The language intervention approach that has been adopted rests on several assumptions:

1. The acquisition of *communicative competence* is the primary goal.
2. The notion of communicative competence is *multi-faceted,* implying competencies in at least three interrelated dimensions:
   (a) social (pragmatic) competence (*language use*)
   (b) representational competence (level of abstraction)
   (c) linguistic competence (language structure—syntax/semantics)
3. The child acquires effective communication skills mainly through exercising these skills with adults who are effective communicators and particularly in situations in which the child is able and motivated to engage (i.e., intentionally) in the interaction with the adult.

Thus, the language development approach is focused at the level of "critical skills" (i.e., successful communication in situations where the child really wants to communicate), with the awareness that there are specific prerequisites for success. Teachers learn to apply the approach in any potential interaction with children. In this way they can capitalize on those situations and activities that happen to motivate individual children. In addition, teachers can use the approach in planning cohesive sequences of class activities and projects according to particular needs and constraints.

Teachers are given inservice training and consultative help in assessing children's needs, setting objectives, planning and implementing activities that will stimulate particular kinds of communication, and in evaluating their own interactions with the children. For example, an early aim in staff training was that teachers would use informative (vs. directive) language with children in 75% of their verbal interactions. To help teachers acquire understanding of this basic distinction, a didactic session handout (see Table 7.5) at the beginning of the year presented definitive and illustrative examples.

At the end of the didactic session, a worksheet quiz (Table 7.6) assessed staff understanding of the concepts presented. As teachers reached a criterion of 80% on didactic quizzes, observations began in the classroom to assess their application of the information—sharing/eliciting strategy. Each week, teachers were asked to surpass their previous week's performance by 25%, until they had reached a criterion of 75% informative language in interactions with children.

Table 7.6

Informative/Information Processing and Eliciting

Information language has the quality of stimulating thought, and often a verbal reply. It shares an idea with a child, or asks for his own ideas to influence the child's behavior; this language requires something more than blind obedience. It requires the child to think out at least part of what he is to do by himself. If directing language aims at behavior, informative language aims at thought and communication.

Examples:

Can you hear the story if you are talking? How do you need to be to hear the story?
Well, it has four legs and fur, and it barks...what do you think it is?
How does it make him feel when you call him that?
Where do the blocks belong now?

Directive Language

Directive language asks a child to start or stop something. It is used mainly to manage behavior. It rarely asks for any verbal responses from the child. No words, no thinking — just action: this is the essence of directing or "administrative" language.

Examples:

I need you to be quiet.
Point to the dog. Find me the dog, please.
No more name-calling.
You need to put the blocks on the shelves.

There are obviously many situations in which directive language is called for. If a child is playing in the middle of a busy street, a teacher would not say "There are cars coming. What might happen if you stay in the street?" Our goal of 75% Informative language implies that there *should* be an overall 25% Directive language. We set this goal because research has shown roughly this amount of information sharing language in families with communicatively sophisticated children. Some times and activities in a preschool day might really require an adjustment of the goal.

Table 7.7
(Sample) Worksheet: Classifying Informative/Directive Language

Just to check up on our understanding, let's try to classify these bits of teacher language taken from classroom language in the past two weeks. Mark Informative Language (I) and Directive Language (D) and we'll see what percentage of utterances we agree on.

Pull up your underpants first.   _____
What color is this shape?   _____
Walk quickly on the curved line.   _____
Skip on the straight line.   _____
Can you find me one like this?   _____
Could you walk back to the other table, please?   _____
Who has blue shoes on? How about black shoes?   _____
What did you trace on your paper?   _____
Don't pull your plate like that. Pull it to you.   _____
You won't grow up big and strong if you don't eat your greens.   _____

When teachers had reached the 75% informative, non-directive objective, the focus became a particular linguistic function *within* the larger "informative language" category—specifically, one of seven social functions of language identified by Joan Tough (1976): See Table 7.9 on p. 169 for a presentation of Tough's framework.

Once teachers had mastered the framework so that they could reliably classify adult and child language according to its categories, consultants helped them to select objectives to work on in the classroom each week, and guided them in devising activities that would help children reach the objectives set.

Objectives Developed with the Day Care Staff in Communication Skill Development

Following our review of linguistic research, we began to develop an approach in which teachers agreed to:

1. Learn to classify language according to two major categories: information sharing/eliciting, and directive.
2. Learn to classify language according to seven categories within information sharing/eliciting: self-maintaining; directing; reporting; logical reasoning; predicting; projecting; imagining. (Tough, 1976).
3. Demonstrate at least 75% informative language in verbalizations to children.
4. Demonstrate ability to model and elicit language in each of Tough's 7 categories of informative language: (see 2 above).
5. Set short-term objectives for children to reach in specific categories of language use (given long-term objectives set by language consultants to the classrooms).
6. Devise activities to stimulate language in specific categories of communicative use (given advice and assistance in developing materials by language consultants).
7. Learn to assess "quality of response (for age level)" in children's language—in specified categories of language use (reporting for the 3-year-old class; reporting, logical reasoning, predicting, and projecting for the 4-year-olds), given a consultant-developed rating scale to guide assessments.
8. Provide each child daily with at least 3–5 minutes of private conversation.
9. Read and discuss a story, poem, picture sequence, or other written material with each child daily in 1:1 or very small group sessions.
10. Elicit a number of active verbal responses from each child daily. (Number variable from child to child).

At present, consultants meet weekly with teachers for 2 hours to assist them in mastering the approaches developed and to help with plans and activities for the following week. Working from the language uses classification system developed by Tough, the consultants wrote criterion-referenced objectives for each strategy within four of the seven categories of language use: reporting, (pre) logical reasoning, predicting, and projecting. The criteria were based on estimates of what the 3 and 4-year-old groups would be able to achieve; the estimates were guided by results of half-hour language samples done early in the fall on each child, using a series of wordless picture stories as stimuli for questions requiring reporting, (pre) logical reasoning, predicting, and projecting responses. A sample criterion-referenced objective for year-end achievement in (pre) logical reasoning for the 4-year-old group is the following:

> Child can explain a 5-step process, including and correctly sequencing all 5 steps; and using explicit, clear references:
>   -in a present experience, with picture cards to aid recall
>   -in an immediately preceding experience, without picture cards to aid recall
>   -in a recent experience, with verbal reminder of a key incident or detail
>   -in a remote experience or potential situation

In weekly planning sessions with the language consultant, teachers select one or more long-term objectives as a focus for the next week's activities in the classrooms. Activities that will stimulate the particular language use selected for focus are proposed and planned for.

A sample weekly Plan Sheet (Table 7.8) will illustrate the translation of objectives into activities for the classroom: Consultants conduct observations in the classrooms following the planning meeting to monitor teachers' interactions, children's responses, and the progress of activities. The data resulting are prepared and discussed with the teachers in the next week's meeting, as a guide to setting new objectives and preparing new activities.

INTELLECTUAL AND LINGUISTIC RESULTS OF THE ABECEDARIAN PRESCHOOL INTERVENTION

In order to evaluate the relative impact of the Abecedarian Program with its particular curricular emphases, a variety of standardized and experimental measures are administered at periodic intervals. Typically, the performance of the day-care-attending children is compared as a group, with that of the randomly assigned control group mentioned earlier. Under the logic of the randomly constituted day care and control groups, differences between the two can reasonably be ascribed to the variables that have been manipulated—namely the day care pro-

Table 7.8

Trip to CCF Farmer's Exchange to buy seeds for classroom garden this week   Week of 3-26-79

Plan Sheet: Language/Communication

WHO	WHAT CHILD/TEACHER WILL DO	WITH WHAT MATERIALS	WITH WHAT DIRECTIONS	HOW OFTEN
All 4's	Reporting 1, 2, 5 on trip to CCF to buy garden seeds	Seed packets, plants, etc., at CCF store and verbal cues from teacher.	What do we call these seeds/plants? What color are these?	Monday – before and after trip
All 4's	Reporting 1, 2, 3, 4 when planting seed	Seeds, dirt, etc., & planting guide cards – for first 3 days; then without cards on Day 4	(Repeat previous questions) Let's see who can remember what we need to do when we plant our seeds	Daily for 4 days
All 4's	Directing 2, 3	In planting experience with cards and teacher prompts on Day 1, only cards on Day 2; without cards – directing another child by Day 3	1) Look at the cards and tell me what you have to do; I'll help you 2) The guide cards will tell you what to do 3) Today we will be teachers, we will help each other remember how to plant seeds	Daily – with variations – for 4 days

(Continued)

167

Table 7.8 (Continued)

Trip to CCF Farmer's Exchange to buy seeds for classroom garden this week

Week of 3-26-79

Plan Sheet: Language/Communication

WHO	WHAT CHILD/TEACHER WILL DO	WITH WHAT MATERIALS	WITH WHAT DIRECTIONS	HOW OFTEN
All 4's	Prelogical Reasoning 5 and Predicting 1, 2, 4, 5	Garden plants	Let's try to predict what will happen to our plants: -which will come up first? -which will come up biggest? -which will be smallest?	On Friday when survey chart is done
All 4's	Projecting 1, 2, 3	With *My Friends & Me* curriculum lesson: non-destructive ways of dealing with unpleasant feelings	See curriculum	Tues. (Part I) Thurs. (Part II)
All 4's	Reporting 3; Predicting 1, 6; Prelogical Reasoning 5	With *My Friends & Me* curriculum lesson: Non destructive ways of dealing with unpleasant feelings	What did _____ do? How do you think s/he felt – why? What might s/he do next or what do you think s/he did?	Tues. (Part I) Thurs. (Part II)

*Note: Objectives are keyed to Tough's categories or language use and the numerals (e.g., Reporting *1*) refer to strategies under each category. Refer to Table 7.9 for a full listing of these.

Table 7.9

Uses of Language: Tough's 7 Categories of Language Function

Self-Maintaining	Directing	Reporting	Prelogical Reasoning	Predicting	Projecting	Imagining
Tell about own needs, wants; criticize, threaten others to protect own interests; seek attention for self. "I want ice cream". "That's *my* truck!" "Teacher look at me!"	*Give instructions,* feedback to self and others on "how to do"	*Tell about* event, Incident in story, real experience, objects: *color, size, shape, what happened, compare / contrast; tell sequence* of events.	Explaining *why* a thing happened, what caused it; what made you think so, "*how come?*"	Say *what is likely to happen* next, in future, or in some possible situation; *what a character will say or do*— in overt words or actions.	Say what a person *feels, wishes for, would like* also, how a person probably *has felt* or *would feel* in a future situation or some other situation than the present.	Making up a story/ possible imaginary situation (I am the Mamma, you are the Daddy; let's pretend we live at the North pole and we can have all the toys; we're fishes and we can't talk, only swim and wave our fins).
Strategies:	*Strategies:*	*Strategies:*	*Strategies:*	*Strategies:*	*Strategies:*	*Strategies:*
1. Referring to physical and psychological needs and wants	1. Monitoring own actions	1. Labelling the components of the scene	1. Explaining a process	1. Anticipating and forecasting events	1. Projecting into the experiences of others	1. Developing an imaginary situation based on real life
2. Protecting the self and self interests	2. Directing the actions of the self	2. Referring to detail (e.g., size, color, and other attributes)	2. Recognizing causal and dependent relationships	2. Anticipating the detail of events	2. Projecting into the feelings of others	2. Developing an imaginary situation based on fantasy
3. Justifying behavior or claims	3. Directing the actions of others	3. Referring to incidents	3. Recognizing problems and their solutions	3. Anticipating a sequence of events	3. Projecting into the reactions of others	3. Developing an original story
4. Criticising others	4. Collaborating in action with others	4. Referring to the sequence of events	4. Justifying judgments and actions	4. Anticipating problems and possible solutions	4. Projecting into situations never experienced	
5. Threatening others		5. Making comparisons	5. Reflecting on events and drawing conclusions	5. Anticipating and recognizing alternative courses of actions		
		6. Recognizing related aspects	6. Recognizing principles	6. Predicting the consequences of		
		7. Making an analysis using several of the features above				
		8. Extracting or recognizing the central meaning				
		9. Reflecting on the meaning of experiences, including own feelings.				

gram and its associated curriculum. As a conclusion to this chapter we will review two examples of results from the Abecedarian program which we believe indicate that the program is accomplishing its goal of preventing retarded development in intellectual and linguistic performance.

Intellectual Results

Ramey and Campbell (1979) have presented results from intelligence tests for the day care and control groups administered at 12, 24, 36, and 48 months. The scores at 12 months were obtained from the Mental Development Index of the Bayley Scales of Infant Development. At the other three ages the scores are from Stanford-Binet assessments. Figure 7.1 contains a graphic portrayal of the mean scores by groups. Statistical analyses indicated no differences between the two groups at 12 months. At each measurement occasion thereafter, the two groups differed significantly. The difference between the two groups is due to a decline from normality in the control group which reached a mean IQ of 81 at 48 months. Further, for each child in the day care group who scored below 80 at 48 months, six children scored below 80 in the control group. Thus, the day care program appears to be *preventing* developmental retardation in this high-risk sample of disadvantaged children. As a beginning effort to analyze what particular intellectual abilities were affected by our intervention program, we performed item analyses of the Binet protocols. Item analyses of these protocols revealed that 17

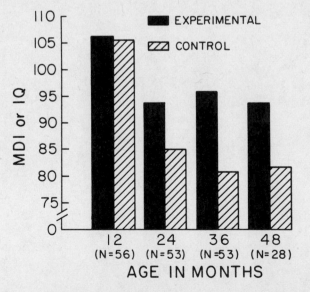

FIG. 7.1 Trends in Bayley MDI and Binet IQ between 9 and 48 months for preschool Experimental and Control.

items at 48 months significantly discriminated between the two groups. Of the 17 items, 10 were language items. Thus, language seems to be an important aspect of the general intellectual decline.

Linguistic Results

To pursue this language deficit possibility more closely, the McCarthy Scales of Children's Abilities, which yield a separate verbal subscale, were administered at 30 and 42 months of age to the day care and the control groups (Ramey & Campbell, 1979). There was a significant difference in the Verbal Scale Index between the two groups at 30 months. This difference persisted at 42 months with the day care group scoring at the national average and the control group below average. These findings lead to the conclusion that:

> Early educational experience did result in accelerated language development [as measured by the McCarthy Verbal Subscales] which was apparent before age 3. By age 42 months, the difference in language development still existed... Earlier development of language competence in center-attending children relative to their non-center-attending controls is supported by these results.'' (Ramey & Campbell, 1979, p. 184)

SOCIAL POLICY IMPLICATIONS FOR PRESCHOOL INTERVENTION PROGRAMS

Tbe educational program of the Carolina Abecedarian Project has altered the educational ecology of disadvantaged children from birth, and has apparently succeeded in *preventing* a significant amount of developmental retardation during the preschool years. There are a few, but only a few, other demonstrations of successful preventive programs in the research literature. By far, the most famous of those programs is the pioneering work of Skeels (1966) with institutionalized infants who were subsequently adopted after being transferred to a ward where they were cared for by retarded adolescent girls. In comparison to a group of infants who did not have the additional attention bestowed by these additional caregivers and who were not adopted, the adopted children were markedly superior in achieving normal adult status. Recent work by Scarr and Weinberg (1976) on the transracial adoption of black infants from disadvantaged homes who were adopted by advantaged white families also supports the positive power of major ecological change on intellectual development. Finally, this preventive thesis is also supported by a recent research report from France by Schiff, Duyme, Dumaret, Stewart, Tomkiewicz, and Feingold (1978). They reported that working-class children who were adopted in upper-middle-class homes were superior intellectually to their subsequent biological siblings who were reared by their natural mothers.

The Skeels (1966), Scarr and Weinberg (1976), and Schiff et al. (1978) studies all relied on a drastic ecological intervention (adoption) to prevent intellectual retardation. This form of intervention surely raised fundamental issues in social ethics and social policy concerning disadvantaged families. Thus, while they make excellent theoretical contributions to our understanding of the malleability of intelligence, they offer relatively little help in solving the problems of a large segment of the disadvantaged population in this country.

It is at the pragmatic level of working with disadvantaged families that we believe the Abecedarian Project can make a meaningful contribution for disadvantaged families who are at high risk for producing a developmentally retarded child. If one accepts, as demonstrated, that significant amounts of developmental retardation can be prevented through a relatively limited ecological intervention, then the major practical questions become: (1) how can we improve the effectiveness of such programs; (2) how can equally effective but less costly programs be developed; and (3) how do we optimally match various facets of successful programs with the needs of individual families? We think that research and development into these questions deserves a high priority on the public agenda for the 1980s.

ACKNOWLEDGMENTS

The Abecedarian Project has been supported by grants from the National Institute of Child Health and Human Development, the North Carolina Department of Human Resources, the Spencer Foundation and the Carnegie Foundation. We gratefully acknowledge the assistance of Marie Butts, Pam McPherson, and John Bernard in the preparation of this manuscript.

REFERENCES

Berko-Gleason, J. Fathers and other strangers: Men's speech to young children. In D. P. Dato (Ed.), *Developmental psycholinguistics: Theory and application.* Georgetown University Round Table on Languages and Linguistics Monograph, 1975. Washington, D.C.: Georgetown University Press, 1975.

Bernstein, B. Social class and linguistic development: A theory of social learning. In A. H. Halsey, J. Flond, & C. A. Anderson (Eds.), *Education, Economy, and Society.* New York: Free Press of Glencoe, 1961.

Blank, M. *Teaching learning in the preschool: A dialogue approach.* Columbus, Ohio: Merrill, 1973.

Bruner, J. S. *The relevance of education.* London: Allen & Unwin, 1971.

Caldwell, B., Heider, J., & Kaplan, B. *The inventory of home stimulation.* Paper presented at the annual meeting of the American Psychological Association, New York, September, 1966.

Cazden, C. B. *Child language in education.* New York: Holt, Rinehart & Winston, 1972.

Cazden, C. B. The role of parent speech in the acquisition of grammar. *Project Literacy Reports,* No. 8. Ithaca, N.Y.: Cornell University, 1967, 60-65.

Davis, D. E. *My friends and me*. Circle Pines, Minnesota: American Guidance Service, 1977.

Dunn, L. M., Chun, L. T., Crowell, D. C., Dunn, L. M., Avery, L. G., & Yachel, E. R. *Peabody Early Education Kit*. Circle Pines, Minn.: American Guidance Service, 1976.

Farran, D., & Ramey, C. Social class difference in dyadic involvement during infancy. *Child Development*, 1980, *51*, 254–257.

Gahagan, D. M., & Gahagan, G. A. *Talk reform: Exploratives in language for infant school children*. London: Routledge & Kegan Paul, 1972.

Greenberg, P., & Epstein, B. *Bridges to reading*. Morristown, N.J.: General Learning Corp., 1973.

Harms, T., & Cross, L. *Environmental provisions in day care*. Day Care Training and Technical Assistance System, Chapel Hill, N.C., 1977.

Hess, R. D., & Shipman, V. C. Maternal influences upon early learning: The cognitive environment of urban preschool children. In R. D. Hess, & R. M. Bear (Eds.), *Early education*. Chicago: Aldine, 1966.

Karnes, M. B. *GOAL program: Mathematical concepts*. Springfield, Mass.: Milton-Bradley, 1973.

Kolers, P. A. Three stages of reading. In H. Levin & J. P. Williams (Eds.), *Basic studies in reading*. New York: Basic Books, 1970, 90–118.

Levenstein, P. *Cognitive growth in preschoolers through verbal interaction with mothers*. Paper presented at the annual meeting of the American Orthopsychiatric Association, New York, N.Y., 1969.

Loban, W. D. *The language of elementary school children*. National Council of Teachers of English Research Report #1. Champaign, Illinois: National Council of Teachers of English, 1963.

Maratsos, M. Nonegocentric communication abilities in preschool children. *Child Development*, 1973, 44, 697–700.

Nelson, K. *Structure and strategy in learning to talk*. Society for Research in Child Development Monograph (Serial No. 149). February–April, 1973.

Phillips, J. Syntax and vocabulary of mothers' speech to young children: Age and sex comparisons. *Child Development*, 1973, *44*, 182–185.

Ramey, C. T., & Campbell, F. A. Parental attitudes and poverty. *Journal of Genetic Psychology*, 1976, *128*, 3–6.

Ramey, C. T., & Campbell, F. A. Compensatory education for disadvantaged children. *School Review*, 1979, *87*(2), 171–189.

Ramey, C. T., Collier, A. M., Sparling, J. J., Loda, F. A., Campbell, F. A., Ingram, D. L., & Finkelstein, N. W. The Carolina Abecedarian project: A longitudinal and multidisciplinary approach to the prevention of developmental retardation. In T. Tjossem (Ed.), *Intervention strategies for high-risk infants and young children*. Baltimore, Maryland: University Park Press, 1976, 629–665.

Ramey, C. T., Farran, D. C., & Campbell, F. A. Predicting IQ from mother-infant interactions. *Child Development*, 1979, *50*, 804–814.

Ramey, C. T., & Haskins, R. The causes and treatment of school failure: Insights from the Carolina Abecedarian project. In M. Begab, H. C. Haywood, & H. Garber. Psychosocial influences in retarded performance (Vol. 2). Baltimore: Maryland: University Park Press, 1982, 89–112.

Ramey, C. T., Holmberg, M. C., Sparling, J. J., & Collier, A. M. An introduction to the Carolina Abecedarian project. In B. M. Caldwell & D. J. Stedman (Eds.), *Infant education for handicapped children*. New York: Walker and Co., 1977, 101–121.

Ramey, C. T., Mills, P., Campbell, F. A., & O'Brien, C. Infants' home environments: A comparison of high-risk families and families from the general population. *American Journal of Mental Deficiency*, 1975, *80*, 40–42.

Ramey, C. T., & Smith, B. Assessing the intellectual consequences of early intervention with high-risk infants. In *American Journal of Mental Deficiency*, 1977, *81*, 318–324.

Ramey, C. T., Stedman, D. J., Borders-Patterson, A., & Mengel, W. Predicting school failure from information available at birth. *American Journal of Mental Deficiency*, 1978, *82*, 525–534.

Rieke, J. A. Communication development. In N. G. Haring & A. H. Hayden (Eds.), *Behavior of exceptional children*. Columbus, Ohio: Merrill, 1975.

Rieke, J. A., Lynch, L. L., & Soltman, S. F. *Teaching strategies for language development*. New York: Grune & Stratton, 1977.

Scarr, S., & Weinberg, R. IQ test performance of black children adopted by white families. *American Psychologist*, 1976, *31*, 726–739.

Schiff, M., Duyme, M., Dumaret, A., Stewart, J., Tomkiewicz, S., & Feingold, J. Intellectual status of working-class children adopted early into upper-middle-class families. *Science*, 1978, *200*, 1503–1504.

Shaftel, G., & Shaftel. F. *Role playing for social values*. Englewood Cliffs, N.J.: Prentice-Hall, 1967.

Shantz, C. U. The development of social cognition. In E. M. Hetherington (Ed.), *Review of Child Development research*, Vol. 5. Chicago: University of Chicago Press, 1975.

Sigel, I. An inquiry into inquiry: Question-asking as an instructional model. In. L. G. Katz (Ed.), *Current topics in early childhood education* (Vol. 2). Norwood, N.J.: Ablex Publishing, 1979.

Skeels, H. M. *Adult status of children with contrasting early life experiences*. Monographs of the Society for Research in Child Development, 1966, *31*(3, Serial No. 105).

Smilansky, S. *Effects of sociodramatic play on disadvantaged school children*. New York: Wiley, 1968.

Snow, C. E. Mothers' speech to children learning language. *Child Development*, 1972, *43*, 549–565.

Stein, A. *An analysis and comparison of mothers' and fathers' speech to young children in a story-telling situation*. Unpublished paper, Boston University School of Education, 1973.

Streissguth, A. P., & Bee, H. L. Mother-child interactions and cognitive development in children. In W. W. Hartup (Ed.), *The young child: Reviews of research* (Vol. 2). Washington, D.C.: National Association for the Education of Young Children, 1972, 158–181.

Tizard, B., Cooperman, O., Joseph, A., & Tizard, J. Environmental effects on language development: A study of young children in long-stay residential nurseries. *Child Development*, 1972, *43*, 337–358.

Tough, J. *Focus on meaning: Talking to some purpose with young children*. London: George Allen & Unwin, 1973.

Tough, J. *Listening to children talking*. London: Ward Lock Educational, 1976.

Tulkin, S. R., & Kagan, J. Mother-child interaction in the first year of life. *Child Development*, 1972, *43*, 31–42.

Ward, M. C. *Them children: A study in language learning*. New York: Holt, and Winston, 1971.

Wechsler, D. Wechsler Adult Intelligence Scale. The Psychological Corporation, New York, 1955.

8 The Role of Communication in the Socialization of Certain Handicapped Children

Richard R. Kretschmer, Jr.
Laura W. Kretschmer
University of Cincinnati

Contemporary sociolinguistic research has begun to provide some interesting insights into the conditions that promote the acquisition and development of communication in normally developing children (Cross & Morris, 1980; Howe, 1980; Snow & Ferguson, 1977; Waterson & Snow, 1978). Children's first language development should be considered as the result of the interaction between social, cognitive, and linguistic experiences (Bloom & Lahey, 1978). Children begin to understand their world by engaging primary and secondary caretakers in social/communication exchanges; exchanges that in turn facilitate the child's expression of his cognitive awareness. To fully understand normal child language acquisition, consideration must be given to the social and learning environment provided the child as well as the linguistic interactions that occur in that environment.

A question of interest to many people who deal with children who may have special needs is whether the process of language acquisition and development is altered by the presence of cognitive, sensory, and/or social-emotional handicaps. Research on normal child language development provides us with a rich variety of concepts and research techniques that can be applied to the study of children with handicaps to determine the effects such conditions have on their language acquisition processes.

If different handicaps have noticeably different effects on communication learning, those differences can provide direction for the social, linguistic, and educational management of handicapped children. It would be important to know whether instructional programs based on information from the child language literature are as efficacious as they appear to be, or whether the language acquisition and development process in handicapped children is so different that our contemporary observations about learning and socialization of normal children is

175

of limited value in program development. Do we need to develop different types of programs for different types of handicapping conditions? Does a sensory/ cognitive handicap alter language learning and social use of language in ways that are distinct from a physical movement handicap?

To examine these questions, the remainder of this chapter will focus on two specific groups of children, namely: children with early onset of severe hearing impairment and children with significant delay in first language onset. The latter group of children does not have observable sensory or cognitive handicaps, other than delayed appearance of language expression. The research to be discussed examines the cognitive and social bases of language growth in hearing impaired and in language delayed children. The studies reported have been conducted primarily by graduate students in Special Education or Speech and Hearing at the University of Cincinnati, or by the authors themselves.

Descriptions of mother–infant interactions have reported many characteristics of the verbal component of these interactions. The mother's contribution has been generically tagged as motherese or mother register (Snow & Ferguson, 1977). When mothers talk to infants and/or young children, they systematically alter their speech and language to make it conform to the linguistic/ communication needs of their children. Although it is not entirely clear how these alterations relate to language growth, there is evidence to suggest that at least some aspects of motherese are important in aiding children to segment and to make sense of what is being said to them (Cross, 1978; Cross & Morris, 1980). The question of whether motherese is altered or varied when the child-partner is known to be linguistically handicapped has intrigued us.

To investigate this question, Bondurant (1977) observed two groups of children as they interacted with their primary caretaker—who in most cases was a mother. One group consisted of 14 children whose expressive language was tested 1 to 2 years delayed relative to their chronological age and the other group consisted of 14 children whose expressive language was considered age appropriate. Both groups of children were judged to be normal in physical, personal, intellectual, and educational development as determined by the Developmental Profile (Alpern & Boll, 1972), a scale which uses the mother as the informant. The subjects ranged in age from 2 years to 5 and were matched in age between groups.

Each mother was asked to interact with her child in two distinctly different communication situations. In the first situation, the unstructured communication condition, the mother and child were seated on the floor with various toys arranged about them. The mother was instructed to play naturally with the child for a 15-minute period. In the second situation, the mother was asked to direct the child in constructing a replica of a model farm which the child could not see, but which could be constructed from the available toys and blocks accessible to both communication partners. This condition was referred to as the structured communication condition.

The language produced by the mothers under both conditions was analyzed using descriptors such as: total number of utterances; mean length of utterance; utterances per minute; numbers of reports, comments, questions, directions; number of maternal utterances repeated; number of maternal expansions of the child's utterances; number of verbs produced by the mother as an index of syntactic complexity; number of accepting and rejecting utterances produced by the mother.

Using multivariate techniques, four variables were found to significantly differentiate mothers of normally developing children from mothers of language delayed children. Mothers of normally developing children generated longer sentences, used more questions and fewer directives, and produced more accepting utterances. In contrast, mothers of language delayed children used mostly short imperative sentences and provided much less positive verbal reinforcement as they interacted with their children. The communication setting, that is, whether it was structured or unstructured, was not a significant variable. These findings are consistent with those reported by Wulbert, Inglis, Kriegsmann, & Mills (1975) using a less detailed observational procedure as well as reports by Buium, Rynders, and Turnure (1974) for mothers of mentally retarded children and by Greenstein, Greenstein, McConville, & Stellini (1975) and Wedell-Monnig and Lumley (1980) with regard to mothers of hearing impaired children.

Such results might be used to argue that the altered linguistic and social behavior of the mother is contributive to the delays in language acquisition evidenced in their children. Since the same behaviors are observed in mothers whose children have communication problems because of organic handicaps, it is probably more reasonable to suggest that mothers are only being realistic about their children's comprehension and expression of language even though these limited capabilities may be disquieting to the parent. Indeed, there is ample evidence to suggest that variations in linguistic environments do not in themselves produce delay in language. A study by Field and Pawlby (1980) illustrates this point. Language interactions between middle class and working class British and American mothers and their children were reported. Their description of working class mothers' linguistic and social behaviors was similar to those described by Bondurant (1977) for the mothers' of language delayed children. The working class children in the Field and Pawlby study all developed language, albeit at a slower rate than the middle class children. While data on the mother register of a variety of handicapped children still need to be gathered, the research presently available suggests that *variation* in linguistic environment alone may not be the cause of significant language delay in otherwise normal children.

As stressed, linguistic/social factors and cognitive development must be recognized as playing an important role in the development of communication in young children. Research on the cognitive underpinnings of early language has centered around attempts to specify the semantic/cognitive categories underlying single words and two word productions of children (Bloom & Lahey, 1978; Brown, 1973; Greenfield & Smith, 1976; Leonard, 1976). These research efforts suggest that children learning different natural languages develop and express comparable semantic/cognitive categories and relations at the one and two word stages. More specifically, it is generally agreed that, regardless of the language being learned, children show understanding of the concepts of existence, non-existence, disappearance, and recurrence of objects and actions, and an appreciation that objects (actors) can act upon other objects (patients) in prescribed locations during the earliest stages of language development.

Another line of research investigating the cognitive underpinnings of language has examined the symbolization process in general in order to determine what cognitive/social prerequisites might be necessary for the development of symbolic systems such as language or play (Bates, 1979; Corrigan, 1978; Miller, Chapman, Branston, & Reichle, 1980).

Accordingly, it has been of interest to us to investigate cognitive development in language delayed children, by considering their ability to symbolize in systems other than language, specifically through play. We are not yet prepared to argue that language and play spring from a common base, but only that disturbances in language symbolization are frequently accompanied by disturbances in symbolic behavior such as play.

Williams (1977) investigated the quality of play observed in children diagnosed as language delayed. She observed the play of 15 language impaired and 15 normally developing children matched on mean length of utterance, as well as chronological age, sex, race, and socioeconomic class. The children who ranged in age from 36 to 55 months of age, were screened using the Preschool Attainment Record (Doll, 1966) to eliminate those children demonstrating educational problems, other than language delay.

After an initial interview to allay concerns about the experimental situation, each child was provided with toys while the investigator conversed with the mother in another room. Each child was then videotaped for 9 minutes. The number of occurrences of relational play acts and the number of occurrences of symbolic play acts that appeared during this 9-minute segment was calculated. Relational play was defined as using materials without any apparent attempt at pretense. Relational play could be non-accomodative, which was defined as using materials together that do not "normally" go together such as putting spoons in the playdough, putting the teapot lid on a block, or accomodative, which was defined as using materials together that do "normally" go together such as putting lids on the margarine tubs, stacking blocks, or putting a spoon in a cup. Symbolic acts were defined as those acts that involved pretense, or making use of objects or body movements to signify states other than the concrete functions normally expected with the materials being employed. Examples of symbolic play would be using blocks as cars, using a cardboard tube as a musical instrument.

Analysis of the data indicated that children described as normal language users engaged in twice as many symbolic acts as did the language delayed children. Apparently, some children with difficulty in performance in one symbolic system (language) might be expected to have difficulty in another symbolic system (play). Longer samples of behavior in a more socialized context might have shown fewer differences among the subjects in Williams's study. The present results still suggest that some language delayed children may have more than one kind of symbolic difficulty, an observation worthy of continued investigation. If further research substantiates this possibility, it could then be asked: Can therapeutic or educational programs to develop one symbolic system be beneficial in the development of another symbolic system? Can play "therapy" improve language performance, or vice-versa, in children with significantly delayed onset of language?

On another level, previous studies on semantic/cognitive performance of language delayed children have suggested that their expressive productions reflect semantic categorization that is similar to that of younger normally developing children (Freedman & Carpenter, 1976; Leonard, Bolders, & Miller, 1976). Unfortunately, the value of these studies is somewhat diminished by the fact that they all concentrated on oral language samples collected over a short period of time, specifically, 300 utterances over a 2 week period in one study and 50 utterances collected during a single session in the other. In an attempt to establish a clearer picture of the growth of semantic categories expressed by language delayed children, Prendeville (1978) with Person (1978) collected language samples on three language impaired children, three mentally retarded children, and three normally developing children matched on mean length of utterance (between 1.25 and 1.90 morphemes per utterance). The language delayed subjects were chosen from a therapy program for children with communication disorders. Thirty minute language samples from each child were collected twice a month over a 4-month period. During each videotaped sample, the child's mother interacted with her child as normally as possible, using different sets of play materials. The play materials for each session was held constant for all children. All intelligible, non-imitated two-word productions were transcribed along with the linguistic and non-linguistic context surrounding the production of each utterance. The context was critical in interpreting the child's underlying semantic/communicative intentions.

An analysis system developed prior to initiation of the study was used to describe the semantic categories/relations expected in the two-word productions of children. The system was based on the then current literature on semantic/cognitive categories/relations observed in children's utterances (Bloom, 1970; Bowerman, 1973; Brown, 1973; Duchan & Erickson, 1975; Edwards, 1973; Greenfield & Smith, 1976; Leonard, 1976). The system included expected categories of cases and relations consistently reported in the literature, as well as categories of cases and relations whose appearance was controversial or whose appearance was not substantiated from the two-word stage data reported in the literature. As the study progressed, some utterances appeared which had not been accounted for beforehand, especially the expansion of notions about time, manner, reason, and intensity.

Both the normally developing and the two language delayed groups demonstrated a major increase in mean length of utterance during the second half of the sampling, with the language delayed group demonstrating greater change than the normally developing or moderately retarded children. There were no significant differences in the absolute number of different semantic categories/relations expressed by the three groups of children during the test sessions. However, as the sampling progressed, the language delayed group began to produce many instances of semantic categories/relations not represented in the normally developing children's language samples. Of particular interest was the exclusive use by the language delayed children of experiencer-verb relationships like *think* and *love* as well as a highly developed adverbial system which included adverbs of reason, time, and intensity.

The development of longer utterances and the expression of more varied semantic categories/relations by the language delayed children did not support a conclusion that the underlying semantic/cognitive structures of language delayed children were similar to younger normally developing children. Given that language delayed children have more living experience by virtue of being older, it seems reasonable to find that such children are more cognitively and socially mature. Further, it would seem reasonable to assume that once language expression is begun, language delayed children would express their semantic maturity when compared to younger, normally developing children who are only linguistically equivalent and not necessarily cognitively equivalent.

The child with significantly delayed language seems to have an inability for some reason to connect a spoken language system to his or her cognitive knowledge even at the most basic level, but once the process of language use is activated, many language delayed children soon use language in ways that reflect his or her greater social and cognitive maturity.

One additional finding of interest in the Prendeville (1978) study was that the language delayed children used more tag questions than did the normally developing subjects. Those question forms seem to represent the language delayed child's strategy for encouraging their mothers to acknowledge the correctness or clarity of their productions, a cue, if you will, to the mother to indicate if the child could be understood. Even within the limited syntactic competence of the language delayed children in Prendeville's study, establishing social exchange and conversational contact with others seemed to be an important function.

A second group of children with significant language handicaps are those with severe hearing loss of onset early in life. Like children with language delay, hearing impaired children in their social interactions with their parents, have received some research attention. Wedell-Monnig and Lumley (1980) found mothers of hearing impaired children to be more dominating in their communicative and social interactions than mothers of normally hearing children, with the result that the hearing impaired children under study tended to be more passive and less involved in interactions. The need for independence and activity may be especially critical to the hearing impaired child whose primary difficulty is not lack of hearing, but limited information and experience with communication. The study by Greenstein et al. (1975) underscored the point that mothers of linguistically successful hearing impaired children tended to be less possessive of their children, that is, they permitted their children more freedom to explore the environment than did mothers of linguistically less successful hearing impaired children. The hearing impaired child's learning difficulties unfortunately lie not only in the area of communication. A lack of acceptance of the handicap by the child's parents may interfere with those adults' ability to establish normal bonds, whether affective or communicative, with the hearing impaired child. The importance of social bases for the development of communication seem to be as important as the cognitive and linguistic ones (Corson, 1973).

Study of family dynamics surrounding the social and communication development of normally hearing children of deaf parents deserves attention as a way of understanding the factors involved in language acquisition. Does the deaf mother have a mother register? Does the use of a nonvocal communication system alter the socialization process so critical to language acquisition? Does the extreme environmental variation of nonspeaking adults serve to significantly alter the language development process in their children who have normal hearing?

In answer to the last question, Bard and Sachs (1977), Cicourel and Boese (1972), Jones (1976), Prinz and Prinz (1979), Sachs and Johnson (1976), and Todd and Aitchinson (1980) have considered the process of language acquisition, whether spoken or signed, in children with normal hearing whose parents are deaf. These studies, with the exception of Todd and Aitchison (1980), have examined a sample of expressive language from one or more children to determine its relation to "normal" communication development. Although the language acquisition process is apparently unaltered in some situations and altered in others, these studies leave questions about the establishment and development of social interactions and motherese in a family structure where deaf parents and their normally hearing children interact.

To consider this specific topic, Johnson (1980) focused on the use and development of parent-infant interactions during the first year of an infant's life, a time in which infant behavior is ordinarily thought to be interactive but symbol free. The focus of the study was one infant, Dot, who was normally hearing and the second child of parents who were profoundly hearing impaired and who preferred to communicate using American Sign Language. Dot's mother was capable of speaking, but her primary means of communication was American Sign Language. This situation, though not uncommon in American society, poses an interesting problem. Published interactional studies of early infancy have focused on dyads in which the adult spoke. In Johnson's situation, the primary medium for communication exchange was visual and when a linguistic system was employed, it was a language distinctly different syntactically, semantically, and conversationally from English (Wilbur, 1979). Are interactions formed when the medium of communication is visual, not auditory/oral, similar to those observed in parent-infant interactions where both participants can hear and at least one can speak normally?

Johnson videotaped Dot and her parents, primarily her mother, interacting in their home. Taping was accomplished every 2 weeks for about one hour over a 16 month period. Taping was initiated when Dot was 3 months of age and concluded when she was 18 months old. Only results from the first 24 tapes, those collected from 3 to 14 months of age, were reported in the 1980 study.

Using an ethnographic approach (Boese, 1968; Erickson & Schultz, 1977), definite patterns of socialization were identified in Dot which appeared to be related in part to changes in the mother's perception of Dot's emerging capabilities for interaction and for communication. Table 8.1 summarizes a pattern of socialization that occurred between Dot and her mother along one dimension of behavior. As we can see, the period between 3 months and 6½ months was characterized by a lack of visual synchronization, that is, a lack of establishment of mutual gaze (m/g) or eye-to-eye contact. During this period of establishing mutual gazing, the mother began to introduce sound effects such as *boom, boom, boom* as she engaged in activities with her daughter. The child's response to these efforts was to produce gross body movements which were interpreted by the examiner as the child's being aware of her mother's verbal attempts at attention-getting.

At approximately 6 months of age, topical gaze, that is, mutual attention to external objects, occurred for both subjects. There continued to be a lack of visual syncronization even topically, however, until approximately 7 months of age. At that time, both the mother and Dot engaged in either meaningful mutual gaze or topical gaze patterns, but never both in the same session. Concomitant to the establishment of consistent visual syncronization patterns was the introduction by the mother of consistent vocalizations in addition to sign language. The mother began to communicate verbally with Dot. Most of these productions tended to be directives. Dot's response initially was to vocalize and reach as a way of responding to her mother's directives. By 8 months of age, Dot's vocalizations actually seemed to trigger her mother's vocalizations, or to occur simultaneously with her mother's vocal efforts.

By 10 months, Dot and her mother engaged in equal use of mutual and topical gaze patterns, and by 12 months, Dot was vocalizing without her mother's vocalizations, during reaching, pointing, or gesturing behaviors. By 1 year of age, Dot's mother shifted from using directives to the use of question-forms in interactions.

Table 8.1

Summary of Interactional Strategy Change Points

Infant's Age	Session	Gaze Behavior	Vocalization Behavior	
			Mother's	Infant's
3 months	1	m/g fluctuating visual synchronization		
4 months	2		non-linguistic (sound affect) before & after infant's vocal.	during m/g during gross body movement 0.0 to 1.0 sec. following mother's vocal.
	3			
	4			
5 months	5			
6 months	6			
	7			
	8	introduction of t/g		

(Continued)

Table 8.1 (Continued)
Summary of Interactional Strategy Change Points

| Infant's Age | Session | Gaze Behavior | Vocalization Behavior | |
			Mother's	Infant's
7 months	9			
	10	stabilization of visual synchronization	70 vocal.	15 vocal. during reaching behavior
8 months	11		linguistic (directive) before infant's vocal. with a m.c.	before and during mother's vocal.
	12			
9 months	13			
	14			
10 months	15	equal use of m/g and t/g		during t/g
	16			

11 months	17		
	18	31 vocal.	11 vocal.
	19	linguistic (questions) too few to compare	during both m/g and t/g without mother's vocal. during reaching, pointing, & gesturing
	20		
12 months	21		
	22		
13 months	23		
	24	8 vocal.	33 vocal.
14 months			

CODE: m/g = *mutual gaze;* t/g = *topical gaze;* m.c. = manual component; vocal. = vocalization

Taken from: Johnson, H., 1980. A longitudinal constitutive ethnographic investigation of the development of interactional strategies by a hearing infant of deaf parents. Unpublished Doctoral Dissertation, University of Cincinnati.

Johnson's data were seen to indicate that Dot developed an appreciation of her mother's interactional strategies and learned to incorporate her mother's behaviors into her own approaches to interaction. Changes in the mother's patterns of interaction were understood to reflect her perception of Dot's increasing interactional competence. That is, the mother's behavior was considered to indicate that she viewed Dot as changing from a nonlinguistic, inconsistently communicative partner, to an interactionally competent individual who was capable of understanding the various language/communication systems of the home and who actively engaged the mother in interactions over a variety of topics.

Such sensitive perception on the part of the mother and the child indicates that socialization can occur when mutual respect and sensitivity are present between partners regardless of the communication system. Ability to judge communication competence and to revise that judgment as needed was observed in Dot's mother, even though she was unable to hear Dot's vocalization and thus did not respond to them in the standard way.

Next we consider investigations of play and early utterances produced by children with hearing impairment as we have already with language delayed children.

Gorrell (1971) studied the social interactions that occurred between triads of hearing impaired preschool children and triads of closely matched normally hearing preschool children. Each triad was placed in a television studio constructed to resemble a nursery school setting. All the children were told to play together until the examiner returned. Interactions were videotaped for a period of 30 minutes.

Using a rating scale that emphasized identification of the contact and non-contact times that occurred between the subjects, it was found that hearing impaired children attempted fewer direct contacts with each other and more importantly responded less favorably when direct contacts were attempted by other members of their triad. Self-directed or self-stimulatory behaviors were observed exclusively within the hearing impaired triads. Deaf children in that situation acted differently than their normally hearing counterparts by approaching each other less, responding less to each other's social overtures, and paying more attention to themselves as opposed to others or to the environment.

In Gorrell's study, all of the subjects in all the triads were strangers to each other which may have had an inhibiting effect, especially for the hearing impaired subjects. However, Higginbotham and Baker (1981) investigating the free play behavior of hearing impaired children enrolled in a preschool program, found the instances of cooperative play to be low when compared to normally hearing children of comparable age.

It would appear then that some hearing impaired children lack the socialization skills and probably the communicative ability to establish social contacts with others, even when they are familiar with others in the environment. Even if hearing impaired children possess esoteric or home manufactured gesture systems, this does not appear to be sufficient to allow them to interact meaningfully with others, even other hearing impaired children. Clearly it is a question of the less you have the less you get from an interactive standpoint.

In a second investigation, using the nursery school setting previously described, Kretschmer (1972) studied the initiation of play in preschool children left unattended with a variety of toys. Sixty-three hearing impaired and 63 closely matched normally hearing children were videotaped individually in a nursery school setting and encouraged to play until the investigator and parent returned. Each child's behavior was videotaped for 15 mintutes. Hearing impaired children primarily engaged in visual and tactual scanning of the environment which, at best, suggested minimal symbolic activity. Most normally hearing children began to relate with materials on a symbolic play level before the first 5 minutes had passed. The hearing impaired subjects apparently had difficulty structuring themselves or had a need to verify the security of the situation since they spent their time in environmental exploration rather than play of any type. A longer sample of behavior may have shown the hearing impaired subjects beginning to play. However, Higginbotham and Baker (1981) reported similar reduced levels of symbolic play in observations they made of hearing impaired children over a 6-week period.

These results point to disturbances in symbolic behavior in hearing impaired children; the obvious disruption of language/communication and the less frequently considered disturbance in another form of symbolic expression, play.

In general, hearing impaired children can be said to show the effects of disturbed communication development not only in a variety of cognitive/symbolic processes, but in development of socialization as well. Their socialization problems do not appear to be a consequence of deafness per se, since the appearance of synchronized behavior between deaf parent and normal hearing infant can be demonstrated (Johnson, 1980). The socialization disturbances considered in this chapter are a clear consequence of communication disorder. By the age of three or four, many deaf children already show some effects of atypical communication development through their restricted social and symbolic behavior. The need to establish, or re-establish social interaction with parents and others through early identification of the handicap and energetic parent/child management programs seems obvious.

In summary, we have reviewed the ways in which understanding of the development of communication in normal children has been and will continue to be of help in understanding the communication and the social development of handicapped children. Indeed, therapeutic and/or educational programs for handicapped children, especially those who are language delayed and/or hearing impaired, can be reasonably based on data drawn from the study of normal children. Any such efforts, of course, should be undertaken with the understanding that linguistic, cognitive, and social experiences are all critical to the establishment of functional communication. Regardless of the ways in which society changes, the ability to communicate with others continues to be fundamental to each child's social maturation in that society.

REFERENCES

Alpern, G., & Boll, T., 1972. *Developmental profile*. Indianapolis: Psychological Developmental Publications.

Bard, P., & Sachs, J., 1977. *Language acquisition patterns in two normal children of deaf parents*. Paper presented at the Second Annual Boston University Conference on Language Development.

Bates, E., 1979. *The emergence of symbols: Cognition and communication in Infancy*. New York: Academic Press.

Bloom, L., 1970. *One word at a time*. The Hague: Mouton.

Bloom, L., & Lahey, M., 1978. *Language development and language disorders*. New York: Wiley.

Boese, R., 1968. *Towards an ethnography of the deaf*. Unpublished Master Thesis, University of California at Santa Barbara.

Bondurant, J., 1977. *An analysis of mothers' speech provided to children with normal language as compared to mothers' speech provided to children with delayed language*. Unpublished Doctoral Dissertation, University of Cincinnati.

Bowerman, M., 1973. *Early syntactic development: A cross-linguistic study with special reference to finnish*. Cambridge: Cambridge University Press.

Brown, R., 1973. *A first language: The early stages*. Cambridge: Harvard University Press.

Buium, N., Rynders, J., & Turnure, J., 1974. Early maternal linguistic environment of normal and Down's syndrome language learning children. *American Journal of Mental Deficiency, 79,* 52-58.

Cicourel, A., & Boese, R., 1972. The acquisition of manual sign language and generative semantics. *Semiotica, 7,* 225-256.

Corrigan, R., 1978. Language development as related to stage 6 object permanence development. *Journal of Child Language, 5,* 173-190.

Corson, H., 1973. *Comparing deaf children of oral deaf parents and deaf parents using manual communication with deaf children of hearing parents on academic, social, and communication functioning*. Unpublished Doctoral Dissertation, University of Cincinnati.

Cross, T., 1978. Mothers' speech and its association with rate of linguistic development in young children. In N. Waterson & C. Snow (Eds.), *The Development of Communication*. New York: Wiley.

Cross, T., & Morris, J., 1980. Linguistic feedback and maternal speech. *First Language 1,* 98-121.

Doll, E., 1966. *Preschool attainment record*. Circle Pines, MI: American Guidance Service.

Duchan, J., & Erickson, J., 1975. Normal and retarded children's understanding of semantic relations in different verbal contexts. *Journal of Speech and Hearing Research, 19,* 707-716.

Edwards, D., 1973. Sensory-motor intelligence and semantic relations in early child grammar. *Cognition, 2,* 395-434.

Erickson, R., & Schultz, J., 1977. *When is a context? Some issues and methods in the analysis of social competence*. Unpublished Manuscript, Harvard University and University of Cincinnati.

Field, T., & Pawlby, S., 1980. Early face-to-face interactions of British and American working- and middle-class mother-infant dyads. *Child Development,* 51, 250-253.

Freedman, P., & Carpenter, R., 1976. Semantic relations used by normal and language-impaired children at Stage I. *Journal of Speech and Hearing Research, 19,* 784-795.

Gorrell, S., 1971. *An investigation of the social interactions occuring among comparable groups of normal hearing and hearing impaired children, using an interactional scale*. Unpublished Master Thesis, University of Cincinnati.

Greenfield, P., & Smith, J., 1976. *The structure of communication in early language development*. New York: Academic Press.

Greenstein, J., Greenstein, K., McConville, K., & Stellini, L., 1975. *Mother-infant communication and language acquisition in deaf infants*. New York: Lexington School for the Deaf.

Higginbotham, D., & Baker, B., 1981. Social participation and cognitive play differences in hearing-impaired and normal hearing preschoolers. *Volta Review, 82,* 135–149.

Howe, C., 1980. Learning language from mothers' replies. *First Language, 1,* 83–97.

Johnson, H., 1980. *A longitudinal constitutive ethnographic investigation of the development of interactional strategies by a hearing infant of deaf parents.* Unpublished Doctoral Dissertation, University of Cincinnati.

Jones, M., 1976. *A longitudinal investigation of question formation in English and American Sign Language.* Unpublished Doctoral Dissertation, University of Illinois at Champaign.

Kretschmer, R., 1972. *A study to assess the play activities and gesture output of hearing handicapped preschool children.* Final Report, Project No. 95-2109, Office of Education, Bureau of Education for the Handicapped.

Leonard, L., 1976. *Meaning in child language.* New York: Grune and Stratton.

Leonard, L., Bolders, J., & Miller, J., 1976. An examination of the semantic relations reflected in the language usage of normal and language disordered children. *Journal of Speech and Hearing Research, 19,* 371–392.

Miller, J., Chapman, R., Branston, M., & Reichle, J., 1980. Language comprehension in sensorimotor stages V and VI. *Journal of Speech and Hearing Research, 23,* 284–311.

Person, C., 1978. *The semantic cases and relations reflected in the two-word utterances of normal and trainable mentally retarded children.* Unpublished Master Thesis, University of Cincinnati.

Prendeville, J., 1978. *The semantic cases and relations reflected in the two-word utterances of normal and language-delayed children.* Unpublished Master Thesis, University of Cincinnati.

Prinz, P., & Prinz, E., 1979. *Acquisition of ASL and spoken English in a hearing child of a deaf mother and hearing father.* Papers and Reports on Child Language Development 17:139–146.

Sachs, J., & Johnson, M. 1976. Language development in a hearing child of deaf parents. In W. von Raffler-Engel & Y. Lebrum (Eds.), *Baby Talk and Infant Speech.* Amsterdam: Swets and Zeitlenger.

Snow, C., & Ferguson, C. (Eds.), 1977. *Talking to children.* Cambridge: Cambridge University Press.

Todd, P., & Aitchison, J., 1980. Learning language the hard way. *First Language, 1,* 122–140.

Waterson, N., & Snow, C. (Eds.), 1978. *The development of communication.* New York: Wiley.

Wedell-Monnig, J., & Lumley, J., 1980. Child deafness and mother-child interaction. *Child Development, 51,* 766–774.

Wilbur, R., 1979. *American sign language and sign systems: Research and Applications.* Baltimore: University Park Press.

Williams, R., 1977. *Play behavior of language handicapped and normal speaking preschool children.* Unpublished Doctoral Dissertation, University of Cincinnati.

Wulbert, M., Inglis, S., Kriegsmann, E., & Mills, B., 1975. Language delay and associated mother-child interactions. *Developmental Psychology, 11,* 61–70.

9 Fostering Peer Relations in Young Normal and Handicapped Children

Edward Mueller
Boston University

Joan Bergstrom
Wheelock College

The first goal of this chapter is to outline the important roles of peer relations in child development. The second goal is to outline how adults can aid in the early development of play relationships between children. We will stress the structuring of the physical environment and the important role of the caregiver. Most of the ideas presented here derive from the recent explosion of research on the growth of early peer relations. A third goal of the chapter is to consider the relevance of this work for children with special needs. Research on the peer relations of normal children and those with special needs will be discussed.

WHY ARE PEER RELATIONS IMPORTANT?

Early peer relations enrich the experience of young children; they aid in the development of social intelligence, that is, those skills which allow children to predict and control the behavior of other people (Mueller & Brenner, 1977); they foster higher levels of toy play (Rubenstein & Howes, 1976); they differ from parent-child relationships in fundamental ways (Mueller, 1979). In these ways, early peer relations are "enriching." This term is intended to contrast with the term *necessary*. There is no evidence that early peer relations, those in the period before entry into school, are *necessary* for normal social development. It may be of critical importance to be able to form friendships by the age of 12 or 14 (Sundby & Kreyberg, 1968), but not by age five. Therefore, in discussing the importance of peer relations, it would be a mistake to limit our discussions only to the first few years after birth. The early years simply have the potential for beginning socioemotional relations with peers; this type of relation, in turn, we shall try to show, will be of lifelong importance.

Three basic positive aspects of personality have been linked to peer relations. They are cooperativeness, playfulness, and friendliness. Taken together they constitute such important personal characteristics that they would justify the fostering of peer relations throughout the lifespan. Because they are so important, we briefly outline how each one has been linked to peer relations. Before saying how to foster early peer relations, we seek to show why they are worth fostering.

The idea that peer relations are the fundamental source of a child's *cooperativeness* and sense of justice stemmed from Piaget's (1965) famous study of moral judgement. All moral acts, he suggested, stem either from feelings of duty or cooperation. Just as parent-child relations yield the morality of duty, so peer relations are responsible for the morality of cooperation:

> . . . the rule of justice is a sort of imminent condition of social relationships. . . And as the solidarity between children grows we shall find this notion of justice gradually emerging in almost complete autonomy.
> . . . [this] sense of justice . . . is largely independent of these [adult] influences, and requires nothing more for its development than the mutual respect and solidarity which holds among children themselves. (p. 198)

It follows from Piaget's theory that school age children need not be taught to be cooperative by their parents. Indeed it is far more instructive that they experience the sense of equality of control of interaction that is fully possible only in relations with a true equal, a peer. It is regrettable that during the period of his life when Piaget was studying communication and cooperation for preschool children, he was convinced of the validity of the rather encompassing cognitive construct called "egocentricism." It led him to believe that no real cooperation, empathy, or true friendship was possible between young children because each required a sociocentric rather than egocentric child. During the last decade, several psychologists (e.g., Borke, 1971; Mueller, 1972) have challenged the relevance of egocentricism in developing an adequate theory of the origins of children's cooperation and friendship. Many now believe that egocentricism has proved to be too global a concept which has inhibited efforts to reveal the extent of cooperation and friendship even between 1-year-olds (Mueller & Lucas, 1975).

Even at these early stages it is being discovered that peer relations may be providing for the child a sense of equal participation in a relationship which in turn affects the initially unequal parent-child relationship. Evidence in this regard has recently been provided in a series of studies by Vandell and her colleagues (Vandell, 1977; 1979). Studying mother-toddler play in a university play room, Vandell found that mothers initiated much more social interaction than did their offspring. Some of these toddlers, however, also participated in daily playgroup with their peers while others received no peer experience (controls). Later in the year, it was found that the playgroup children, but not the controls, had significantly increased their role in initiating interactions with their parents. In other words, peer experience was facilitating the beginnings of "equality of participation" in parent-child relations. Of course this is an equality on the level of action rather than of representation. It will be some time before the child can "understand" (at the level of reflection) just which of his/her relations are truly equal.

In summary, the main point is that even in the toddler period, peer experience fosters equality of participation in social communication. This equality appears to be an essential step in any theory of the development of cooperativeness.

Alongside cooperativeness, *playfulness* is a second highly valued developmental outcome in our culture. Psychological research has linked playfulness to problem solving ability (Sylva, Bruner, & Genova, 1976), knowledge acquisition processes (Baldwin, 1911), creativity (Singer, 1973) and both to the proper methods and aims of psychotherapy (Anthony, 1968; Winnecott, 1971). By playfulness we mean what Anthony means:

> . . . I tend to view the world and its events in the framework of play; and by this, I do not mean recreation, repetition, compulsion, rehearsal for life, surplus energy, or football and baseball; I mean an element in the organism that tends to express itself joyously and spontaneously. Nietzche has reminded us that, "As soon as a man can apprehend himself as free and able to use his freedom, then his activity, whatever it is, is play [p. 299]."

The initial development of playfulness occurs long before a baby can understand his/her first peer; it originates in a healthy, joyful parent-child relationship (Brazelton, Koslowski, & Main, 1974). Yet as the child grows and the mother's focus is more on socializing and teaching her child, the maintenance of play falls increasingly on other relationships. The father may take an increasing role in play; in an informal survey, a group of college students rated their fathers as more playful than their mothers. But dad may not be around very much, and as children grow, they come to rely more and more on their peers for maintaining their sense of joy and spontaneous expression. Roberts and Baird (1971) reported that 6-11-year-old American children spent more time outside school playing with their friends than in any other activity, including television. Bronfenbrenner (1967) showed that this is a culturally variable pattern. In Germany, for example, the family appears to remain at the heart of socialization influence through these years; and in the U.S.S.R., the peer group is explicitly utilized in socializing adult approved values. Bronfenbrenner's studies focus on values such as honesty, loyalty, and hard work rather than on values like democracy and autonomy where peer relations may have their important impact. Tizard (1977) for example, has suggested that such values are a product of the play culture of childhood:

If we think it is important that children should be happy (and this is very much a contemporary belief: in former times it was thought more important that they should be good, or useful) then play is clearly preferable to rote drill as an educational method . . .

Free play is also likely to appeal to people who may not have any knowledge of psychological theories but who have a strong belief in the importance of individuality, autonomy, creativity, and intrinsic motivation . . .

. . . What we are saying implicitly . . . is that it is more important for the child to act as an individual . . . than that he learn new skills, learn to cooperate with other children, or learn to do or make things because they are needed by somebody else. (p. 203)

Unlike Tizard, we believe that playfulness will be found to be of central importance in learning new skills and learning to cooperate; nevertheless we agree that play is a cultural technique for producing people who are democratic, autonomous, and individualistic. Too often in America, we stress only the negative aspects of peer relations forgetting their central role in socializing treasured national values.

The relationship between peer relations and play is mediated by *friendship*. It is friends, not merely "any old peer," that are important in both play and mental health. The most compelling support for these assertions is Sundby and Kreyberg's (1968) longitudinal study of mental health in Norway. Between 1950–1954, 124 neurotic children were examined in a psychiatric hospital. Over two-thirds were 7–14-years-old; the remainder were 3–6. Although they were labeled as "neurotic" one might also simply view them as having serious problems. For example, one 12-year-old girl had refused to go to school for 4 months and did not dare let her mother out of sight. A boy, also 12, was admitted for repeated stealing and truancy. Based on EEG and clinical tests, a small proportion of these children were also diagnosed as suffering from "organic brain damage." During their stay in the hospital, only a few of these children received any treatment; most were there only for "observation and assessment." These were extensive and became the basis for a set of "prognostic factors" for predicting adult mental health. A few examples of the many factors assessed included social class, family integrity, duration of the "neurosis" in childhood, and tested IQ.

In 1965, some 11 to 15 years after the initial assessment, these same people, now mostly young adults, were re-evaluated in terms of present mental health and grouped as showing good, fair, or poor health outcome. Of all the child prognostic factors studied, child friendliness was among the most important in predicting adult adjustment. A child was considered as showing good friendship capacity if either: (1) the psychiatrist could establish a "true and durable contact (p. 84)" or (2) the child was found to have a "best friend" among his peers.

In summary, this study suggests that friendliness is a personal characteristic developed during the childhood period. When it is well established, even children with problems serious enough to require psychiatric attention stand an excellent chance of becoming healthy, emotionally stable adults.

In this section we have stressed the positive or "prosocial" importance of peer relations. Obviously peers are also important in the development of aggression, competitiveness, and leadership (Blitsen, 1971; Hartup, 1970). Each of these relationships, however, is inevitably unequal. In aggression and competition there must be losers. For leadership, there must be followers. Such unequal relationships are common throughout our lives: with parents, teachers, employers, etc. All these relationships, separate from peer relations, play central roles in developing these personal features. We have focused on the *special* contributions which stem from the inherently equal nature of friendship and peer relations.

Extending Peer Relations to Children with Special Needs

Current research findings regarding the topic of early peer relations, also supported by observational reports and anecdotal data from infant–toddler specialists, early childhood educators, psychologists and others, have specific implications for the practitioner working with young children, both normal and those with special needs. Furthermore, these research findings, observational reports and anecdotal data, provide insights as to the role of parents, educators and other adults in planning a setting which encourages early peer relationships. Each will be discussed in this chapter. In addition, a philosophical orientation for planning group experiences and peer play for young children will be explored.

For very young children early peer relations cannot be taught by primarily using words because some children understand peer relations before they understand words. Before 18 months, toddlers given the proper opportunity, can form specific friendships with one another. Such friendships are marked by two children reciprocally seeking each other out in a larger group and engaging in more frequent positive interactions than other children (Vandell & Mueller, 1980). Furthermore, it has been learned that the messages in toddlers' social interactions occur at the remarkable rate of one message every 2 seconds and each message is composed of up to five or six coordinated behaviors. After one appreciates the complex social skills and competence of young children, we find it difficult to understand why the child psychology literature is so dominated by concepts such as "dependency" and "egocentricity." The literature also creates a sense of confusion for the practitioner who observes young children engaging in early peer interaction and can find few research studies to assist him/her to understand these interactions.

Programs for young children with special needs have focused primarily on the parent-child relationships and the planning of specific activities to assist the child to develop specific motor skills and competencies. Often, the overall objectives of many intervention programs and play groups for children with special needs do not encourage opportunities for the children to play and interact with one another for extended periods of time. When young children with special needs are in a program, the children receive a number of specialized services from the educator, physical therapist, speech and language therapist, occupational therapist, and other such specialists. The activities planned by the specialist are conducted outside of the group setting and involve the young child and specialist interacting together around a specific skill or task. Such settings allow for minimum opportunities for peer-peer interaction among the children. It seems probable that if children with special needs have contact with normal young children before the age of three, such experiences could lead to greater group acceptance for these children as preschoolers. In Sweden, for example, every effort is made to integrate young children (infants and toddlers) with special needs into the day nurseries with children who are developing normally. It has been reported by educators, child nurses, psychologists and physicians that when young children with special needs are integrated at a young age into a group setting with normal children they are more likely to develop to their potential (Bergstrom & Gold, 1974). It was also observed that the children are more likely to be accepted, appreciated, and understood by their peers. In Sweden, the parents and professionals stressed the fact that this process did not happen easily and it required the continuous involvement of additional support staff in the day nurseries to insure that the children with special needs functioned to their capacity and interacted with the other young children whenever possible.

On the other hand early peer relations and friendships cannot develop if the children's time together is needlessly disrupted by parents, educators and/or teacher interventions. Adult-child relations inevitably develop earlier than peer relations (Mueller & Vandell, 1979) and often peer and adult relations compete for attention. When this is the situation, the young child is likely to abandon the poorly understood, and in this sense difficult, peer interaction for the better understood, and hence simpler, relationship with adults.

Therefore, the curriculum for fostering peer social interactions and skills has at its core, periods of adult silence and observation mixed with needed guidance. Adults learn from observing the children at play, and in order for this philosophical orientation to be a reality, the play setting must be equipped with specific materials and equipment that allow the children to interact more easily with one another. Observation clearly reveals that adult relationships are different from peer relationships. Research comparing the two (Mueller, 1979; Vandell, 1979) shows that early peer relations do not develop simply as a generalization from parent-child relations. Instead, parent-toddler relations and peer relations utilize different communication modes—language for the parent and direct action for the child. They focus on different content—shared object reference for the parent and run-chase for the child. They also involve different patterns of dominance or control. Generally, the world of early peer relations has no or few words as we know them.

The issue of when to intervene in early peer aggression warrants further investigation. In playgroup, our teacher-observer decided to sit and watch the interaction which took place as one child hit another over the head with an eraser. It can be clearly seen on video tape that instead of crying or hitting back, the 23-month-old child responded verbally, "Hit—Hit—Hunch—No!" As he was saying this, he was shaking his head "no" and the message he was conveying was "Don't hit." Indeed, he was not hit again and even succeeded in getting the eraser away from the other child. Thus, the child had to try several times before verbalizing the negative aspect of the message. If the adult had intervened, the child could not have practiced the proper wording for such an occasion! Both children would not have realized the conflicts were resolvable without adult involvement.

On the other hand, sometimes adult involvement is necessary. A philosophical orientation which values silence and observation is not a hands-off attitude. Adults are involved in guiding the children. One toddler with three older siblings often sought to physically intimidate other playgroup children. Even when he sought to initiate prosocial exchanges such as run-chase, the child approached was apt to misconstrue his intent and run away rather than play with him. In this situation, the teachers intervened with statements like "Don't hit," "Be gentle" and (to the recipient) "Chuckie just wants to play." An observational attitude assists adults in developing awareness of each child's particular needs for intervention and assistance.

Much of the research cited regarding early peer relations was derived from Playgroup Project, a 3-year study at Boston University of toddler peer relations. The children were studied in a group care setting. During each year there was a playgroup composed of six children who were together every week-day morning across the entire academic year (Sept.–May). There were two teachers with the children; no other adults were permitted in the playroom. Of course, parents were involved as they dropped off and picked up their children. The playgroup teachers followed the philosophical orientation as previously outlined. For a major portion of the 4 hours, the children engaged in free play. Everyday the children's peer play was recorded on video tape using two cameras and split-screen video system.

EARLY PEER RELATIONS AS A SOURCE OF COMPETENCE

We know that during the early years formal tests of intelligence have low predictive validity. (McCall, 1977). Intelligence may be too broad or global a term for appreciating how children differ from each other across the various domains of cognitive functioning (Ginsburg & Opper, 1979). We do better, it seems, to ask and assess the extent to which a child's skills are relevant to particular objects or situations. Clearly, peers present the young child with one kind of "social object" requiring mastery and we can ask how skillful any given toddler is in interacting with agemates.

Suppose you have a child in a toddler playgroup and you would like our estimate of his/her "peer skill quotient." We would videotape your child in peer play with familiar playmates across several days. We would discard the tapes from any day when we had reason to think your child was tired, ill, or hungry. Young children vary immensely from one day to the next. From the remaining tapes we would analyze each message that your child delivered to other children, deriving three major summary measures:[1]

Measure 1: -How often does the child coordinate his/her social messages into complex units? For example, a child who is able to call to another child while banging a stick on the table will score higher than a child who merely watches his agemate and bangs on the table imitatively. This stress on the coordination of actions derives from Piaget's theory of early intellectual development; its application to early peer skill is discussed in more detail by Mueller (1979).

Measure 2: -What is the average length of interaction in which the child participates? A skilled child will sustain longer interactions with most of the available toddler partners.

Measure 3: -What is the diversity of content or "meaning" that the child seeks to communicate? For example, in playgroup some children understood the meaning of peek-a-boo, rough and tumble, and naming things while most did not.

Your child's peer social skill would be a composite of these three measures. Such a measure of skill clearly meets the criterion of ecological relevance because it is gathered from samples of his/her natural play. Data concerning the construct validity of its component parts appear in Mueller (1979). By 16 months there are wide situationally stable differences among normal toddlers in peer skills. These differences also maintained individual rank stability across time.

The IQ testing movement and Piaget's interest in play with physical objects has come to dominate our views of intelligence. Given recent progress in conceptualizing early communication skills, the formulation of predictively useful tests for social skills prior to language should be just around the corner. However, teachers and parents can begin to observe that children's social acts are just as reflective of achieved skill as is their object play.

---

[1]No such formal test actually exists. The measures chosen here are exemplary of ones whose importance is supported in several studies. Another candidate for inclusion in this list would be number of successful interaction initiations.

Applications to Children with Special Needs

One special needs group where this approach to social intelligence is being tested is childhood autism. One can ask whether 3- 12-year old autistic children resemble much younger normal children in their social skill processes. Perhaps it is possible to identify where individual autistic children stand in the normal sequence of early social skill development (Mueller & Lucas, 1975). Frank Curcio, at Boston University, is carrying out such studies with children enrolled in a school for the autistic. Using a series of original teacher-administered communication probes, Curcio found that autistic children perform at one of three levels; the levels are only partly related to chronological age. The lowest group coordinates only 13% of its social messages into complex units and using Measure 3 (above) almost all these acts are of a single content (the sign for "eat"). The highest group coordinates 71% of their messages and uses varied message content.

The identification of such groups suggest that a normal developmental model may be useful in understanding communication skill development in autistic children. It also points toward concrete goals for communication training for children functioning at each level. For example, Curcio observed that level three children are quite good at requesting things but showed little ability to point or otherwise "reference" objects of interest. Thus, the training goal for level three children is teaching pointing and reference skills.

Efficacy and Early Peer Relations

How do young children acquire the social skills described in the previous section? Mueller's research on normal children suggests that children learn peer skills because they venture forth and are willing to *participate* with strange peers before they understand them (Mueller & Brenner, 1977). One child, for example, offered another a toy truck with no intention of letting go when the agemate tried to take it. Initially children appear to be experimenting with one another! Rather than understanding that they can "share" social events like "object exchange" or "peek-a-boo," they seem to be asking: "What can I make this 'thing' do?" From many such bold little experiments, young children develop a reciprocal sense of what works (Mueller & Lucas, 1975); they come to understand what kinds of meaning can be sustained among them (Brenner & Mueller, 1979). Motor copy or imitation play, for example, was among the most successful type of social play developed between the playgroup toddlers.

In this section, we wish to focus the discussion on a development of a definition for the term "sense of efficacy." Yarrow (1979) has described a similar phenomenon which he refers to as "motivation for mastery." He has stated that "motivation for mastery" is central for the future development of theory and development of intervention programs. He cites the need for the development of sensitive and valid measures in this area. Adopting Rotter's term, we will label as "sense of efficacy" a child's curiosity or willingness to engage with novel objects. An efficacious person, says the dictionary, is one having the power to produce a desired effect. Yet such a definition seems more reflective of skill, the endpoint of the mastery process, than of curiosity. A skilled child, for example, has already learned that the trapeze affords swinging up-side-down by the knees while the playground swing affords swinging right-side-up by the seat of the pants. Some time earlier in life, the same child had to learn these properties of the different kinds of swings. The general idea of how to approach the two kinds of swings could be learned by watching older children. But the actual skill of swinging required active and daring participation with an initially difficult and partially uncontrolled object that swings through the air. This daring participation with new objects is what we mean by efficacy.

Lewis (in press) has played a central role in introducing the concept of efficacy into the study of children's early social development. He suggested that infants derive a generalized sense of efficacy chiefly from early participation in interaction with caregivers. Institutionalized children are distinguishable from normal children not so much on the basis of skill as on the basis of passivity and unwillingness to practice skills and thus learn new ones. Learning theorists, after Seligman, employ the term "learned helplessness" to describe the behavior of rats in situations where nothing they do can effect the series of reinforcements they will receive. This term seems like a useful antonym and we will use it in discussing the growth of both normal and handicapped children. Its use, however, does not imply that the acquisition of skill through participation in interaction is reducible to any simple theory of reinforcement.

Before turning to application, a further qualification about the concept of efficacy must be added: The study of early social development will not progress by making of efficacy another personal trait akin to egocentricity or attachment. Rather than assigning a child a sweeping "efficacy quotient", we must determine those situations in which a given child is efficacious and those where the same child is relatively helpless. Situations, in turn, should be understood both in terms of the behavioral setting or ecology and in terms of the child's *state*. One preschooler, for example, seemed highly efficacious both in the home and the preschool environment. When she fell down or otherwise lost physical control however, she became helpless and dependent for several minutes in both situations. The role of "situational" control of social development is outlined in Cairns' (1979) useful perspective overview of the social development literature.

Among the 30 normal children studied in Mueller's toddler playgroups he has observed signs of learned helplessness in two or perhaps three children. These children spent considerable time sitting and watching their agemates play. Occasionally, they ventured forth, stimulated by an interaction in progress. Yet they stood at the periphery of play, not seeming adventurous enough to join in. After the interaction ended and the children dispersed, they sometimes went to the toys just used and imitated the play of their just departed peers. So far, our identification of learned helplessness is limited to this informal clinical assessment. It is not based simply on the child who scores the lowest in social participation because in some playgroups no children were identified as low in peer efficacy.

Helplessness could originate in the playgroup context itself, or could stem from earlier developmental factors and thus be present at the very start of playgroup. For one child seen as low in peer efficacy we had numerical data on social participation at the start of playgroup. This child was found to have participated in fewer social interactions from the start. This was true both when he was observed with one other child at a time (dyadic situation) and when observed with the entire playgroup. In the dyadic situation he also produced fewer socially-directed behaviors of any kind (simple, coordinated and unsuccessful initiations) than any other child and ranked at or near the bottom on a variety of measures of social participation. Such results agree with our clinical guess that peer helplessness may reflect developmental events prior to the start of playgroup. In such instances, toddler participation in playgroup should allow truly "early intervention" to adopt the overused phrase. Sometimes the parents are concerned about their own relationship with their child. And then playgroup allows the teachers to offer the parents simple practical suggestions about relating to the toddler. In some instances clinical referrals may be needed, but it is necessary to remember that many clinics do not know what to make of problems involving such young children. We can also try to help the less experienced child understand how to participate more effectively with peers. For example, in research now in progress, adults are teaching young children a set of games which seem particularly effective in fostering peer relations.

Applications to Children with Special Needs

Wedell-Monnig (1977) has shown that deaf children of hearing parents decrease in social efficacy as they approach their second birthday. Over 90% of deaf children, incidently, have hearing parents. The mothers were seen as highly devoted to and involved with their deaf offspring. The mother-child pairs were videotaped in free play interaction in four sessions across a 2 month period. A control group of normally hearing children with their mothers was included for comparison. The video tapes were analyzed for 38 direct measures of mother and child interactive behavior.

This detailed analysis showed that the deaf children were similar to the hearing children *only* in their *responsiveness* to mother initiated interaction. Beyond this finding, deaf children were found to initiate fewer interactions while their mothers seemed forced to dominate the play session by initiating many more social interactions than the mothers of hearing children. By their second birthday, the deaf children looked dependent; they required their mothers to go with them around the playroom or moved away from their mothers only briefly to retrieve a toy which was then used while in close proximity to the mother. They showed a greater tendency to simply sit near their mother doing nothing and waiting for her to lead. Wedell-Monnig's overtime analysis suggested that these tendencies were increasing with age. This work strongly supports the need for the early identification of children's deafness and beginning of communication training programs for the parents of deaf infants and toddlers.

Vandell (1977), from whom Wedell-Monnig derived some of her interactional measures, studied peer communication in hearing, deaf, and mixed pairs of familiar preschool-aged children. Hearing children relied chiefly on simple verbal messages while deaf children combined touching, gesturing and nonlinguistic vocalizations in seeking to interact with peers. When placed together in mixed pairs, these different communication styles resulted in hearing children rejecting deaf children's social initiations an average of 10 times in each 15-minute session. A few hearing children, however, did communicate effectively with their deaf peers; thus, Vandell is trying currently to identify their exceptional competency with the hope of training other hearing preschoolers in these skills. The success of mainstreaming would appear to depend on the development of effective interventions that consider more than the teacher-child relationship.

ALTERING THE ENVIRONMENT FOR EARLY PEER RELATIONS

Without intruding, how can adults provide environments which encourage and enhance the growth of early peer relations? We would like to explore three major areas which we believe warrant the attention of people involved in planning and implementing programs for young children. In this chapter, the three major areas to be investigated are: the role of toys, play equipment and materials; the role of the adults; and the role of space and the size of the group.

Role of Toys, Play Equipment and Materials

Children Developing Normally.   At the simplest level, "novel toys" compete with "novel agemates" for attention. Most children, high in developed efficacy, operate with the following rule: "I will divide my attention among every novel object present, trying to control and understand everything." From this rule it follows that the more novel toys present, the less time available for exploring peers. Experimental evidence supporting such a rule has been obtained both for infants (Vandell, Wilson, & Buchanan, in press) and toddlers (Eckerman, 1979). Thus, it seems wise to reduce the number of competing toys present during periods aimed at fostering social relations. Remember, however, that there is no such thing as an object-free environment (DeStefano, 1976). The research literature consistently shows that even when all toys are removed, children still use objects in their social play. For toddlers, physical objects seem so important that when all objects are removed, they take off their shoes to create toys or imitate each other's stamping on the floor. Also, the more bizarre becomes the setting, as when all objects are removed, the less likely will children feel the safety for exploration engendered by familiarity. Therefore, while the available recent work stresses object presence versus absence, the more profitable question will be how objects influence peer relations.

The work to date suggests a rapidly shifting developmental picture across the first years of life. During infancy, Mueller and Vandell (1979) suggest a growing interest in peers after the onset of sitting and crawling. Vandell et al. (in press) found that most peer interactions from ages 6-12 months consisted of pure smiling and vocalization, activities involving *no* object mediation. During this same period, however, "object-related social acts" were among the few behaviors that grew in frequency. In terms of our previous analysis of children's social skills, infants begin to "coordinate" toys and agemates in complex but unified messages. They look expectantly at a peer while simultaneously banging the radiator grating with a stick. Through this coordination of banging and looking, the act is transformed into a "message." The child seems to ask: "What will you do if I do this?" The agemate teaches him/her that she/he will probably either imitate the act or try to take the stick! The key to developmental progress relates to sufficient active experience with both toys and peers. Explanations in terms of the maturation of attention span seem overly simplistic (for a differing position see Jacobson, 1979) because even among toddlers, understanding or skill is what normally controls attention and not the reverse.

In the United States many babies are isolated from other children until after their first birthday; this is especially true of first born (Lewis, Young, Brooks, & Michalson, 1975). They have had over a year to become familiar with toys, yet know nothing of how to interrelate with peers. In these circumstances, it should surprise no one that toddlers' initial contacts with one another take on an "object-centered" quality (Mueller & Lucas, 1975). Place an attractive new toy in the room, and all the children present in a playgroup will cluster around it, but will not know just how to react to each other's presence (Mueller & Rich, 1976). Among child developmentalists, this object-centered play with the same or similar toys has long been called "parallel play." Its paradoxical quality ranks it among the intriguing phenomena of early childhood: Children come together physically but seemingly do not relate to one another socially. The view of parallel play as an inescapable feature of early peer relations is based on a theory of some universal cognitive problem often labeled "egocentricity." Such a theory is not supported by recent studies showing complex peer relations and even friendship formation during the earliest years of childhood (e.g., Vandell & Mueller, 1980). Alternative explanations of parallel play are therefore needed. Part of the explanation may rest in children's differential experience with toys versus peers just outlined. Yet there is also "para-social" quality to parallel play which suggests that much more is involved. For example, it may be that parallel play represents a primary social contract, often established using visual gaze alone, allowing two children to share a well demarcated "place."

Whatever its ultimate meaning, Mueller and Brenner (1977) supported the claim of the founder of peer research, Charlotte Buhler, that object-centered contacts are the initial basis of sustained social interactions among young children. Because they are brought together physically, children find themselves having to accommodate to one another socially. Jacobson (1979) pinpointed 12 months as a transitional point regarding this critical role of toys in early social development. After this age social interaction frequency among peers continued to develop *only* in an object-centered context. Before this age, the growth of interaction showed no relationship to toy context. This is the first evidence that toy related social play will remain important even among children becoming at least somewhat familiar with one another before their first birthday. No one has yet tested the hypothesis that children who are highly familiar with one another by their first birthday should be able to reduce their object-centered play.

To this point we have treated toys as if they were all alike. We had little choice because the much needed research on the social-facilitory nature of *particular toys* has yet to be conducted. A study by DeStefano (1976), however, suggested major differences between the effects of small "possessible" toys and large non-portable play equipment. Play equipment was shown to foster positive social interactions while small toys fostered object possession struggle. Small toys, like the removal of *all* objects, was shown to maximize physical intrusive play marked by negative emotions like crying or "mad face." Studying the same sample of boy toddler play, Brenner and Mueller (1979) found that object possession struggle and object exchange, both dependent on the presence of small toys, were two of the three most common types of content shared by boy toddlers. (The third was motor copy.) Therefore, removing most small objects from a toddler playgroup should radically shift the composition of possible shared meaning among toddlers. Object possession struggle would be reduced; regrettably motor copy and object exchange could also suffer reduction. Nevertheless, it seems worthwhile trying such a manipulation if one's playgroup seems overly dominated by fighting over toys.

Little is known about how large play equipment supports prosocial interaction. Perhaps slides, tunnels and rocking boats are ideal "spacing" devices. One child goes into the tunnel while the partner climbs on top and peeks in. The children are together socially while maintaining some barrier to direct physical intrusion. Big objects allow easy "escape" around the "other side" when and if needed. All these ideas concerning the role of toys are easily subject to further testing in the home or center. This is a way for parents and educators to stimulate their own curiosity about how the environment they create effects their children's early social development.

Children with Special Needs.   There are a variety of toys, play equipment and materials that provide opportunities for normal young children and children with special needs to socialize and develop early peer relationships. We consider materials and equipment that foster motor development and peer-social development. Other materials are discussed which encourage expressive development and peer-social development. Materials specially related to fostering dramatic play and peer-social development are explored. Finally, small and large group experiences encouraging early peer relations are illustrated.

Most early peer relations between young children focus on fine and gross muscle activities. For example, the process of pouring is an activity which encourages fine motor development and one observes several children together spilling, pouring, or mixing water or sand. Other examples of activities appropriate for both groups of children are climbing a jungle gym, sliding, crawling through a barrel and painting with water. Equipment fostering these activities include slides—double or triple width, ladders designed for two children to climb simultaneously, ramps, mats, rocking boats, balls, wagons and other small push carts, and blocks designed specially for young children. Some of these materials have to be adapted and still others have to be provided to accommodate young children with special needs. A list of some equipment that can be used to foster peer-peer interaction and include children with special needs is provided in Table 9.1.

Toddlers with special needs can play together on the jungle gym when ramps are built along two of its sides. The ramps enable the child with physical handicaps to pull up or crawl up to the top of the jungle gym. If the ramps are two levels high and there is a flat level in between, both normal toddlers and those with physical handicaps can play together on the jungle gym. Ramps with holes some 6 inches apart, allow for children to crawl along them. As children put their fingers into the holes and pull along, they experience a sense of mastery. At times, one child can climb the jungle gym and another can crawl up a ramp, side by side.

The rocking boat is enjoyed by normal young children and those with special needs. The boat encourages children to interact as two children are needed to balance the weight which moves the boat. A low birth weight, small 2-year old child was observed sitting and being rocked in the boat by his friend. Children with prosthetic limbs can usually maneuver themselves to sit in the boat and can then enjoy rocking with another child. Also, a child who was delayed in language was observed singing as she was rocked by other children in the boat.

Blocks which can be designed for all children (hollow, light in weight, bright in color, special sizes and dimensions) can be used in endless numbers of ways. In the process of building and playing with block creations, social interaction takes place. A child with balancing difficulties was encouraged to sit and interacted with the other children who were building with these blocks.

All children enjoy making and using bubbles. Children who have physical handicaps can develop motor skills as they play with their normal peers. The children can blow bubbles which helps control their breath pressure, follow the bubbles with their eyes (visual tracking), pop them (eye-hand coordination), and

Table 9.1
Summary of Equipment for Children with Special Needs Fostering
Peer-Peer Interaction*

Equipment	Description
1. RAMP	This piece of equipment enables the child to move from one level to another. It should be about 1½ - 2 feet wide, with low railings or sides, and hand holes about every 6 inches.
2. CORNER SEAT	This piece of equipment consists of three triangular pieces of wood fitted together to form a corner. It can have a strap that crosses the hips and is used to assist the child in maintaining a sitting balance.
3. STANDING BRACE	This piece of equipment is a brace often prescribed for a child with spina bifida. It consists of a platform with molds for the feet and padded steel supports for the ankles, knees, hips and chest. It holds the child in a standing position and can be bent for sitting on a low stool.
4. STANDING BOARD	This piece of equipment is designed by the physical therapist to support a child with cerebral palsy in an upright position when appropriate. It has straps to support the feet, hips and chest. Wedges can be provided to support the child's legs in a natural position.
5. ADAPTIVE CHAIR	This piece of equipment has a 3 cornered back support for the trunk. Foot supports are provided to maintain the child's legs in a natural position. It may also have a special rounded seat (tube seat) to further assist in positioning the legs.
6. SCOOTER BOARD	This piece of equipment is a rectangular piece of wood, covered with carpeting, with four caster wheels and a belt. The child who is nonambulatory uses it to move around the room independently.
7. PROTECTIVE HELMET	This piece of equipment can either be purchased commercially (hockey helmet) or through an adaptive equipment supplier. The helmet should fit the child properly and protects the child with hydrocephalus or seizure disorder from further head injuries.

*The educator must consult with the appropriate specialist about usage of all of this adaptive equipment.

reach up, down and to the side (range of motion). The children enjoy the bubbles together and obviously are not aware that they are developing skills.

Children can play together at a large activity board which includes a variety of manipulative materials. This board stands about 2½-3 feet high and about 2-3 feet wide. It includes a range of activities such as small doors that are opened by one child to see another child on the other side; cutout holes to drop blocks through with a cup on the back to catch them and cylinders that are socially manipulated from either side of the board. If the board is placed close to the floor, all of the children will be able to reach it, including those on scooter boards.

Expressive experiences and peer-social development are facilitated when young children use materials such as crayons, chalk, markers, collage, paint (to use with brushes as well as fingers), clay, and play dough. Sand or water are among other materials useful for expressive and interactive development. Such experience allows young children to experiment, create and interact as they work together.

When normal children and children with special needs work together at a wall easel, (one allowing several children to stand beside each other) they can paint on either a large piece of paper or on individual sheets. A long wall easel facilitates a shared expressive experience between the children present, normal and handicapped. Finger painting on the table covered totally with paper, allows for all children to create in a peer-social context. This was vividly illustrated when a child who was hydrocephalic was wearing a protective helmet and was observed spending a block of time painting at a table, mixing colors, talking, laughing and enjoying himself. As he was laughing, he painted the nose of a friend sitting beside him; the friend responded by painting his helmet. This was the first time that the child with special needs had painted and it was related to a natural opportunity for him to interact with another child.

The sand table or sand pit is a natural setting for young children to interact with one another, express themselves and develop competencies. A child with a brace could find it especially satisfying to sit inside the sand area or sand pit and experiment with the sand and other props. At times, the adult may decide to allow the child to take off his/her brace and play at the water table where peer-peer interaction is also facilitated.

Again, there are some pieces of equipment that could be especially appropriate for facilitating peer-peer interaction at the sand and water table. For example, the child who has a physical handicap can use pieces of equipment such as a standing brace, a standing board, or an adult size chair with a belt to assist the child to stand or sit at the table and play with the water. Such pieces of equipment could be used to encourage children who have cerebral palsy or spina bifida to engage in sand play at the table with other children. The educator should work closely with the physical and/or occupational therapist to be certain that the equipment is used appropriately.

In addition to motor and expressive experiences, dramatic play also fosters early peer social development. Children need the opportunity to explore roles, in both reality and fantasy, and to interpret the wider social world around them. To encourage this play, there are a variety of props appropriate both for normal and special needs children. Some examples are hats (soft and hard), large beads, telephones, dolls (male and female) and large rectangular mirrors. Such mirrors allow children to stand and view themselves in relation to others. All young children should be encouraged to explore their body movements and facial expressions; this experience allows for the recognition of individual characteristics especially since a child without sensation in his/her legs or arms may not realize that he/she has legs or arms. Such experiences help children to develop a positive self image as well as an awareness of others while interacting. Hats as a prop easily allow young children to initiate dramatic play and to interact with others.

Houses and tents are natural ways to encourage dramatic play among children who are normal and those who have special needs. The tent allows the child room to be alone or with peers and therefore provides children the opportunity to experience privacy as well as socialization. This type of space also has an advantage in that it is usually large enough to naturally accommodate all children despite any handicaps. Children with special needs can come into the dramatic play area using such equipment as a standing brace or a standing board which assist the child with physical handicaps to reach the table, sink, put on hats and engage in dramatization with his/her peers.

A large cardboard storage box is another favorite place for two toddlers to play together. Two toddlers were observed in a game; it involved one child going inside and closing the "door" while the other child waited and listened outside the door. When the child inside would call out, the child outside would open the door and they both giggled. They continued this game and did it six to eight times; it seemed to last for several minutes.

Children who have physical handicaps can use scooter boards to get themselves around the classroom without the help of an adult. (A scooter board is made from a rectangular piece of plywood covered with carpeting; it has four caster wheels and sometimes a belt). Freedom to move from one space to another increases the likelihood that the child with handicaps will interact with his/her peers.

Small and large group experiences such as singing, eating and meeting together and going on short field trips encourage young children to interact and develop peer-peer relations. Such experiences assist children to become more aware of one another, and in some instances they begin to see themselves as part of a larger group. For example, with puppets or singing, adults and children can share their emotions or feelings. While singing the song, *If You're Happy and You Know It...*, a group of young children have the opportunity to express a range of emotions and they are usually able to do so. The song has other possibilities for encouraging interaction of all young children. Songs can be adapted so that the activity being sung about is one where all the children may participate and the special needs of a child can be considered as one suggests a special action song.

The snack time is another example of a social setting for young children. While eating, the names of the foods and the children are two examples of topics likely to be of interest to the group and can initiate responses from individual children.

Role of Adults in Early Peer Relations

Traditionally in attempting to foster peer relations, adults have had desirable and undesirable effects. They provided the security from which children first explored each other, yet they could hardly resist intervening in the fragile peer relation. Sometimes they were so much the focus of child interest and attachment that peer relations became impossible. While not having studied adults' roles systematically, we cannot simply pass over them. These brief observations are merely suggestive of possible adult influences.

When parents rotated the task of leading the playgroup, the child whose parent was in charge was sometimes noted to be more upset than his peers and requested more attention from his parent. In one memorable incident, a mother tried to create a pleasant peer play atmosphere by playing her guitar softly. Yet her musical activity was itself an interesting new event in the room and several toddlers gathered around and even tried reaching up to pluck the guitar strings. Her son, however, was not willing to share his mother and began to push the other children away. They, of course, could not understand this type of treatment by their agemate and eventually the mother found herself intervening on behalf of the other children, which merely added to her son's distress.

A more frequent problem in playgroup was that adults did not realize that a play sequence was beginning between two children and the adults began interacting with the children themselves. When this happened the children were easily distracted from the unfamiliar peer by the better understood adult communication. In the early stages of developing our work on peer relations, we were just as insensitive as anyone. Only when we reviewed our own videotapes did we come to realize that we had interfered with beginnings of interactions. Thus we suggest a curriculum of observation for part of each play session and we believe that the adults must be supported and assisted in learning to observe. During the free play time the children can learn how to relate to each other and the adults can observe how effective the environment is for the children.

In educating infant-toddler specialists at Wheelock College, a specific strategy has been developed to assist specialists to become more sensitive to the peer-peer interactions taking place among young children in group settings. While reading the literature and observing videotapes on the topic of peer-peer interactions, a scheme for observing peer-peer interactions has been developed. Here the students observe the children, 24–36-months-old, in a playgroup setting. The interactions that the children have with one another (peer-peer) are recorded. The materials that facilitated the interactions and the role of the adult at the time of the interaction is also described. Efforts are made to record the approximate length of the interaction and the activities that the children engaged in immediately following the interaction. Following the observation, efforts are made to understand the role of the parent, teacher, and/or educator who was with the group of toddlers and types of educational materials and equipment that enhanced such interactions.

To conclude, adults have it within their power to influence the environment of early peer relations. They determine the setting, its designs, the adult-child ratio, the objects present, and the social atmosphere.

Adults are also playing an important positive role in early peer relations. Midway through a long peer vocal interaction, for example, a toddler looked at the caregiver with a bright happy expression. He seemed to be saying, "See. Aren't I smart! Look what I can do with him!" Of course, there are many interpretations of this behavior. We have seen it so often however, that we suspect that adults play a supportive role as the child explores the strange new peer.

Children in day care seem to realize that teachers are just as able as parents to meet their needs for comfort, food and intervention when events become frightening. Toddlers learn that if a peer gets too aggressive, one can simply run to the teacher. After picking a fight by hitting his agemate with a stick, one toddler ran to the teacher and gave him (it was a man) his "weapon." The teacher had little choice but to intervene when the adversary, now himself armed with a stick, approached. Adults appear to be understood both in terms of their trustworthiness and power and all these features come to play roles in the formation of peer relations.

Children with Special Needs.   Young children with special needs generally receive the services of a therapist or multi-disciplinary team from a local hospital or rehabilitation center. These specialists are usually available to provide consultation with the educator in planning for handicapped children's participation in group activities, and can, in turn, use the information which the educator can provide about the child's interactions with their normal peers. The team of specialists meets at regular intervals with the parents to plan a program for the children. The program establishes goals for the children in the areas of socialization, cognition, language, fine and gross motor and self-help skills. The objective of the plan is to encourage the children's total development focusing on strengths as well as weaknesses.

The educator can have a very important role in this planning since he or she will have the primary responsibility to be certain that the goals of the program are being implemented. Educators will provide two kinds of information for the multidisciplinary team. First, they will listen to the goals of the specialists and identify activities which would encourage development of the skills needed. For example, the occupational therapist identifies that a child who has poor fine motor skills, needs to work on grasping and releasing with fingers. The educator plans some group activities using play dough, silly putty, and throwing foam scraps which all of the children will enjoy together, and which will encourage the child with special needs to open and close his or her fingers. The educator will also identify, for the team, activities in which he or she has observed that the child needs some special support in order to participate with peers. For example, the educator observes that a child who has poor trunk control seems to enjoy playing with a drum with his friend, but needs his hands to balance himself in sitting. The physical therapist may observe the child in the play group setting and recommend that a corner seat be provided or may give the educator a positioning cue which will help improve the child's balance. Then the child is free to enjoy making music with his friends. Planning in this manner provides for the mutual development of peer-peer relations and assists the child to develop motor, cognitive and language skills within the group setting.

As with normal children, the role of the adult is critical in facilitating and providing the setting for early peer relations. Equally important, adults working with the children must understand the needs of all of the children and simultaneously provide the setting for peer-peer interaction to occur among the group. For example, in one instance, a 2-year-old child who, due to a neurological problem at birth, had difficulty walking without support, was frequently given by the other children, a piece of equipment which could most appropriately be described as a small wooden bench with four wheels. When turned over by the other children, the bench would be pushed over and given to the child with special needs. The child would use the bench to support herself as she pushed it and walked from one place to another in the playroom. In conversation with the staff, it was realized that the children had learned from the educator, who had consulted with others such as a physical therapist, to support this child by handing her this particular piece of equipment at certain times. The educator also observed that this piece of equipment encouraged interaction between other children in the day care center. After some investigation and discussion of this matter, a decision was made by the educators and other specialists to obtain other pieces of equipment that could be used in a similar way. Hence, two different carts were selected. One cart, with an L-shaped handle, could be easily pushed around and also supported the handicapped child as she walked around the center. This cart was low and thus allowed the children to get in and out of it easily; the children also pushed one another, a favorite toy or doll in it. The other cart selected was more difficult for some of the children to get into; it was made of heavy plastic and was rectangular in shape. Again, the child with special needs was often helped into the cart and two to three children would push it around.

Another setting in which children who were developing normally and children with special needs were together, was a playgroup where the children met for 5 days a week, 3 hours a day. Triplets, three brothers who were visually impaired at birth, attended this program. They were 3-years-old and often preferred to play with and interact with children younger, 2 years of age. As we observed the group of children over a period of a week, it was evident that one of the triplets was determined to learn how to crawl through a large, barrel-type plastic cylinder. He soon learned to crawl through two and then three of them. The educator who supported the child in this venture observed that the child appeared to especially enjoy crawling through the large barrels when another child was ahead of him, and making some sounds as they crawled along. From observing, one soon realized that the child who was visually impaired, frequently went over to the location where the barrels were placed and waited for his friend. The two children had developed a friendship and the large barrels allowed them to play with one another and to interact with each other. The two children were communicating as they made various noises and crawled through the barrels. In both settings, the role of the adults was critical. The adults were involved in the process of observing and planning and provided the children with special equipment that allowed the children to engage in peer-peer interactions.

The Play Environment and Group Size

Children Developing Normally. The children of Playgroup Project experienced a group care environment. In nearly all their activities, whether free play, snack time, rest time or visits to a local playgroup, they were together. If playgroup experience had an impact on their peer social skills, and we have reason to believe that it did (Mueller & Brenner, 1977) then this was from the group situation. In order to study the children's spontaneous peer interaction in the playroom, we made several 30-minute video tapes of the group play each week. The cameras focused on each child for 5 minutes insuring equal and representative study of all playgroup participants. For purposes of comparison, we also studied the peer play of each possible pair of children (six children result in 15 pairs) when separate from the other children. This was accomplished by closing a sound proof folding wall that divided the playroom in half. The pair of children to be videotaped accompanied by one of the two teachers played for 15 minutes by themselves. Each child spent about 1¼ hours in this "dyad situation" across the course of each 30 hours of playgroup participation. Thus the *group* situation was the much more familiar one and it might have been expected to better reflect the growth of peer interaction and skill occurring in playgroup.

In reality, however, Vandell and Mueller (1977) showed that the growth of peer skill was much more readily observable in the *dyad* situation. In research based on the second playgroup only, little difference between the two situations was found at the start of the playgroup. In two later comparisons, however, interaction frequency and duration was increasing in a linear fashion in dyads but not growing at a significant rate in the group situation. Had we only assessed the group situation we might have concluded that no significant growth of peer skill occurred as a result of toddler playgroup participation.

It appears then that the interactional competencies being developed in the group situation could be more readily expressed in the dyad situation. We do not know what features of the dyad situation facilitated this expression of peer skills. It is possible that the absence of distracting group activity allowed the children to be more attentive to one another. Perhaps the educators conveyed subtle cues that "now was the time to play with each other." Whatever the correct interpretation, the results suggest that group care settings be so designed to allow children access to each other in spaces separate from the larger group.

Toddlers do not spontaneously engage in group interactions. Klein and Wander (1933) were the first to note that group interactions, those involving three or more children, occurred only among 2-year-olds. At this age language allows one child to summon the entire group with expressions like "hey you guys" which we have once heard used by a playgroup child not yet 3-years-old. These few results hardly settle the question of optimal group size for toddler relations. Two children playing without others present could suffer from a lack of choice in their partner. Our playgroup had to be designed without partitions so the video cameras could observe the children everywhere. A natural playroom presumably would be more partitioned allowing a division of the group into smaller units.

Children with Special Needs.   In the environment, the space within each play area should be large enough so that two or three children come together and interact easily; each area must be planned so that children with special needs can move in and out on scooter boards. An environment which is divided into several sections can become too restrictive for some handicapped children. Whenever possible, small empty spaces can be set up to be appealing places for two children to go off and be together, and if a curtain is available, the place becomes a more private one and additionally, two children can easily play peek-a-boo. A note of caution—large, empty spaces and long corridors create problems since children are likely to run around in them aimlessly.

The ratio of children to educators in such a setting should be approximately two or three normal toddlers to one adult. Generally, a smaller group is more desirable. In planning the size of the group consideration should be given to the types and degree of handicaps that the children have. Perhaps two children with special needs is the maximum number that should be integrated into a group. In order for the experience to be meaningful for all of the children, support staff is needed to assist in facilitating the peer-peer interactions. Sufficient numbers of adults are necessary to support, guide and facilitate interaction among the children.

Summary

The chapter shows how to foster early peer relations among children who are developing normally and those with special needs. After outlining the importance of peer relations in human development the chapter focuses on peer relations as a source of competence. Early peer relations are shown to foster both specific social skills and a general sense of efficacy. To foster early peer interaction, the specific ways in which an environment can be planned is outlined in detail. Recommendations are provided regarding the role of toys, play equipment and materials, the role of the adults, and the size of the groups. Special attention is given to the equipment needs and special experiences which assist in integrating and encouraging peer-peer interaction for the young child with special needs.

ACKNOWLEDGMENTS

Many of the innovative ideas for toys, materials and adaptive equipment which encourage peer-peer interactions among toddlers were provided firsthand by educators involved in working with young children in group settings.

Special thanks to Rita Chrappa, Teacher, Two Year Old Group, Wellesley College Child Study Center; Eileen Kirwin, Clinical Nursery Teacher and Martha Shea, Infant and Toddler Specialist. We also thank Deborah Vandell for access to some unpublished data.

REFERENCES

Anthony, E. J. Reflections on twenty-five years of psychotherapy. *International Journal of Group Psychotherapy*, 1968, *18*, 227–230.

Baldwin, J. M. *Thought and things, volume 2, interest and art*. London: George Allen, 1911.

Bergstrom, J. L., & Gold, J. R. *Sweden's day nurseries: focus on programs for infants and toddlers*. Washington, D.C.: The Day Care and Child Development Council of America, 1974.

Blitsen, D. R. *Human social development*. New Haven: College and University Press, 1971.

Borke, H. Interpersonal perception of young children: egocentricism or empathy. *Developmental Psychology*, 1971, *5*, 263–269.

Brazelton, T., Koslowski, B., & Main, M. The origins of reciprocity: the early mother-infant interaction. In M. Lewis & L. Rosenblum (Eds.), *The Effect of the infant on its caregiver*. New York: Wiley, 1974.

Brenner, J., & Mueller, E. *Toddlers dictionaries of social shared meanings*. Paper presented at the summer institute on the Origins and Development of Communication Skills, Newark, Del., 1979.

Bronfenbrenner, U. Response to pressure from peers versus adults among Soviet and American school children. *International Journal of Psychology*, 1967, *2*, 199–207.

Cairns, R. B. *Social development*. San Francisco: Freeman, 1979.

DeStefano, C. T. *Environmental determinants of peer social behavior and interaction in a toddler playgroup*. Unpublished doctoral dissertation, Boston University, 1976.

Eckerman, C. O., Whatley, J. L., & McGehee, L. J. Approaching and contacting the object another manipulates: a social skill of the 1 year old. *Developmental Psychology*, 1979, *15*, 585–594.

Eckerman, C., & Whatley, J. *Toys and social interaction between infant peers. Child Development*, 1977, *48*, 1645–1656.

Ginsburg, M., & Opper, S. *Piaget's theory of intellectual development*. (2nd ed.) Englewood Cliffs: N.J.: Prentice-Hall, 1979.

Hartup, W. W. Peer interaction and social organization. In P. M. Mussen (Ed.), *Carmichael's manual of child psychology*. (3rd. ed., Vol. 2). New York: Wiley, 1970.

Jacobson, J. *The role of inanimate objects in early peer interaction*. Paper presented at the meetings of the Society for Research in Child Development, San Francisco, 1979.

Klein, R., & Wander, E. Gruppenbildung im zweiten lebensjahr. *Zeitschrift für Psychologie*, 1933, *128*, 257–280.

Lewis, M. The infant and its caregiver: the role of contingency. *Allied Health and Behavioral Sciences*, in press.

Lewis, M., Young, G., Brooks, J., & Michalson, L. The beginnings of friendship. In M. Lewis & L. A. Rosenblum (Eds.), *Friendship and peer relations*. New York: Wiley, 1975.

McCall, R. B., Eichorn, D. M. & Nogarty, P. S. Transitions in early mental development. *Monographs of the Society for Research in Child Development, 1977, 42*, No. 3, (Serial No. 171).

Mueller, E. The maintenance of verbal exchanges between young children. *Child Development*, 1972, *43*, 930–938.

Mueller, E. (Toddlers plus toys)=(an autonomous social system). In M. Lewis & L. A. Rosenblum (Eds.), *The child and its family*. New York: Plenum, 1979.

Mueller, E., & Brenner, J. The origins of social skills and interaction among playgroup toddlers. *Child Development*, 1977, *48*, 854–861.

Mueller, E., & Lucas, T. A developmental analysis of peer interaction among toddlers. In M. Lewis & L. A. Rosenblum (Eds.), *Friendship and peer relations*. New York: Wiley, 1975.

Mueller, E., & Rich, R. Clustering and socially-directed behaviors in a playgroup of 1-year-olds. *Journal of Child Psychology and Psychiatry*, 1976, *17*, 315–322.

Mueller, E., & Vandell, D. Infant-infant interaction: a review. In J. D. Osofsky (Ed.), *Handbook of infant development*, New York: Wiley, 1979.

Piaget, J. *The moral judgment of the child*. New York: Free Press, 1965.

Roberts, J., & Baird, J. L. *Parent ratings of behavioral patterns of children*. Vital and Health Statistics. Data from the National Health Survey (Ser.11, No. 108) Washington, D.C.: U.S. Government Printing Office, 1971.

Rubenstein, J., & Howes, C. The effect of peers on toddler interaction with mother and toys. *Child Development*, 1976, *47*, 597–605.

Singer, J. *The child's world of make-believe*. New York: Academic Press, 1973.

Sundby, M. S., & Kreyberg, P. C. *Prognosis in child psychiatry*. Baltimore: Williams & Wilkins, 1968.

Sylva, K., Bruner, J. S., & Genova, P. The role of play in the problem-solving of children 3–5 years old. In J. S. Bruner, A. Jolly, & K. Sylva (Eds.), *Play-its role in development and evolution*. New York: Basic Books, 1976.

Tizard, B. Play: the child's way of learning? In B. Tizard & D. Harvey (Eds.) *Biology of play*. Philadelphia: Lippincott, 1977.

Vandell, D. L. *Boy toddlers' social interaction with mothers, fathers, and peers*. Doctoral disertation, Boston University, 1977.

Vandell, D. L. Effects of a playgroup experience on mother-son and father-son interaction. *Developmental Psychology*, 1979, *15*, 379–385.

Vandell, D. L., & Mueller, D. *The effects of group size on toddlers' social interaction with peers*. Paper presented at the meetings of the Society for Research in Child Development, New Orleans, 1977.

Vandell, D. L., & Mueller, E. Peer play and friendships during the first two years. In H. Foot, T. Chapman, & J. Smith (Eds.), *Friendship and childhood relationships*. London: Wiley, 1980.

Vandell, D. L., Wilson, K. S., & Buchanan, N. R. Peer interaction in the first year of life: an examination of its structure, content, and sensitivity to toys. *Child Development*, in press.

Wedell-Monnig, J. *Child deafness and mother-child interaction*. Paper presented at the Boston University Child Language Conference, 1977.

Winnecott, D. W. *Playing and reality*. New York: Basic Books, 1971.

Yarrow, L. J. Historical perspectives and future directions in infant development. In J. Osofsky (Ed.) *Handbook of infant development*. New York: Wiley, 1979.

THE CROSS CULTURAL PERSPECTIVE

10 Internal State Words: Cultural and Situational Variation in Vocabulary Usage[1]

Maryl Gearhart
Hampshire College

William S. Hall
University of Maryland at College Park

INTRODUCTION

The purpose of this chapter is to describe a set of procedures for coding words of internal report. The motivation for the development of this set of procedures was to apply them to a corpus of data assembled by William S. Hall on language used in ten temporal situations by young children (4½ to 5 years of age) and those with whom they conversed during the course of a two day period (see Hall, 1978). The data from the children were audiotaped in their homes and in their schools. The total number of subjects recorded was 40. One-half of the subjects (hereafter referred to as target children) were black and the other half white. The children were divided equally in both racial groups into middle and lower social classes.

As originally designed, the Hall study (Hall, 1978) focused on nine questions. The particular hypothesis guiding the work behind the development of this set of coding procedures was that cultural variation in vocabulary usage has certain consequences for children's cognitive development and for their performance in school. Thus these coding procedures were designed to capture important differences in the kinds of cognitive activities that characterize the everyday worlds of home and school for the children in the study.

The procedures developed here are concerned with a single domain of vocabulary items which may have critical functions in cognitive activities—those words

---

[1]The listing of authors for this paper is alphabetical. The preparation of this paper was a joint enterprise.

representing mental states and perceptual experiences. These words are of considerable interest in view of current theories of ''meta'' cognition which assume that consciousness of one's knowledge, of cognitive processes, of attentional processes, of perceptions, and of feelings can play a critical role as higher-level ''executor'' of lower-level processes.

In sections to follow we describe our procedures for the investigation of variation in use for those words. Immediately following, however, we present a brief discussion of the rationale for studying cultural variation in vocabulary use.

CULTURAL VARIATION IN VOCABULARY USE

Three Consequences of Cultural Variation

Cultural variation in the function and uses of language has important consequences for speakers of variants, particularly with respect to educational performance. Three consequences can be proffered: social, cognitive, and acquisition of school skills.

The *social consequences* of a variant way of using language can affect teacher-pupil as well as peer relationships. The consequences of a teacher's attitude towards a given dialect—including vocabulary differences—are profound. For example, it can affect his or her initial judgment about how smart a child is likely to be, or how he will fare as a learner, how he will be grouped for instruction, and how his contributions in class will be treated. This, in turn can affect the child's attitude about himself as a school learner, his willingness to participate, his expectations about results of his participation, etc. There are also consequences of variation in language use with respect to one's standing with peers. It is often suggested that high status in peer and school settings requires opposing rules for using or not using a variety of speech.

Also at issue in the present work is whether different patterns of language socialization in the home—in this case, vocabulary use—have discernible *cognitive consequences*. Vocabulary differences clearly reflect differences in public access to one's ideas. These differences lead to different opportunities to talk about a given meaning or aspect of meaning, and as a result different speech communities have different access to their members' and others' ideas. At a deeper level, different types of speech might involve different opportunities to engage in certain basic cognitive processes. For example, the process of modification in the case of adjectives or adverbs or the process of subordination in the case of conjunctions could easily be affected by differentially elaborated vocabularies. There is also evidence suggesting that unrecognized differences in vocabulary result in mis-estimates of memory capacity and ''general intelligence.''

The possible consequences of variants from the school register for the *acquisition of school skills* may be illustrated for reading and the ability to deal with a kind of meta-behavioral information. In reading, semantic mismatches between reader's word meaning and author's word meaning may affect children's expectations about the gist of the language that they are reading. Moreover, it is often suggested that different cultures may promote different levels of meta-linguistic awareness, or the capacity to reflect upon language use. Learning to read requires a certain set of meta-linguistic awarenesses, and some cultures may provide vocabulary items which are reasonably isomorphic to these kinds of cognitive processes and which are therefore useful for their development and use in reading. Variation in language socialization may also differentially facilitate or support the child's growing ability to analyze and and make analytical statements about certain kinds of behavior which are not always reflected upon in everyday life. Such "meta" behavioral abilities include perceptual awareness (like the ability to analyze a perceptual array into a set of geometrical or mathematical relationships), as well as, behavioral awareness (such as the ability to analyze the emotions of a person or those of a fictional character). Since such analysis is a hallmark of schooling, it is a prime area for analyzing home/school mismatches (see, e.g., Cole & Scribner, 1973).

Examples of Problems in Communication

The potential communications problems that might ensue across cultural boundaries can be illustrated. We have noted earlier that vocabulary differences among individuals could contribute to variation in ease of public access to one's ideas. Suppose that individual A possesses a more highly differentiated vocabulary within some semantic domain (say color terms) than does B. A knows more types than B. It is possible that B may know and produce much the same set of corresponding meanings (concepts) as does A, but the lexical tools differ. B's reliance on a smaller set of types (and as well on larger syntactic units such as phrases and clauses) to represent a concept is likely to result in ambiguity and vagueness from A's point of view, and in a less explicit mode of communication than A's. A and B may each also have culturally-specific concepts and beliefs, any of which may or may not have a culturally-specific lexical representation. So if A and B should converse, the mappings of tokens to meanings in any interaction will differ for the two individuals, and misunderstandings are likely to result.

A and B can misunderstand one another then, because one has a less explicit mode of communication, because one has a culturally-specific idea to express, because one uses a culturally-specific vocabulary item. Problems of misunderstanding increase directly with the dissimilarity of their two cultures. The less knowledge which A and B share about their social situation, the less they can depend on their knowledge of the broader context of their interaction to make sense of each other despite lexical misinterpretations, and the more likely that one or both of them will fear social censure for exposing a misunderstanding. The listener may fear that he would appear ignorant (in some circumstances) or implicitly critical of the speaker's competence (in other circumstances). Similarly, the speaker, if he suspects that the listener misunderstands him, may fear that publicly "repairing" the misunderstanding would display his initial "incompetence" (in some social circumstances) or implicitly criticize the listener's competence (in other social circumstances).

Consequences for Children

Problems in Communication and Interpretation.   We assume that, even if adults feel constrained from making public their efforts at effecting shared understandings, most adults have cognitive resources for recognizing at least the existence of differences in lexical interpretation, if not for actually determining the nature of those differences. While the pragmatic nuances may be missed, the participants can probably at least achieve some primary interactional purpose. But for a child who is not so adept, differences in lexical meaning could be more serious obstacles to effective communication. There is considerable evidence (Glucksberg, Krauss, & Higgins, 1975; Shantz, 1975) that young children often interpret communications from their own perspective without recognizing that others may have alternative interpretations. They also appear to have difficulty reassigning an interpretation; even if the child's interpretation of one utterance doesn't make much sense in view of what else the speaker appears to have said, the child has difficulty stepping back and rationally and flexibly making sense of the discrepancy. These kinds of difficulties would be exacerbated in a situation where participants are from different cultural groups. A child may "misinterpret" or be unable to assign *any* interpretation to a word, and if that happens too often, she/he may just tune out of the interaction. It is of concern to us that this may happen for many children in school.

The Home-School Transition.   One implication of cultural variation in vocabulary use is that a child from a minority culture may well have to master the majority's vocabulary usage. Children will have to learn both the vocabulary characteristic of their homes and that of the school. The school environment generally requires of the child knowledge of fairly conventional, middle-class, "literal" meanings for many words. A school child needs to understand and use these words in the same way that the teacher does if she/he is to learn from participation in any teacher task. The transition from home to school for majority children may be far easier than for minority children, who have more to learn.

In fact, there is considerable support in the literature on acquisition of language that children's early language use is situation-specific. Several investigators (cf. Nelson & Brown, 1978; Shatz, 1978) report that children first learn language as limited routines with familiar others in familiar situations. With regard to vocabulary growth, a child's early lexical knowledge should then be organized in terms of the familiar situations in which he and familiar others use the words. Nelson's research on semantic development supports this view that children initially represent words according to their roles or slots in episodes and only gradually construct a semantic system decontexted from personally experienced events. Litowitz (1977), in reporting on children's abilities to define words, notes that children initially know words according to the particular situations and uses they have encountered and only gradually construct a system organized through taxonomic and modification relations. Hall and Dore (1978) invoke this explanation in explaining similarity in performance between children on an intelligence (vocabulary) task; when mothers administered the task and supplied their own definitions for the vocabulary items. there were neither ethnic group nor social class differences among the children's intelligence scores.

VOCABULARY GROWTH AND COGNITIVE GROWTH

It is not unreasonable to suppose that a child's exposure to some optimal diversity of vocabulary types within a domain would have the following cognitive consequences. For one, such a child has more opportunity to learn that concepts can be represented by words, that words have the function of representing concepts. This "metalinguistic" awareness of words as units is quite important for early reading development. Further, when she/he is engaged in the process of learning a new word, since she/he is likely to know words already which share critical conceptual bases, the child may well learn it by a process of differentiating it from other related lexical types already known, and therefore will become aware of the commonalities and differences among word meanings. Thus the child will be more likely to learn that there are domains of meaning and that these correspond to interrelated sets of lexical items. Awareness of possible organizations for knowledge would appear to be important for the learning of certain memorial and problem-solving strategies.

A child's growing knowledge of the lexicon and its organization would also be facilitated by specific experiences identifying, defining, and categorizing words as units. There is some controversy as to whether semantic organization of the type which Litowitz (1977) and Nelson and Brown (1978) describe is necessarily the most complex or "mature" of all possible organizations but it is clear, in any case, that not all cultures find this kind of organization particularly functional. Litowitz's "socially shared" method of defining words according to taxonomic and modification relations may in fact be a method "shared" primarily by the middle class. A working-class child may be learning how words and their referents can be used to accomplish specifiable tasks in the world. (Analyses of our mothers from Hall's study administering the Peabody Picture Vocabulary

Test to their children support this claim. Lower-class white mothers, in particular, generally defined words in terms of the function of their referent, (see Hall & Dore, 1978). Working-class children, then, may not spontaneously produce or recognize certain kinds of hierarchical relationships, because they have not often been asked to do so. It will take greater effort on their part than for a middle class child to make sense of the "standard" definitions in terms of classes and categories in school. A spontaneous tendency to organize lexical knowledge in terms of referent functions may have consequences for the processes by which they acquire new words. If nothing else, they will be relatively unfamiliar with the procedures of hierarchical categorization which they will be asked to use in school.

WORDS AS INDICATORS OF COGNITIVE PROCESSES: THEORETICAL RATIONALE FOR STUDYING INTERNAL STATE WORDS

One way to investigate the relation of vocabulary growth to cognitive growth is to select particular vocabulary types within one conceptual domain. "Internal state" words can be shown to map onto the domain of "meta" cognitive processes.

The prefix "meta" is used to refer generally to such cognitive phenomena as consciousness of one's knowledge as well as capacities to analyze, plan, and evaluate one's mental activities. An analogy is often made to the executor in a computer program, which is that component responsible for allocating lower-level resources for task accomplishment, overseeing task progress, and evaluating task completion. Brown (1977), in a review of the literature concerned with metacognition, acknowledges that the proliferation of "meta" terms as prefixes for virtually any psychological term (metacognition, metabehavioral, metamemory, metalinguistic, metacomprehension, metacommunication . . .) leads one to question whether there is anything new—or at least coherent—being offered in the term. She argues that there is, that the term represents a new perspective on human intelligence. What is new is the assumption that the "essence of intelligent activity" is "conscious executive control of the routines available to the system." Intellectual functioning—for example, "deliberate learning and problem solving"—is the topic of interest, not human intelligence defined primarily in terms of its contents or its products. The "basic characteristics of efficient thinking in a wide range of learning situations" include: predicting and planning outcomes, checking and monitoring task progress, testing the reality and internal consistency of outcomes. Flavell (1977) makes the same argument—that the topics for study are "active monitoring and consequent regulation and orchestration of these processes in relation to the cognitive objects or data on which they bear—usually in the service of some concrete goals or objectives."

Internal state words are concerned with mental processes and states. The use of any such word (e.g., think, remember, feel, listen, etc.) is not necessarily associated with any sort of metacognitive process; nor is the verbalization of metacognitions dependent upon a lexical correlate. Nevertheless, in as much as lexical representations of mental processes and states are often used to express (if not to organize) metacognitive activities, these vocabulary types seem critical to examine. There is also a small set of words which either represent or require "meta" linguistic knowledge about words—for example, "call," "name," and "mean." Locating uses of these words helps us locate occasions where a word is defined or paraphrased, or, where a definition is provided and a word is solicited. On such occasions words are objects for analysis, and defining words is an identifiable conversational task.

Children's lives are filled with requirements for using internal state words. For example, a quick glance through just one reading series (Scott, Foresman, revised: "Reading Unlimited") makes it clear that the ability to interpret these kinds of metacognitive and metalinguistic words is critical for a child's successful participation in classroom interaction. Consider these suggestions for teacher instructions and for the teacher's role in text discussions at the first grade reading level:

Find the *word* that rhymes with
Find the *word* that tells how a
Find the *word* that *names* something
Find the word that *means*
Can you find a *word* in the second column that *looks* almost *like* your word in the first column?
What do you *call* a (definition—soliciting a word)
What do you *see* in this picture that tells you that
What are (   ) doing that makes you *think* that
Why do you *suppose*
How does (   ) make you *feel*?
How would you *feel*?
Read the line that tells you how (   ) *feels*.

And so on . . . . It is reasonable to assume that if a child comes to school having had experience with these words and with these kinds of uses for these words, he will be at an advantage for school success.

In conclusion, we would like to suggest a specific hypothesis with regard to internal state words: that the use of internal state words, in conjunction with particular kinds of tasks in which these words play critical roles, can facilitate the acquisition of metacognitive processes and help the child to become an active seeker, interpreter, and user of information. Certain of our procedures are designed to provide evidence for this hypothesis.

PROCEDURES

Types and Tokens: The Basic Units

Table 10.1 lists the vocabulary types that we are investigating. This list is not meant to be exhaustive of the words in these domains which can be found in our corpus; but the listing should clarify for the reader which words are of concern to us.

Making Comparisons

A coding procedure is only useful if it answers questions relevant to the investigator's concerns. One of our concerns is to make appropriate comparisons across different groups and situations. We now turn to a description of how our procedures work in this regard.

Proportions are the appropriate data with which to make comparisons across speakers and situations, since not all taped situations are of equal length and

Table 10.1
Categories of 'Internal State' Vocabulary
With Examples of Possible Types

Verbs	Nouns	Adjectives
Cognitive		
know	knowledge	certain
know how		
think	thought	thoughtful
believe	belief	believable
understand (see) (get)	understanding	understanding
wonder		
imagine	imagination	
guess	guess	
make sure		sure
suppose		
doubt	doubt	doubtful
remember	memory	
recall		
forget		forgetful
realize		
(pretend)		
(learn, pick up)		
remind	reminder	
dream	dream	
(appear)	(appearance)	
(seem)		

(Continued)

Table 10.1 (Continued)
Categories of 'Internal State' Vocabulary
With Examples of Possible Types

Verbs	Nouns	Adjectives
Perceptual		
see	sight	
look	look	
(appear)	(appearance)	
(seem)		
watch		
hear		
listen	sound	
touch		
(feel)		
taste	taste	
smell	smell	smelly
Affective		
frighten	fear	afraid, scared
	anger	angry
like	like	
love	love	loving
hate	hate	
bother		
(feel)	feeling	
hope	hope	hopeful
(stand)		
	comfort	comfortable
	(bad) mood	
	concern	concerned
		sorry
	worry	worried
		upset
A 'Metalinguistic' Category: Lexical Definition		
(call)		
(name)	name, word	
(mean)		
(stand for)		

since speakers produced different amounts of talk. In the illustrative data in Table 10.2, we determined the proportion of each speaker's total tokens which were 'internal state' tokens. We see in Table 10.2 that our speakers used internal state words about 1 to 3% of the time. Although these proportions and the differences among them are small, they need not be too small for examining group differences. We did not pursue proportions for each particular internal state domain

Table 10.2
Distribution of Internal State and Lexical Definition
Tokens for ROG and TOH Speakers at Home (Dinner) and at
School (Directed Activity), With Proportion of Total
Internal State Tokens Over Total Tokens for Each Speaker

	Situation	Vocabulary Domain	Speaker		
			Child	Mother	Teacher
ROG[a]	Dinner	cognitive	3	28	
		perceptual	21	5	
		affective	0	5	
		(lexical)	(0)	(0)	
	Total internal state tokens/ Total tokens		$\frac{24}{1036} = .02$	$\frac{38}{1576} = .02$	
	Directed Activity	cognitive	1		8
		perceptual	6		11
		affective	1		0
		(lexical)	(1)		(1)
	Total internal state tokens/ Total tokens		$\frac{8}{451} = .02$		$\frac{19}{92} = .02$
TOH[a]	Dinner	cognitive	5	28	
		perceptual	14	18	
		affective	4	28	
		(lexical)	(2)	(0)	
	Total internal state tokens/ Total tokens		$\frac{23}{1222} = .02$	$\frac{74}{2199} = .03$	
	Directed Activity	cognitive	1	10	
		perceptual	5	12	
		affective	4	2	
		(lexical)	(0)	(0)	
	Total internal state tokens/ Total tokens		$\frac{10}{693} = .01$	$\frac{24}{1154} = .02$	

[a]Code names for subjects.

(cognitive, perceptual, affective) since in these case examples there were too few tokens in each domain to warrant even an illustrative analysis. Another way to examine specific domains is illustrated instead in Table 10.3. In this table we have determined, for each speaker (eventually by group) in each situation, the relative proportion of his/her total internal state tokens in each particular internal state domain. Table 10.3 indicates that, at home, both TOH's mother and TOH used words from all three domains with roughly equal frequency. ROG's mother tended to use primarily cognitive words, and ROG perceptual words. While TOH and ROG both used perceptual words more than either cognitive or affective

Table 10.3
For Each Speaker (x Situation), the Proportion of
Total 'Internal State' Tokens in Each Particular
'Internal State' Domain (Cognitive, Perceptual, Affective)

ROG	Situation	Vocabulary Domain	Speaker		
			Child	Mother	Teacher
	Dinner	cognitive	.13	.74	
		perceptual	.87	.13	
		affective	.00	.13	
			(N = 24)	(N = 38)	
	Directed Activity	cognitive	.12		.42
		perceptual	.75		.58
		affective	.12		.00
			(N = 8)		(N = 19)
TOH	Dinner	cognitive	.22	.38	
		perceptual	.61	.24	
		affective	.17	.38	
			(N = 23)	(N = 74)	
	Directed Activity	cognitive	.20		.42
		perceptual	.50		.50
		affective	.40		.08
			(N = 10)		(N = 24)

words, the greater extent to which TOH diverged from a "preoperational" concern with external appearances and perceptual experiences appears related to the greater diversity across domains by TOH's mother as compared to ROG's mother. At school, both boys' teachers looked quite alike in this analysis, with about equal concern for cognitive and perceptual words; TOH's teacher did use a couple of affective words, ROG's teacher none, a modest difference at best but one which corresponds to differences between TOH's and ROG's mothers. The greater use of perceptual words by teachers than by mothers makes sense in view of teacher's interest in encouraging sustained attentional involvement in some fairly focused task.

The data on diversity of tokens among these three categories corresponds to the data on diversity of *types* within as well as across all three internal state domains (see Table 10.4). There was substantially a greater diversity of affects expressed both at home and at school for TOH than for ROG, and greater diversity across all three domains as well. These data correspond to differences between TOH and ROG. The two teachers differ in this type analysis with regard to the diversity of cognitive words used: ROG's teacher used only one cognitive word ("know") yet used it just about as often (from the token data in Tables 10.2

Table 10.4
Distribution of Internal State Types for ROG and TOH Speakers
at Home (Dinner) and at School (Directed Activity)

	Situation	Vocabulary Domain	Speaker		
			Child	Mother	Teacher
ROG	Dinner	cognitive	2	6	
		perceptual	3	4	
		affective	–	4	
		lexical	–	1	
		TOTAL	5	15	
	Directed Activity	cognitive	1		1
		perceptual	4		4
		affective	–		–
		lexical	–		–
		TOTAL	5		5
TOH	Dinner	cognitive	3	9	
		perceptual	5	5	
		affective	3	11	
		lexical	–	1	
		TOTAL	11	26	
	Directed Activity	cognitive	1		5
		perceptual	3		4
		affective	1		2
		lexical	–		–
		TOTAL	5		11

and 10.3) as all five types used by TOH's teacher. We argued earlier that exposure to a number of different types could facilitate the child's construction of differentiated and flexible domains of lexical knowledge. TOH's mother and his teacher appear to provide that kind of environment for TOH. In contrast, ROG's teacher appeared to be constricting ROG's experience with words of internal state. Whereas both teachers are using fewer types of words than are the mothers (as would be expected from the rather focused nature of the directed activities which were taped), ROG's teacher provided virtually no diversity at all. We might also point out that ROG's mother shows in this analysis a fairly even distribution of type diversity among the three categories, even though her token data (Tables 10.2 and 10.3) showed a preponderance of cognitive tokens. This is because several affective and perceptual words were used only once. Data like these point to the importance of looking at the data on diversity of type together with data on the frequency of use. As Keith Nelson (1977) has argued, the character of the adult's interactions with a child as the occasion for a child's learning language may be just as important as the frequency of use. A new word

could be acquired on one occasion if it was important to the child and to the success of the interaction that she/he use it and have some kind of understanding for it. Nevertheless, it is also not unreasonable to expect that frequency of a type's use facilitates its acquisition.

TOH's mother was more concerned with feelings, emotions, and attitudes than was ROG's mother. Similarly, TOH's teacher displayed at least some concern with affect—ROG's teacher none. These data correspond, as one would predict, to the children's vocabulary. TOH used words concerning affects both at home and at school—ROG neither. Would a child whose mother and teacher were concerned with affects and attitudes be at any advantage when he entered school? At first one might think that these affective concepts are essentially irrelevant to traditional academic tasks and to our concern with metacognitive processes. But there are two ways in which they are quite fundamental to school performance. The first has to do with the child's growing concepts of personal attitudes towards tasks and accomplishments. A child who is learning about internal states and their relation to external states and interactions has opportunity to learn to recognize and evaluate his own motivations for doing things. School, then, could be experienced and "accomplished" in a more personal, independent, and self-defined way for such a child than for a child who is less knowledgeable or aware of feelings and motivations. The second has to do with critical school skills related to reading comprehension. While "learning to read" might seem a dry, impersonal school task, in fact what is asked of a child are complex interpretations of characters' thoughts, feelings, and intentions. Having learned to recognize these in himself and those close to him would facilitate his learning to do so for characters in stories. Such a child would more easily interpret "beyond the information given" and concern himself with underlying personal and interpersonal dimensions of characters' actions. Our data for TOH, then, suggest that he will be at an advantage for these kinds of interpretive school tasks as compared to ROG. This would be the case even if it were not for the additional burden upon ROG, much of the time, to *transform* the story content from themes predominant in the majority culture to ones that are familiar and interpretable to him. If anything, ROG needs a teacher with particular concern to develop his skills for these kinds of affective and intentional interpretations, and instead he has a teacher who (in these data) shows no concern with such tasks.

Semanticity: The Second Step

Once tokens are located, they are then coded for what we have glossed as "semanticity," i.e., the relation of the word's meaning to the utterance meaning as a whole.[2] These codes can be seen in Table 10.5. The general motivation for

---

[2]The "semantic—pragmatic" distinction introduced here is intended more as metaphor. We recognize that semantic (structural or grammatical aspects of meaning) and pragmatic (inter-sentential and contextual aspects of meaning) factors operate in the use and interpretation of *any* utterance.

Table 10.5
"Semanticity" of Usage For Internal State Words

Cognitive

'Semantic' uses

A. *Reflections,* assertions, and requests for reflections upon one's knowledge, beliefs, cognitive processes, capacities, etc. . . . These uses are usually coordinated with topic development. That is, the reflection upon mental states or processes is the focus of a proposition which contributes to the topical organization of one or more conversational sequences.

B. *Genuine expressions* of knowledge, beliefs, cognitive processes, capacities, etc. which support some other interactive task and are not used to establish a topic concerned with cognitive states or processes.

'Pragmatic' uses

C. *Hedges; dubitatives; etc.* Especially 'think' but also other of the more general verbs in this category are used with predicate complements to express some attitude toward the complement proposition, but the use for such expression may be better characterized as a 'pragmatic' use rather than a genuine expression of some internal state. Often the 'main clause' (e.g., "I think") is not the focus of the utterance. It could even be deleted and the utterance would still make sense; some essential purpose of the utterance would remain stable; topical organization would remain coherent, and so on. These may also be constructed as tags ("e.g., . . ., I think" or ". . ., I guess").

D. *Exam questions.* Many examination questions have the form of a yes-no request for information about the hearer's knowledge—for example, "Do you know what this is?" but in fact are conventionally used as WH-requests.

E. *Conversational devices* – for example:
1. speaker-selection techniques, such as tags (". . . you know?", ". . . do you know?", ". . . remember?", ". . . do you believe?").
2. acknowledgements and back-channel responses—("mm I know", "I see").
3. mannerisms—scattered throughout a speaker's turn, functioning as pause-fillers or as minimal (probably unconscious) efforts to maintain listener's attention (". . . you know . . .").

Perceptual

'Semantic' use

A. *Reflections* (assertions and request for reflections) upon one's perceptual and sensory experiences and processes. These uses are usually coordinated with topic development. That is, the reflection upon mental states or processes is the focus of a proposition which contributes to the topical organization of one or more conversational sequences.

B. *Genuine expressions* of perceptual and sensory experience which support some other interactive task and are not used to establish a topic concerned with same.

'Pragmatic' uses

C. *Attentional devices* (request for attention)—e.g., "look," "watch," "listen."

(Continued)

Table 10.5 (Continued)
"Semanticity" of Usage For Internal State Words

D. *Conversational mannerisms*—scattered throughout a speaker's turn, functioning as pause-fillers or as minimal (perhaps unconscious) efforts to maintain listener's attention (e.g., ". . . see . . .," ". . . look . . .").

Affective

'Semantic' uses

A. *Reflections* (assertions and requests for reflections) upon one's affective states and processes. These uses are usually coordinated with topic development. That is, the reflection upon affective states or processes is the focus of a proposition which contributes to the topical organization of one or more conversational sequences.

B. *Genuine expressions* of affective states and processes which support some other interactive task and are not used to establish a topic concerned with same.

'Pragmatic' uses

C. *Conversational devices*—Primarily acknowledgements and back-channel responses ("let's hope so" or "I feel that way too").

---

these codes is the following question: If you examine the word in the context of the utterance, how critical is it that the child interpret *any* meaning for the word in order to assign a reasonable interpretation to the utterance? There are what we are calling "pragmatic uses" for these words, in which the semantic content concerned with internal states is not contributing to the topical focus of the proposition, and so the utterance meaning may be quite interpretable without understanding the internal state words. Consider such common "pragmatic" uses for the cognitive verbs "know" and "think" as exam questions ("Do you know what this is?"), dubitatives ("I don't think the elevator's running"), and indirect requests ("Do you think you could just take the garbage out?").[3] Similarly, there are conversational devices for cognitive verbs, such as rhetorical questions ("You know what?") or tags (". . ., you know"), which have an interactional function in securing and maintaining a listener's involvement, and that interactional function overrides any topical concern with the listener's internal states. For vocabulary representing perceptual processes and experiences, there are also "pragmatic" uses, for example, attentional devices. Even though attentional devices must be understood by the listener as requesting a certain kind of attention, they are not likely to be occasions for the listener to reflect upon perceptual processes—upon listening, looking, touching, and so on. For vocabulary representing affective states, there are "pragmatic" uses designed to mitigate requests, offer excuses, and so on: for example, "I'm afraid I didn't think

---

[3]Actually, criteria for a "pragmatic" usage include paralinguistic cues and the context of the utterance as well as its syntactic form. However, these examples are such that the reader can quite easily imagine these utterances being used as described.

of it,'' where the speaker's fear is hardly at issue. (There do not appear to be any pragmatic uses for lexical definition vocabulary, and therefore these vocabulary types are not included in these analyses.)

In general, it is unusual for discourse in which pragmatic uses occur to display any grammatical orientation to the (standard) meanings of the internal state words used. Accordingly, we would not expect pragmatic usage to do much in the way of facilitating the child's understanding of mental processes or states.

In contrast, *semantic uses* are codes for those utterances in which internal state words are intended to contribute topical content. *Reflections* are those uses which appear to call explicitly for metacognitive abilities—for example, ''How did you know . . .'' or ''I realized that if I could just remember . . . .'' When internal state words are used as reflections, generally their content (thinking, remembering, knowing, . . .) contributes to the discourse topic. ''Genuine expressions'' of internal states also contribute substantial content, yet it is usually the object of the internal state which becomes the topic (*what* one was thinking about).

Coding a ''pragmatic'' use for words of internal state in hedges, examination questions, attentional devices, and many conversational devices is not tantamount to arguing that these words carry no ''meaning.'' Determining precisely *what* and *how much* meaning such a word conveys requires a fuller account of the speaker's purposes in the discourse; paralinguistic cues (stress, condensation) accompanying the utterance are often critical devices for signaling the focus of the proposition. The extent to which a lexical item carries semantic meaning is multidetermined and should ultimately be viewed more as a dimension of semanticity than the semantic versus pragmatic dichotomy we have introduced here.

Nevertheless, the distinction between 'pragmatic' and 'semantic' usage should prove quite useful in comparing our four groups. The codes make possible a variety of analyses. Consider as illustrations some data from the two children we described earlier. Table 10.6 indicates, for each speaker, the proportion of his/her internal state tokens which were coded as having a *semantic,* as opposed to a *pragmatic,* function. In other words, the table describes, for each speaker, the frequency with which, roughly-speaking, a ''literal'' meaning for the internal state word was essential to an utterance's meaning. There are consistent differences between the children's teachers. The TOH data show these speakers primarily using these words to express some literal meaning. The ROG speakers were using these words for *pragmatic* functions almost as often as for *semantic* functions.

These differences can be seen as well when we look at *speaker turns.* Table 10.7 reveals the proportion of speaker's turns which contained at least one word of internal state (or lexical definition) used in any way (i.e., without regard for semantic ''versus'' pragmatic usage). The TOH data, as compared to the ROG data, show the greater frequency with which these words were included in the turns of TOH speakers as compared to ROG. Table 10.8 displays the frequency

Table 10.6
Proportion of Internal State Tokens (For Each Speaker) Which
Were Semantic Uses, i.e., Genuine Expressions or Reflections

ROG		Speaker		
	Situation	Child	Mother	Teacher
	Dinner	.25 (N = 24)	.58 (N = 38)	
	Directed Activity	.50 (N = 8)		.53 (N = 19)
TOH				
	Dinner	.83 (N = 23)	.75 (N = 74)	
	Directed Activity	.91 (N = 11)		.67 (N = 36)

Note. N = total tokens of internal state.

with which a speaker included in his turn an internal state word used "semantically." TOH adult speakers used internal state words semantically in approximately 15–18% of their turns, as compared to 10% for ROG's mother and 6% for ROG's teacher. Correspondingly, TOH used an internal state word semantically in roughly 7% of his turns, as compared to 2–3% for ROG. These data suggest

Table 10.7
Proportion of All Turns (For Each Speaker)
Which Contained at Least One Work of Internal State

ROG		Speaker		
	Situation	Child	Mother	Teacher
	Dinner	.09 (N = 273)	.16 (N = 203)	
	Directed Activity	.06 (N = 174)		.11 (N = 174)
TOH				
	Dinner	.09 (N = 249)	.24 (N = 310)	
	Directed Activity	.08 (N = 143)		.21 (N = 124)

Note. N = total speaker turns.

Table 10.8
Proportion of All Turns Which Contained a Semantic Use
(i.e., Genuine Expression or Reflection) of Some Internal State Word

ROG		Speaker		
	Situation	Child	Mother	Teacher
	Dinner	.03 (N = 273)	.10 (N = 203)	
	Directed Activity	.02 (N = 174)		.06 (N = 174)
TOH				
	Dinner	.08 (N = 249)	.15 (N = 310)	
	Directed Activity	.06 (N = 143)		.18 (N = 124)

Note. N = total speaker turns.

that explicitly expressed concern with mental states and activities is far more frequent in one child's world than in another's. In these data, TOH had more opportunity than did ROG to learn the meanings of words in these domains. These are, then, illustrations of the kinds of cultural differences we intend to examine by group.

Lexical Meaning: Step Three

Dictionary readings. We are currently developing procedures to map "semantic" tokens onto corresponding conceptual domains. One of our methods has been to assign each "semantic" token a dictionary reading. The intent here is to determine first *if* a token can be standardly defined and, secondly, the diversity of readings with which any type is used. We have already discovered that standard definitions are very difficult to assign to these words when they are used "pragmatically." Since "pragmatic" usage does not contribute to the propositional focus, the meaning is often vague or ambiguous. It makes sense, then, just to code "semantic" tokens, and we have found that dictionary definitions can be realiably assigned to these.

However, dictionary definitions have given us only a rough idea of the diversity of meanings for which a word is used and of the relations among these meanings. Lexicography is not really a concern with a theory of meaning nor its psychological reality. For example, how different is one dictionary reading from another? Can a token mean more than one reading in any one utterance? Often more than one reading is consistent with (the coder's interpretation of) the utterance's meaning. This is probably no fault of the dictionary but rather a property of communication, that meanings are as precise as they need be for all practical purposes and that may not be very precise at all (cf. Garfinkel & Sacks, 1970). This method offers at best only a rough indication of the relations among types for any given speaker. One speaker may, for example, use words like "think," "know," "believe," "am certain/sure," or "guess" to express fairly explicit beliefs about his knowledge. At times, however, he may use potentially general words like "think" or "know" to express implicitly as many underlying concepts as our first speaker who does (at times) use explicit types. Still another speaker may use only general words in very general ways and appear to lack the differentiated concepts that characterize the first two speakers. We would predict that a child's potential for learning these concepts, then, would vary correspondingly with the speaker's explicit, implicit, or nonexistent expression of them.

We have described our dictionary method, yet we are not in fact convinced of its usefulness for the lexical domains that we have chosen for this particular vocabulary study. If the method is useful, it may be more suitable for words with tangible referents—physical concepts, spatial, and even temporal concepts which appear to have more clearly articulated meanings than do words of internal states. It does seem that a linguist's or a psycholinguist's analysis of a vocabulary domain would, in any case, be preferable to dictionary entries as sets of possible readings for each type. For words of internal state, dictionary codings proved very time-consuming, multiple codings were common, achieving reliability involved considerable negotiation over the meanings of the dictionary readings. "Internal state" concepts are subtle.

Mental Activities: Toward Higher Level Units

It seems more profitable, for words of internal state, to pursue characterizations of the mental states and activities critical to the ongoing discourse in which a token is found. We can either locate, as a first step, 'semantic' uses of internal state words and then attempt a description of the mental states and cognitive activities for which the word is used. Adults often use these words with children, for example, to get them to engage in some sort of cognitive activity or to interpret for them their current mental state. Or, instead, we can first go through the transcripts and locate candidates for classes of mental activities (whether or not internal state words occur) and then examine what kinds of words are used to communicate and carry out that task. Are words used—for example, "remember," "imagine," "guess"—which help the children construct a concept of that particular mental activity? These two approaches would really be part of more ambitious projects (see Hall, 1978) which are concerned with levels of description higher than the lexical item. Mental activities of course do not necessarily require the use of internal state words, so these kinds of analyses will go far beyond this particular vocabulary study. We offer here from our data illustrative examples of possible categories for the use of mental state words in conjunction with some mental activity. (Note: words *in italics* represent semantic use of an internal state word.)

Mothers:	*Interpreting child's internal state;* occasioned by the child's spontaneous behavior or expression, and therefore mother provides a *lexical match* to child's experience.
Mo/TOH/	That's very neat . . very neat, right T--? You're *concerned* about dirtying yourself.
Mo/TOH's father/	T-- doesn't feel like eating that.
TOH's Bro	You see, now they stink.
Mo	L-- what's the matter? What are you *angry* about? What, are you *angry* with Rachel? Are you *angry* with Rachel?
Bro	Yes.

Mothers:	*Reporting her own internal state in order to acknowledge and praise child* (here, for a practical skill).
TOH	I could open it.
Mo	I *know* you can.
TOH	I did it again.
Mo	oh oh I didn't *see*.
TOH	I opened the door again.
Mo	oh T----. I *know* you can, but there's nothing out there now.

Mothers:	*Attributing knowledge to child?* occasioned by a child's misdeed but *not* by any critical mental activity corresponding to the lexical concept. The *attribution of knowledge* is used *to insist that the child use that knowledge.*
Mo	A napkin what T---?
TOH	I *hate* that word. I'm not saying it.
Mo	You *know* how to ask for something.
Mo(ROG)	Now you don't eat like that an you *know* it.
Mo(ROG)	I think that / remember who's / you keep *forgetting* something (napkin)

Mothers and Teachers: Reporting her own internal state? occasioned by a child's misdeed or non-deed. The 'report' of own internal state (or lack thereof) is used to imply pragmatically what internal state ought to exist but now doesn't—*to request correction of misdeed.*

Mo (ROG)	I didn't *hear* you say thank you.
T(ROG)	I didn't *hear* you sing.
T(ROG)	I can not *hear* you when you—when she's talking.

Mothers: Requesting a cognitive activity (reflection, consideration, recall . . .) in order to *teach a social principle.*

Mo(Bro)   . . . You can do as you please. You can wash your hands or not but just *remember* though, you do have to eat with your dirty hands.

Mo(Bro)	. . . if you have to express yourself in that way, it sounds bad, and everybody's going to be against you, you *know* what I *mean*?
Bro	Yes.

Child: Reflecting upon and reporting an acquired skill (or lack thereof)

TOH:	I don't know how to do dat. (here, a response to a T-request).
T	I'll tell you the letters, okay.

ROG   I *know* how to do mine. Oh, I want a little bit.

ROG   I didn't *know* how to say Pizza Pie Man. I try to say it Pizza Pie Land.

Teachers: Requesting that a child display his knowledge (here, relatively rote recall of information).

T   You know where you live R-? You *know* your address? You live in an apartment house, don't you? ("*know*" was assigned a 'semantic' use on the basis of prior discourse context and stress on "know").

T	*Look* at this and tell me what goes (XXX), and what goes to (XXX)?
ROG	I *know* da da boat.

Teachers: Requesting that the child reflect upon and report his mental state.

T	How did you *look* when you were asleep, R----?
ROG	Sad.
T	You *looked* real sad, why?

Teachers:	*Reporting own internal state in order to extend and elaborate the child's own mental activity,* encouraging child to build upon what he is thinking, feeling, and doing by offering her own interpretations in dialogue with the child.

TOH	Touch him.
T	I'm *afraid*. I don't know if I want to touch him. What's he going to do to me if I touch him?
TOH	He bites and tickles.
T	I'm *scared*. You *frighten* me.
T(TOH)	I can't *believe* your Stanley the snake just ate the dog.
T(TOH)	You *mean*, if I said to you, if you were a servant go jump in the lake, you would go jump in the lake?

This last example is one where a mental activity—recalling a personal experience—defined the conversational purpose, yet words of internal state were not used (e.g., "remember," "recall," "memory") to name that activity. Nor were words of internal state used to explore personal attitudes and feelings toward the experience.

Mo(ROG)	She's on the same floor you was on year before last.
ROG	Ss . . . Seventeen? Seventeen das the one I was on? Wha what hap---
Mo	Why don't you tell Carl about the time you was in the hospital. An tell Carl . . . tell Carl what was goin in you hand.
ROG	Needle.
EXP	Is that right?
ROG	Yep. an eh yep, I w' cryin.
EXP	I can believe that. I'd be crying too.
ROG	I was screamin
Mo	Tell tell Carl they had you layin on this cold thing. And they call that the ice mattress, right?
ROG	Yeah dey had to do everything. I I was gonna sit up an pop it, an smack em in na mouth.
Mo	No you wasn't gonna do that . . . the doctors was tryinna help you, right?
ROG	no-o, it's stupid.
Mo	I couldn't say the doctors are stupid.

It will be of interest to determine the occasions in which mothers and teachers introduce and use specific lexical items. Of critical interest will be those occasions in which: a lexical item is a *match* (ideal for learning) or a *mismatch to some corresponding mental activity;* the *occasion for a lexical item is the child's spontaneous mental activity;* a lexical item is used to *misrepresent a mental state or activity* (the child's or anyone else's).

Table 10.A
Dinner—ROG—Mother

COGNITIVE	SEMANTIC		PRAGMATIC			
	Genuine Reflections	Genuine Expressions	Hedges; Dubitatives	Conversational Devices	Exam Questions	Others
forgetting		1				
know		4		4		1
know (how to, the way to)		1				
remember		3				
see		1		4		
think		4	3	1		
thought		1				

(Continued)

Table 10.A (Continued)
Dinner—ROG—Mother

	SEMANTIC		PRAGMATIC		
	Genuine Reflections	Genuine Expressions	Attentional Devices	Conversational Mannerisms	Others
PERCEPTUAL					
hear					1
look			1		
looks like		1			
see		1			
watch		1			

	SEMANTIC		PRAGMATIC		
	Genuine Reflections	Genuine Expressions	Hedges	Conversational Devices	Others
AFFECTIVE					
comfortable		2			
hope					1
like		1			
sorry					1
				17	

21
.58%
are genuine expressions
semantic usage

LEXICAL		
call	1	

| | SEMANTIC | | PRAGMATIC | | | |
COGNITIVE	Genuine Reflections	Genuine Expressions	Hedges; Dubitatives	Conversational Devices	Exam Questions	Others
know how to thought	1?	1				1

| | SEMANTIC | | PRAGMATIC | | |
PERCEPTUAL	Genuine Reflections	Genuine Expressions	Attentional Devices	Conversational Devices	Others
hear	3				
hears					1
look			2		
look like		1			
see		1	4		10
					18

6
.25%
are genuine expressions
semantic usage

Table 10.B
Dinner—TOH—Mother

COGNITIVE	SEMANTIC		PRAGMATIC			
	Genuine Reflections	Genuine Expressions	Hedges; Dubitatives	Conversational Devices	Exam Questions	Others
forget		4				
know		3		2		
know (how to)		2				
make sure		1				
mean		2		1		
realize		1				
remember		1				
see		3		3		
think		1	1			
thought		1				
understand		2				

PERCEPTUAL	SEMANTIC		PRAGMATIC		
	Genuine Reflections	Genuine Expressions	Attentional Devices	Conversational Mannerisms	Others
heard		4			
listen			4		
look		1	2		1
see		4			1
watch		1			

COGNITIVE	SEMANTIC		PRAGMATIC			
	Genuine Reflections	Genuine Expressions	Hedges; Dubitatives	Conversational Devices	Exam Questions	Others
forgot		1				
know		1				
know how to		2				
thought		1				

PERCEPTUAL	SEMANTIC		PRAGMATIC		
	Genuine Reflections	Genuine Expressions	Attentional Devices	Conversational Devices	Others
hear		1			
heard		1			
look			4		
saw		1			
see		2			
taste		1			
watching		4			

(Continued)

Table 10.B (Continued)
Dinner—TOH—Mother

	SEMANTIC			PRAGMATIC	
AFFECTIVE	Genuine Reflections	Genuine Expressions	Hedges	Conversational Devices	Others
afraid		1	2		
anger		6			
angry		1			
bad mood		1			
bothers		1			
concerned		1			
excited		1			
feel		1			
like		9			
love					1
pleasant		1			
sorry					1
upset		1			
worry		1			
LEXICAL					
call	2			19	

55
75%
Genuine expressions
Semantic usage

	SEMANTIC		PRAGMATIC		
AFFECTIVE	Genuine Reflections	Genuine Expressions	Hedges; Dubitatives	Conversational Devices	Others
hate		1			
like		2			
scared		1		4	
		19			
		.83			

Table 10.C
ROG—Directed Activity—Teacher

COGNITIVE

	SEMANTIC		PRAGMATIC			
	Genuine Reflections	Genuine Expressions	Hedges; Dubitatives	Conversational Devices	Exam Questions	Others
know		1				
knows		1		1	5	

PERCEPTUAL

	SEMANTIC		PRAGMATIC		
	Genuine Reflections	Genuine Expressions	Attentional Devices	Conversational Devices	Others
hear		4			
listen		1			
look	1				
looked	1		1		
looking			1		
see		1	1		
	10 .53 genuine 'semantic' usage			9	

LEXICAL

	Genuine Reflections
called	1

COGNITIVE

	SEMANTIC		PRAGMATIC			
	Genuine Reflections	Genuine Expressions	Hedges; Dubitatives	Conversational Devices	Exam Questions	Others
know		1				

PERCEPTUAL

	SEMANTIC		PRAGMATIC		
	Genuine Reflections	Genuine Expressions	Attentional Devices	Conversational Devices	Others
listening	1		2		
look			1		
see		1	1		
watch					

AFFECTIVE

	SEMANTIC		PRAGMATIC	
	Genuine Reflections	Genuine Expressions	Conversational Devices	
like		1	4	
	4 50%			

Table 10.D
TOH—Directed Activity—Teacher

COGNITIVE	SEMANTIC			PRAGMATIC	
	Genuine Reflections	Genuine Expressions	Hedges; Dubitatives	Exam Questions	Others
believe		1			
know	1	4	1	1	
mean	1				
think			2		

PERCEPTUAL	SEMANTIC			PRAGMATIC	
	Genuine Reflections	Genuine Expressions	Attentional Devices		Others
listen			1		
look		2	4		
looks		2			
looking		4			
looks like		1			
see		4	2		
touch		2			
AFFECTIVE					
afraid		1			
frighten		1			1
	24			12	
	67%				

250

	Genuine Reflections	Genuine Expressions	Attentional Devices
COGNITIVE			
know how to		1	
PERCEPTUAL			
look		1	1
see		3	
touch		1	
AFFECTIVE			
like		4	1
	10 91% genuine		

251

ACKNOWLEDGMENTS

The research on which this chapter is based was supported by a grant from the Carnegie Corporation of New York. The preparation of this manuscript was supported by the National Institute of Education under Contract No. US-NIE-C-400-76-0116.

REFERENCES

Brown, A. L. *Knowing when, where, and how to remember: A problem of metacognition* (Tech. Rep. No. 47). Urbana: University of Illinois, Center for the Study of Reading, June, 1977.

Cole, M., & Scribner, S. Cognitive consequences of formal and informal education. *Science,* 1973, *182,* 553–559.

Flavell, J. H. *Metacognitive development.* Paper presented at the NATO Advanced Study Institute on Structural/Process Theories of Complex Human Behavior, Banff, Alberta, Canada, 1977.

Garfinkel, H., & Sachs, H. On formal structures of practical actions. In J. C. McKinney & E. A. Tiryakian (Eds.), *Theoretical sociology.* New York: Appleton-Century-Crofts, 1970.

Glucksberg, S., Krauss, R., & Higgins, E. T. The development of referential communication skills. In F. D. Horowitz (Ed.), *Review of child development research.* Chicago: University of Chicago Press, 1975.

Hall, W. S. *Cultural and situational variation in language function and use: A program of research* (Working Paper No. 15). New York: The Rockefeller University, Laboratory of Comparative Human Cognition and Institute for Comparative Human Development, August 1978.

Hall, W. S., & Dore, J. *Lexical sharing in mother-child interaction: Some cross-cultural variations.* (Mimeo), 1978.

Litowitz, B. Learning to make definitions. *Journal of Child Language,* 1977, *4,* 289–304.

Nelson, K. *How young children represent knowledge of their world in and out of language: A preliminary report.* Paper presented at the 13th Annual Carnegie Symposium on Cognition, Carnegie-Mellon University, May, 1977.

Nelson, K. Personal communication, 1977.

Nelson, K., & Brown, A. The semantic-episodic distinction in memory development. In P. Ornstein (Ed.), *Memory development.* Hillsdale, N.J.: Lawrence Erlbaum Associates, 1978.

Scott Foresman. *Reading Unlimited* (Reading Series). Glenview, Ill., 1977.

Shantz, C. The development of social cognition. In E. M. Hetherington (Ed.), *Review of child development research* (Vol. 5). Chicago: University of Chicago Press, 1975.

Shatz, M. The relationship between cognitive processes and the development of communication skills. In B. Keasey (Ed.), *Nebraska Symposium on Motivation.* Lincoln: University of Nebraska, 1978.

11 Socialization: A Cultural Ecological Approach

John U. Ogbu
Department of Anthropology
University of California
Berkeley

THE LIMIT OF PROCESS-PRODUCT PARADIGM

From the early 1960's to the late 1970's research in childrearing and child development in the United States underwent a phenomenal growth. Much of this research has focused on lower-class and minority children. Moreover, the social and political climate of the period has encouraged improvement research—i.e., research designed to yield information that would be used to improve the life chances of poor and minority children. The underlying assumption is that high unemployment, inadequate employment, and poverty among the poor and minorities in America are due to inadequate education caused by inadequate childrearing practices (Bloom, Davis, & Hess 1965; Hunt 1969; White, Day, Freeman, Hartman, & Messenger, 1973).

The dominant research paradigm has been and continues to be that of process-product (see Denzin; Green & Wallat; and Ramey, McGinness, Cross, Collier & Barrie-Blackley in this volume). These studies are designed to show some causal relationship between family processes, especially parent-child interaction on the one hand and childrearing outcomes—generally the language, cognitive, motivational, and social competencies—on the other. Specifically, these studies provide a wealth of information about the kinds of parental teaching skills or competencies among the poor and minorities and how these differ from those of white middle-class parents. This has generally been interpreted that the parental teaching competencies among the poor and minorities are both deficient and the cause of poor and minority children's inability to develop white middle-class type of language, cognitive, motivational and social competencies which are essential for later school successes. The findings and interpretations are often used as basis for intervention at some point in the lives of the children of the poor and minorities so that they would experience the right socialization process and thereby develop white middle-class competencies for future school success (see Ramey et al. in this volume; Kerber & Bommarito 1965). Although this intervention strategy has at best produced only dismal results, it continues to preoccupy policy-makers and practitioners as the best feasible strategy.

In this chapter we question the usefulness of the process-product model in cross-cultural research on three grounds. First, the correlation between the characteristics of poor and minority children on the one hand and their low academic achievement on the other is not universal even within the United States. For example, there are some non-white immigrant minorities in the United States who do relatively well in school although they were not raised according to white middle-class childrearing practices (Ogbu 1978a, 1978b). Furthermore, in Third World countries one finds groups who do relatively well in Western-type schools although they do not follow the childrearing practices of white middle-class Americans. Of importance is that in such countries "impoverished children" do not experience the same kinds of "educational handicaps" which are attributed to the poor and minority children in America (Heyneman 1979; van den Berghe 1979).

Second, contrary to the process-product paradigm, the products of childrearing—the language, cognitive, motivational, and social competencies which parents and other childrearing agents seek to inculcate in the young— depend on historical and contemporary economic, social, and political realities of the population and not merely on the teaching competencies of its adult members. Childrearing is culturally organized formulae which generally enable parents to successfully teach their children those language, cognitive, motivational and social competencies required to function competently in their culture. The formulae also enable children to acquire those adaptive competencies consciously or unconsciously as they grow up. We know of no culture where parents fail to teach their children successfully what they have to know and be in order to grow up as competent adults because parents lack the teaching abilities or competencies (Ogbu 1979b).

In modern industrial societies the most powerful forces shaping the language, cognitive, motivational and social competencies inculcated in children are the kinds of economic opportunities open to parents and other adults in the population. Adult economic roles and the strategies for obtaining and advancing in jobs both require and encourage the unique patterns of language, cognitive, motivational, and social competencies found in the population, patterns which parents and other childrearing agents have come to value and to foster in their children consciously and unconsciously. Children themselves also strive to acquire these attributes consciously and unconsciously as they grow up.

The above statement is readily acknowledged when referring to geographically separated populations belonging to different societies. But it is equally true of populations within the same society. We shall argue, for example, that the historical and contemporary economic realities of black Americans, especially of ghetto blacks, differ markedly from those of the white middle class. Their different economic realities require and encourage ghetto blacks to inculcate in their children language, cognitive, motivational, and social competencies that differ from those of their white middle-class counterparts. The way in which the language, cognitive, motivational, and social competencies of black Americans (or any other minority) children are related to their social and economic life cannot be fully understood through the prevailing research practice of studying a small number of families because they contain children "at risk" or because they are like white middle-class families (see Ramey et al. in this volume). A more useful approach would study these competencies in the context of black culture and community.

Our third criticism is that contrary to the process-product model, it is probably not the differences in childrearing practices which cause children in different populations to develop different language, cognitive, motivational, and social competencies. The reverse seems to be the case, i.e., it is the anticipated competencies—the nature of the personal attributes to be inculcated in children to prepare them for future adult economic and social participation—which influence parents and other childrearing agents to use particular childrearing techniques in raising their children. We therefore suggest that where two populations differ in both childrearing practices and childrearing outcomes, it makes more sense to first examine the "fit" between the childrearing practices and children's competencies for each population. It would be an error to judge the efficacy of the childrearing practices of one population on the basis of their ability to produce the same competencies found in the children of the other population, *unless we first establish that children in both populations have generally been prepared for the same social and economic realities in adult life*.

In what follows we first review several cross-cultural studies which suggest (1) that the origins of personality attributes or competencies that parents and other childrearing agents seek to inculcate in children lie in the social, political, and economic realities of adult life and (2) that the nature of these competencies influences the choice of childrearing techniques prevalent in a given population. The purpose of this section is to emphasize the point that an adequate approach to childrearing studies must go beyond "purely intrafamilial and interpersonal aspects" of the phenomenon to take into account "the influences of society and the effects of (the social, political and economic systems) on the socialization of the child" (Inkeles 1968b, p. 123, 76). In the concluding part of the chapter we suggest a few framework—a cultural ecological framework—that would enable researchers to go beyond the limitations noted above.

REALITIES OF ADULT LIFE, CHILDREN'S
COMPETENCIES, AND CHILDREARING TECHNIQUES

The work of Barry, Child and Bacon (1959) provides the most explicit statement on the source of competencies which parents seek to inculcate in children and their relationship to childrearing practices. Specifically, they suggest in their study that group differences in adult subsistence activities result in differences in several personal attributes. They examined the personal qualities valued in two types of societies at two different levels of subsistence economy, namely, low-food accumulation societies such as those of hunter-gatherers and high-food accumulation societies such as those of pastoralists and farmers. They found that the first type of societies value adults who are individualistic, independent, assertive, and venturesome; whereas the second type of societies value adults who are conscientious, compliant, responsible, and conservative. The authors suggest that the dominant adult qualities in each type of societies are those functional or congruent with adult economic roles and the requirements of the respective type of subsistence economy. For example, high-food accumulation societies of farmers and pastoralists need "responsible adults who can best ensure the continuing welfare of a society with a high-accumulation economy, whose food supply must be protected and developed gradually throughout the year" (p. 62). Such societies require their members to adhere to routines designed to maintain high accumulation of food. In contrast, societies with low-food accumulation encourage individual initiative "in wresting food daily from nature" in order to survive (pp. 62–63). The authors further suggest that personality traits or behaviors generated by economic roles tend to be generalized to the rest of behaviors (p. 53).

Having identified differences in adaptive adult personal qualities in the two types of societies, the authors proceeded to examine the nature of childrearing practices in each and the relationship of these practices to the adult personal qualities. For example, would the two types of societies follow the same childrearing practices? Barry, Child and Bacon hypothesized that the two types of societies would differ in their childrearing practices in order to produce adults with personality characteristics best suited to their respective economic pursuits. Specifically they state that:

> The kind of adult behavior useful to the society is likely to be taught to some extent to the children, in order to assure the appearance of this behavior at the time it is needed. Hence we predict that the emphases in childrearing will be toward the development of kinds of behavior especially useful for adult economy. (p. 53)

When they rated 104 societies on several aspects of childrearing practices the results generally supported the hypothesis, especially with respect to training in compliance and assertiveness (p. 59).

A second study by an anthropologist, Robert LeVine (1967) has also contributed to our thinking in this chapter. LeVine studied ethnic differences in achievement motivation in Nigeria. His findings led him to challenge the hypothesis of David McClelland with respect to causal relationship between childrearing practices and achievement motivation. In contrast to McClelland, LeVine makes the following points. First, societies may differ in the strategies they approve for achieving higher status or rewards, i.e., in achievement strategies, even though they may not differ in achievement goals, i.e., in aspiration for higher rewards or status. Second, the personal attributes or competencies of people who succeed in gaining these higher rewards through the approved strategies tend to become the admired qualities parents and other childrearing agents seek to foster in the young. LeVine illustrates this second point with two contrasting hypothetical societies. In the first society where adults are rewarded for being:

> utterly loyal, obedient, and useful to their superiors, parents and other childrearing agents would tend to perceive obedience and servility as virtues or personal qualities that would help a person rise socially and gain access to the resources of the world and they would seek to foster these virtues in the young through early and intense obedience training, direct tuition in respect and flattery behavior, punishment for tendencies which might result in antagonizing superiors, and the like. (pp. 17–18)

In the second type of society, the strategy for achieving higher rewards or status is different and so are the personal qualities regarded as virtues. In this type of society individuals achieve higher rewards "through outstanding performance in occupational roles (and) it is possible for someone of humble origins to obtain higher status through his own efforts as an independent producer of goods and services or as a broker who marshals social resources for desired ends." The personal qualities which members of this society will value include independence, initiative, industriousness, foresight and some daring that lead to success. Parents and other childrearing agents will attempt to inculcate these qualities in the young by early training in self-reliance and achievement.

Cohen's (1965) observations among the Kanuri people of Northern Nigeria support LeVine's formulation. Kanuri society fits LeVine's first type of society, where adults achieve higher status and rewards through obedience and servility. The Kanuri describe the relationship between inferiors and superiors metaphorically as the proper father-child relationship, known as *barzum*. Cohen points out that the *barzum* relations are a person's most important "asset" for achieving higher economic, political, and social status. And Kanuri parents perceive the behavioral dimensions of the *barzum* relations, namely, obedience and servility, as virtues to inculcate in their children. As Cohen puts it:

[This] mode of interaction is taught to the child as the proper relationship between a father and his son. Later, the *barzum* relationship is shown to the young child, but most especially to boys, to be the thing that must be used between himself and all his superiors. He is told that his koranic teacher surpasses his father in "fatherness", as does his chief, and the Emir surpasses all. And to all these (superiors) he must use some aspect of *barzum* or disciplined respect. (p. 363)

In a society where different groups follow different economic pursuits or different strategies for achieving social and economic rewards, we find that there are concomitant differences in adult personal qualities as well as in childrearing practices. Such a case is suggested by Maquet's study of the Watusi, Wahutu, and Watwa in traditional Rwanda. Each of these three castes followed a different adult pursuit: The Tutsi who were the dominant caste were warriors, rulers, and herdsmen; the Hutu were peasant cultivators and subordinate to the Tutsi whom they served as porters in times of war; and the Two subsisted primarily as hunters. Members of each caste were characterized by a distinct set of personal attributes which were regarded as appropriate for the caste. The personal qualities dominant within each caste were regarded by members of that caste as virtues to be inculcated in children by the childrearing agents. For example, among the dominant Tutsi caste the admired personal qualities included self-control, personal courage, a sense of superiority, group pride and haughtiness. These were also the qualities Tutsi parents stressed in their childrearing, Tutsi military officers stressed them at camp training as did the royal educators at the court for future courtiers. The subordinate Hutu peasants, on the other hand, required different personal qualities such as external expression of respect and submission, prudence and perspicacity, endurance and dissumulation. And these were the qualities stressed in Hutu childrearing practices (Maquet 1971).

These examples have been taken from anthropological studies outside the United States. However, there are some non-anthropological studies in America indicating that the social and economic realities of adult life determine the competencies that parents and other childrearing agents seek to inculcate in children. We shall discuss three such studies dealing with changes in middle-class economic roles, class differences in economic roles, and sex role differences.

One early study that traced the attributes parents stressed for their children to adult economic roles and suggested that these attributes influenced childrearing practices is that of Miller and Swanson (1958). These authors studied the change from entrepreneurial to bureaucratic economic role among white middle-class Americans and the consequences of such a change for middle-class childrearing practices. They noted that the major personal attributes associated with the older entrepreneurial economic pursuits were self-control and self-denial. And they suggested that the middle class involved in such economic pursuits adopted childrearing practices which produced these qualities. Among these practices were devices for bowel training in the first 6 months; requiring the child to give up breast or bottle at an early age; and refusing to pay attention to the child if he cried "just to get attention" (Miller & Swanson 1958, p. 56).

As American economy changed and became more corporately owned and more bureaucratized, middle-class economic roles also changed, becoming primarily bureaucratic. This change in economic pursuits brought with it changes in personal qualities. For example, the bureaucratic role in a corporate economy no longer required individuals nurtured in self-control and self-denial; instead, it required people who can get along well with others and who can take other people's and their own feelings into account with skill and confidence (p. 55). The adaptive childrearing practices which emerged in the bureaucratic era of economic pursuit are those suited to producing warm, friendly, and supportive individuals; hence, there emerged among the new middle-class parents childrearing practices which encourage children to be accommodating, to allow their impulses some spontaneous expression and to seek direction from the organization programs in which they participate (p. 58).

The study of class differences in economic pursuits and their bearing on personality characteristics and childrearing practices points to similar linkages. Kohn (1969), for example, studied differing economic roles and socialization values and practices of contemporary American middle and working classes. He found that middle-class jobs demand different personal attributes as compared to working-class jobs. For example, middle-class bureaucratic and professional jobs require self-direction and the ability to manipulate interpersonal relations, ideas and symbols. These qualities are virtues among middle-class parents who resort to childrearing techniques facilitating the development of these qualities in their children. These techniques include emphasis on reasoning, isolation, appeals to guilt and other methods which imply a threat to loss of love—i.e., techniques which facilitate internalization of motivations for self-direction and other adaptive qualities.

Working-class jobs, on the other hand, require compliance to external rules instituted by someone in authority; that is, working-class employees are more subject to standardization and direct supervision; and among them, getting ahead depends on collective efforts such as through union organizing, rather than on individual initiative. Furthermore, working-class people's jobs often involve manipulation of things rather than manipulation of ideas, symbols or interpersonal relations. Congruent with these personality and behavioral characteristics demanded by their jobs, working-class people tend to value respect to authority and conformity to externally imposed rules. In their childrearing practices they adopt techniques which more or less encourage their children to develop compliance to externally imposed rules; specifically, Kohn says that working-class childrearing practices rely more on physical punishment than on appeals to the child's internal disposition.

Studies in sex roles and sex-role socialization which have grown enormously over the last decade provide ample empirical evidence to support the contention of this chapter that the competencies or attributes which are fostered in children depend on the requirements of their future positions in the wider social and economic systems. Apart from this empirical support further importance of sex-role studies for our position is threefold. First, there is both folk and intellectual acceptance that role differences, including differences in economic pursuits, exist between the sexes. Second, empirical studies have documented these differences. And, third, we have a near experimental design in that we can study variation in sex roles in different cultures and compare their relationships to childrearing practices.

Focusing on sex role studies in the United States for the moment, many studies show differences in personality and behavioral characteristics between men and women and how these characteristics are related to differences in sex roles within the family, in the economic system and in society at large. Barwick and Douvan (1971), for example, list over 17 such personality and behavioral features (p. 225). Many of the uniquely female qualities arise from the requirements of the woman's subordinate position and subordinate roles in society. Generally, the dominant personality attributes associated with her subordinate roles are conformity, dependence, and manipulation (Weitzman 1975; 1979). These qualities also make up the major dimensions of the attributes Americans stress in the upbringing of their daughters.

Turning to the actual process of upbringing we find that it is heavily influenced by the valued competencies and that for this reason women and men are treated quite differently as children. Oakley (1972) among others, points out that the unique childrearing practices which facilitate development of culturally approved female personality traits and behaviors in America begin as soon as the child is born. Mothers (and parents in general) begin at birth to treat boys and girls differently. They encourage girls to adopt one form of behaviors and boys another; they use different techniques to reward or punish girls and boys; they provide girls with toys, tools, dresses, and other symbols which encourage them to develop culturally approved female qualities. These differential parental child-rearing practices toward girls are reinforced by children's books, school text-books and curricula, by movies and the mass media, advertisement, music and the like (Bardwick & Douvan 1971; Baruch & Barnett 1978; Beloitti 1976; Chodorow 1971; Dweck & Reppucci 1973; Miles 1975; Serbin & O'Leary 1978; Weitzman 1979).

Studies of sex roles and sex-role socialization in other cultures show, however, that there are differences in competencies or attributes of sex roles and that these differences definitely influence sex-role socialization. A classic example is Margaret Mead's study of three New Guinea societies differing from one another and from American society in the allocation of sex roles, in the resulting gender qualities and in childrearing practices toward the sexes. Thus among the Arapesh, men and women are regarded as cooperative, unaggressive, and responsive to the needs of others—qualities which are usually attributed to women in the United States. Among the Mundugumor—the second society—both men and women are regarded as aggressive, unresponsive, and individualistic—qualities which are usually reserved for men in the United States. Finally, among the Tchambuli sex-role assignment is the opposite of what it is in the United States and the resulting personality attributes are also the American opposite. The Tchambuli women are, for example, regarded as aggressive, dominant, impersonal and skilled in management, whereas Tchambuli men are thought to be emotionally dependent and less responsible than the women. All three societies differ in the way their raise their sons and daughters, indicating the influence of valued or functional competencies on childrearing practices.

The studies we have reviewed thus far lead to the following conclusions. First, those personality attributes which parents and other childrearing agents in a society consciously or unconsciously inculcate in the young are qualities required by adult economic, social and other roles. Second, these personal qualities and behaviors may vary from one society to another or from one social group to another whether the latter is based on class, caste, sex and the like. The differences in personality attributes or competencies are particularly large when the groups vary in their adult economic, social, and other important roles. Third, childrearing practices in a given society or its segment generally involve techniques suited to produce the personality attributes or competencies required by adult roles; in other words, childrearing practices are largely determined by the nature of those competencies which children must develop to function effectively as adult members of their society or social group. As Berry (1971) succinctly puts this crucial relationship between adaptive attributes and childrearing techniques:

> One would not expect to discover a society in which independence and self-reliance are conveyed as goals by a harsh, restrictive methods of socialization. Nor, conversely, would one expect to discover societies in which conformity is taught by a method characterized by a stimulation of a child's own interest and of his curiosity. (p. 328)

The implication of our argument for research in childrearing and child development has been partially stated by Inkeles (1968b; see also Aberle 1961; Whiting 1941). Inkeles correctly notes that every society (or its segment if it is stratified) has its role-repertoire which determines the pattern of expected behaviors of adult members. These qualities, i.e., the expected patterns of adult behavior are "what the individuals in the culture must learn and be if they are to meet the role demands set for them by the society—and they are acquired through the processes of childrearing (1968, p. 85). Hence, a first step in studying childrearing practices in a society or its segment is to identify those personal qualities demanded by adult economic, social and other roles. The next step is to study the people's theory and techniques of childrearing and their relationship to the adaptive attributes.

Unfortunately, Inkeles does not follow his own good suggestion when he discusses childrearing and child development among subordinate minorities in the United States such as blacks, chicanos, Indians, and Puerto Ricans. After observing that these minorities do not have some of the personality attributes of the dominant white middle-class which are assumed to be important for "competent participation in the economic, social, and political realms of the larger society," he proceeds to explain their lack as due primarily to the socialization practices of blacks, chicanos, Indians, and Puerto Ricans being different from those of the white middle class. And he concludes by saying that "The challenge for students of childrearing is to show—and explain *how these differences came about as a result of differential socialization practices and experiences*" (1968a, p. 66; emphasis added). Inkeles feels justified to attribute the differences in personality traits and behaviors to differences in childrearing practices because, according to him, legal barriers to minority participation in American life have been removed. As I have argued elsewhere (Ogbu 1978a, 1979a) there is ample evidence that although formal legal barriers have been removed, there are formidable informal barriers which do not yet permit minorities to achieve or experience full participation in American life. Furthermore, through many generations when the formal barriers existed the minorities developed distinct competencies to deal with their social and economic realities. And this adaptive response did not vanish simultaneously with the abolition of the formal barriers. It seems useful, therefore, that we should follow Inkeles' suggestion to begin research on childrearing and child development among these minorities by first identifying their proper adult roles, the types of personality attributes or competencies they may require, and how these qualities may influence the techniques used by these groups to raise their children.

CULTURAL ECOLOGICAL FRAMEWORK FOR STUDYING CHILDREARING

What is needed is an analytic framework that will enable us to incorporate Inkeles' useful suggestion and the insights from the crosscultural studies reviewed earlier. And we think that the ecological, specifically cultural ecological approach, provides such a framework. The framework of cultural ecology will enable us study the linkage between adult adaptations to ecological pressures, personality characteristics and behaviors resulting from such adaptations, and their relationship to childrearing practices. Cultural ecological framework also will enable us both to examine the present interrelationships among these phenomena and to probe their origins, persistence and change.

Following Julian Steward and his students we define cultural ecology as the study of institutionalized and socially transmitted patterns of behavior that are interdependent with features of the environment (Netting 1968; see also Geertz

1962; Goldschmidt 1973). Or, as Bennett puts it, cultural ecology is the study of two related phenomena: one is how a population's use of nature influences and is influenced by its social organization and cultural values; the other is the population's adaptive personality and behavior to its environment; this includes the coping mechanisms devised by members of the population, their ways of dealing with one another and with available resources in order to attain their subsistence goals and resolve recurrent or new problems (Bennett 1969). The adaptive unit on which cultural ecology focuses is the culturally identifiable group or population, not isolated individuals.

Cutural ecology does not deal with the total environment of a given population but only with those aspects of it that directly affect its subsistence quest and protection from threats to its physical well-being; that is, it deals with those aspects of the population's total environment that are relevant to its adaptation. This is called "effective environment" and is defined by the population's technology and knowledge. Technology here refers to both tools and their uses for subsistence exploitation and protection; knowledge includes understanding of the nature of the environment and the necessary techniques for exploiting its resources to satisfy physiological and culturally patterned needs (Netting 1968). With its knowledge and technology a population develops its unique devices for coping with its environment.

Cultural ecologists like Barth (1956) and Bennett (1969) have shown that groups with differing technologies and knowledge can develop different devices for exploiting the same physical environment; consequently, the same elements in a given environment may mean different things to different populations with differing exploitative or coping devices. When such populations co-exist they tend to establish some form of symbiotic relationship. Often, however, the symbiotic relationship involves unequal balance of power so that some groups occupy and exploit parts of the environment which are richly endowed with resources, while the weaker groups occupy and exploit those with marginal resources (Barth 1956; Bennett 1969).

Such symbiotic relationships exist in modern industrial societies, although this has not received the attention of cultural ecologists. The environment to which the populations of modern industrial societies adapt are, of course, not physical but technological, economic, social, and political. Because of the dominant influence of technological and economic portions of this environment we may simply designate the environment of modern industrial societies as technoeconomic. The resources of this environment are not evenly distributed; nor do different populations within the society have equal access to available resources. In the terminology of some economists we may say that the technoeconomic environment of modern industrial societies is segmented into different levels with varying degrees of resources (Edwards, Reich, & Gordon 1975; Piore 1969; 1975). These resources can be thought of as primarily consisting of jobs, wages, opportunities for advancement on the job, social credit, and

the like. Thus some parts of the technoeconomic environment are rich in resources: they contain the more desirable jobs, jobs with stability, good salaries
and wages, and good chances for advancement. Another part of this environment
may be characterized by deadend, peripheral and unstable jobs, low wages, and
little social credit. Still another part may be characterized by almost a total lack
of subsistence jobs and wages, though it contains social resources which include
both other people and care-taker institutions. These hypothetical habitats or
ecological niches of modern industrial societies like the United States are visible
to anyone who cares to look for them.

The distribution of various populations in these differing ecological habitats is
not by choice because traditionally some groups have been forced to occupy and
exploit marginal ones; this is particularly true of minorities, like black Americans. The black history is full of collective struggles, often called civil rights
struggles, intended to advance blacks into parts of the technoeconomic environment with more resources (Scott 1976). These collective struggles have gone on
for nearly 400 years and must be seen as a mode of exploitation of marginal
resources which has made some mark on the personal attributes of blacks.

Another consequence of generations of black restriction to an environment
with marginal resources is that they have been forced to develop many manipulative devices or strategies for exploiting social resources within this environment.
In some historical periods the manipulative strategies consisted primarily of
master-servant or patron-client relationships; a coping mechanism not unlike the
barzum relationship among the Kanuri of Nigeria described earlier. In contemporary urban ghetto patron-client relationships still exist, especially in black relationships with care-taker institutions like the welfare agency. But an important
coping device or subsistence strategy of modern urban ghetto is ''hustling'' in its
various forms.

Many blacks also make it through conventional strategy of the dominant white
middle class, and this has been particularly true since the last two decades
because of civil rights legislations, affirmative action, and the like. But the point
to emphasize is that these black devices for exploiting the marginal resources of
their environment cannot fail to make specific personality and behavioral demands on blacks; that is, they must to some extent affect the competencies
fostered in black childrearing—the qualities which black parents and other childrearing agents consciously and unconsciously try to inculcate in their young.
We have not yet begun to inquire into the nature of these ecological demands.
But until we do we cannot adequately understand why blacks raise their children
the way they do.

Cultural ecological approach also includes the study of what we may call
''ethnoecology''—that is, a study of the people's own view of and knowledge of
the subject matter under study, in this case, their view of childrearing and child
development (see Sutton-Smith in this volume). To incorporate the people's own
perspective on childrearing within the framework of cultural ecology, we pro-

pose a theory of subsistence and status mobility. Simply put, this means the native theory of how one succeeds or how one makes it in their particular environment and status system. By combining information from native theories of how some people make it and about how such theories affect behaviors of childrearing agents with the objective data obtained by the researcher through other instruments, we can come to understand more fully and better the nature of the language, cognitive, motivational, and social competencies which members of a population inculcate in their children and the relationship of these competencies to the particular childrearing techniques prevalent in the population.

REFERENCES

Aberle, D. F. Culture and socialization. In F. L. K. Ksu (Ed.), *Psychological Anthropology,* Evanston: Dorsey Press, 1961.

Barry, H., III, Child, I. L., & Bacon, M. K. Relation of child-training to subsistence economy: *American Anthropologist,* 1959, *61,* 51–63.

Bardwick, J. M., & Douvan, E. Ambivalence: The socialization of women. In V. Gornick & B. K. Moran (Eds.), *Women in sexist society: Studies in power and powerlessness.* New York: Basic Books, 1971.

Barth, F. Ecological relationships of ethnic groups in Swat, North Pakistan. *American Anthropologist,* 1956, *58,* 1079–1089.

Baruch, G. K., & Barnett, R. C. *Implications and applications of recent research on feminine development,* 1978.

Beloitti, E. G. *What are little girls made of?: The roots of feminine stereotypes.* New York: Schocken Books, 1976.

Bennett, J. W. *Northern plainsmen: Adaptive strategy and agricultural life.* Arlington Heights, Ill.: AHM Pub., 1969.

Berry, J. W. Ecological and cultural factors in spatial perceptual development. *Canadian Journal of Behavioral Science Review,* 1971, *3(4),* 324–337.

Bloom, B. S., Davis, A., & Hess, R. *Compensatory education for cultural deprivation.* New York: Holt, Rinehart, and Winston, Inc., 1965.

Choderow, N. Being and doing: A cross-cultural examination of the socialization of males and females. In V. Gornick & B. K. Moran (Eds.), *Women in sexist society: Studies in power and powerlessness.* New York: Basic Books, 1971.

Clark-Stewart, A. *Care in the family: A review of research and some propositions for policy.* New York: Academic Press, 1977.

Cohen, R. Some aspects of institutionalized exchange: A Kanuri example. *Chiers d'etudes Africaine,* 1965, *5(3),* 353–369.

Deutsch, M. The disadvantaged child and the learning process: Some social and developmental considerations. In A. H. Passow (Ed.), *Education in depressed areas.* New York: Teachers College Press, 1963.

Dweck, C. S., & Reppucci, N. D. Learned helplessness and reinforcement responsibility in children. *Journal of Personality and Social Psychology,* 1973, *25,* 109–116.

Edwards, R. C., Reich, M., & Gordon, D. M. (Eds.) *Labor market segmentation*. Lexington, Mass.: D. C. Heath, 1975.

Geertz, C. *Agricultural involution: The process of ecological change in Indonesia*. Berkeley: University of California Press, 1963.

Goldschmidt, W. Introduction: The theory of cultural adaptation. In R. B. Edgerton, *The individual in cultural adaptation: A study of four East African peoples*. Berkeley: University of California Press, 1971.

Heyneman, S. P. Why impoverished children do well in Ugandan schools. *Comparative Education*, 1979, *15(2)*, 175–185.

Hunt, J. McV. *The challenge of incompetence and poverty: Papers on the role of early education*. Urbana: University of Illinois Press, 1969.

Inkeles, A. Social structure and the socialization of competence. In Harvard Educational Review Editors, *Socialization and schools*. Cambridge, Mass.: Harvard University Press, 1968, 50–68. (a)

Inkeles, A. Society, social structure, and child socialization. In J. A. Clausen (Ed.), *Socialization and society*. Boston: Little, Brown, and Co., 1968. (b)

Kerber, A., & Bommarito, B. Preschool education for the developing cortex. In A. Kerber and B. Bommarito (Eds.), *The schools and the urban crisis*. New York: Holt, Rinehart, and Winston, 1965.

Kohn, M. L. Social class and parent-child relationships: An interpretation. In R. Laub Coser (Ed.), *Life cycle and achievement in America*. New York: Harper and Row, 1969.

Levine, R. A. *Dreams and deeds: Achievement motivation in Nigeria*. Chicago: The University of Chicago Press, 1967.

Magnum, G. L., & Seninger, S. F. *Coming of age in the ghetto: A report to the Ford Foundation*. Baltimore: The Johns Hopkins University Press, 1978.

Maquet, J. Rwanda castes. In A. Tuden and L. Plotnicov (Eds.), *Social stratification in Africa*. New York: The Free Press, 1970.

Mead, M. *From the South Seas: Studies of adolescence and sex in primitive societies*. New York: Wm. Morrow and Co., 1939.

Miles, B. Channeling children: Sex stereotyping in prime-time TV. *Women on Words and Images*. Princeton, N.J., 1975.

Miller, D., & Swanson, G. *The changing American parent*. New York: Wiley, 1958.

Netting, R. McC. *Hill farmers of Nigeria: Cultural ecology of the Jose Plateau*. Seattle: University of Washington Press, 1968.

Netting, R. *The ecological approach in cultural study*. Reading, Mass.: Addison-Wesley, 1971.

Oakley, A. *Sex, gender and society*. New York: Harper, 1972.

Ogbu, J. U. *An ecological approach to the study of school effectiveness*. Unp. ms., Washington, D.C.: National Institute of Education, 1978. (a)

Ogbu, J. *Minority education and caste: The American system in cross-cultural perspective*. New York: Academic Press, 1978. (b)

Ogbu, J. *Minority school performance as an adaptation*. Unp. ms., 1978. (c)

Ogbu, J. Social stratification and the socialization of competence. *Anthropology and Education Quarterly*, 1979, *10(1)*.

Ogbu, J. Education, clientage, and social mobility: A study of caste and social change in the United States and Nigeria. In G. D. Berreman (Ed.), *Social inequality: Comparative and developmental approaches*. New York: Academic Press, 1981. (a)

Ogbu, J. Origins of human competence: A cultural-ecological perspective. *Child Development*, 1981, *52*, 413–429. (b)

Piore, M. J. On-the-job training in a dual market. In A. Weber et al. (Eds.), *Public Private Manpower Policies*. Madison, Wisc.: Industrial Relations Association, 1969.

Piore, M. J. Notes for a theory of labor market stratification. In R. C. Edwards, M. Reich, & D. M. Gordon (Eds.), *Labor market segmentation*. Lexington, Mass.: D. C. Heath, 1975.

Scott, J. W. *The black revolts: Racial stratification in the U.S.A.* Cambridge, Mass.: Schenkman Publishing Co., 1976.

Serbin, L. A., & O'Leary, D. How nursery schools teach girls to "shut-up." In J. Williams (Ed.), *Psychology of women: Selected readings.* New York: Norton, 1978.

Weitzman, L. J. Sex-role socialization. In J. Freeman (Ed.), *Women: A feminist perspective.* Palo Alto, Calif.: Mayfield Pub. Co., 1975.

Weitzman, L. *Sex-role socialization.* Palo Alto, Calif.: Mayfield Pub. Co., 1979.

Weitzman, L., Eifler, D., Hokada, E., & Ross, C. Sex-role socialization in picture books for pre-school children. *American Journal of Sociology,* 1973, *77,* 1125–1149.

White, S. H., Day, M. C., Freeman, P. K., Hartman, S. A., & Messenger, K. P. *Federal programs for young children: Review and recommendations.* Wash., D.C.: Dept. of Health, Education and Welfare, 1973.

Whiting, J. W. *Becoming a Kwoma: Teaching and learning in a New Guinea tribe.* New Haven: Yale University Press, 1941.

VI ENDNOTE: THE POLITICAL USES OF CHILDHOOD

12 The Politics of Childhood

Hendrik D. Gideonse
College of Education
University of Cincinnati

I remember starting the fourth grade with glowing anticipation. Miss Crawford seemed to me a happy amalgam of June Allyson and Elizabeth Taylor. (Remember now, at age eight *anything* is possible!) Imagine my dismay, then, when my undeclared and barely savored crush was rudely interrupted by, first, the news and then, the departure of Miss Crawford for Marriage.

Enter Miss Crawford's replacement, a person whose name I have completely suppressed. By the second day our problem was clear; she could not pronounce my name. I can't remember the details of the exchanges we had, only the outcome. I ended up dispatched to the Principal's office over my insistence that my name was pronounced Gideonse, not Gideon-ese!

John Holt tells a different kind of story about an incident he experienced in a supermarket. He had collected the items he needed and went to stand in the checkout lane. Standing in front of him was this tousle-headed child; he reached forward and ruffled the boy's hair. The figure turned around; indignantly looking up at Holt was the mature face of a dwarf! Instantly, Holt was aware that what he had intended as a gesture of affection, was regarded by another adult as a kind of personal invasion, technically, battery.

A third anecdote, this one by E. F. Schumacher. He recalled being seated in a restaurant next to a family of three—mother, father, and a young lad of eight or ten. They all examined the menu in the presence of the waitress. The boy said that he wanted liver and bacon. The father studied the menu as did the boy's mother. Then the father ordered three steaks. The waitress repeated the order,

"Two steaks; one liver and bacon," and departed. The boy looked at his mother and said, "Mommy, she thinks I'm real!"[1]

Finally, a last anecdote. While I did a fair amount of bibliographical research and consulted with peers across the country, I also inquired of my own children. I asked Hendrik, my 6-year-old, if he knew what power was, whether he could give me any examples.

' Oh," he said, "that's easy. Pulling 10,000 tons."

"O.K.," I said, "anything else?"

He thought a minute. "My teacher knows a lot of things."

"Very good!" I said, the neon sign, "Knowledge is power," blinking on and off in my mind's eye. "Anything more?"

"Well, the electric lights are power."

"Great," I said. "Those are excellent examples, Hendrik. I think you really understand what power means. Now let me try another question. Who has power in this family?"

"We ALL do!" There was no hesitation in his response. I remember feeling very proud and wondering whether anybody would believe he'd really said that. I also thought he might be playing with me a bit by providing me with politic answers, so I framed the next question even more pointedly.

"Hendrik, what do you do when you really want to get your way?"

"Oh," he said reflectively, "I let them think about it a few days, and then I ask very politely."

During this exchange, Hendrik's 4-year-old brother, Teddy, had been sitting across the table next to his mother, Sarah. He had been raptly attentive to my dialog with Hendrik. I turned to Teddy to include him, to ask him what he did when he wanted to get *his* way. (I had already formulated a possible answer for him relating to some fairly effective tactical interpretations of civil disobedience he has in his repertoire.)

"Oh," he said without hesitation, "I do it MYSELF!"

These four anecdotes evoke a number of the concerns encompassed by my title, "The Politics of Childhood." In them one can find illustrations of the hegemony of adults over children. One can find differences in status. And one can also find illustrations of the unexpected competence, natural authority, resourcefulness, and power of children.

More than a year has passed since Kathy Borman asked me to give this presentation. At the time I suggested the title I was especially intrigued by the power relationships within the family, what they were, how they manifest themselves, what the external and internal sources of those power relations are, and, finally, what the implications of all that might be for the evolution of public policy about children. In the intervening time I have had to confront my own

---

[1] *The Atlantic,* "Toward an Appropriate Technology," April, 1979, p. 91.

naivete. I discovered, for one thing, that I had stolen a title Norman Denzin had already used for the introductory chapter of his book, *Children and Their Caretakers*.[2] For another, I learned that very little has been done from a political science perspective on power relations in the family. I learned of the outpouring of research and scholarship on matters bearing on childhood and the family. The closer today came, the more anxiety I felt, the more I began to feel outclassed, out-competenced, indeed, like children must often feel in the world of adults. After all, everyone I read or talked with had been at it far longer than I. As a result I sense a feeling of identity with the subjects of my concern. That is probably not a bad frame of mind to be in. We may be beyond our children, but it helps us to understand when we try to think and feel our way back.

What I want to do in this paper is share some speculative thoughts. The organization is not tight; rather than a complete picture it is more like a still-boxed puzzle. The pieces are there but not tightly locked together. Think with me as I spring from a half dozen key terms, spend a few moments with each one, and then draw some implications of those thoughts as they run through the particular policy orientation prism of my mind.

RIGHTS

A good place to start a discussion of the politics of childhood is with the question of the rights of children. As Kenneth Keniston has pointed out[3] the idea of the rights of children as legal persons has begun to engage our attention only in the last two decades. Until recently, the dominant assumption has been that the rights of children were expressed and interpreted by the parents of those children.

Victor Worsfold in Volume II of the *Harvard Educational Review* Special Issue on the Rights of Children[4] developed a philosophical justification of the rights of children resting broadly on John Rawls' *Theory of Justice*. For Worsfold the principles of justice guarantee rights based on the nature of individuals; they are not given to us by anybody. All that is needed is that they be acknowledged, recognized, and respected. Determining who is a member of society, depends to some extent on capability; to participate fully, according to Rawls, one must have reached the "age of reason." But the critical variable for Rawls is not present capability, it is capacity, whether fully developed or not. And clearly children, writes Worsfold, are pre-eminently in this category of

---

[2]Norman K. Denzin, editor. *Children and Their Caretakers,* Transaction Books, New Brunswick, New Jersey, 1973.

[3]*All Our Children,* Harcourt Brace Jovanovich, New York, 1977, p. 184.

[4]Victor Worsfold, "A Philosophical Justification of the Rights of Children," *Harvard Educational Review*. Volume 44, No. 1, February, 1974, pp. 142–157.

having capacity, thus, qualify as members of society, with just claims to fair treatment.[5]

William G. Bartholome in a paper presented to the National Commission for the protection of Human Subjects of Biomedical and Behavioral Research extends the argument a little further.[6] While writing in a medical context, he reminds us that rights are not claims, they are entitlements. They do not have to be recognized to be present. He makes a second point which is especially important in the case of children. Rights are distinct from powers; an entitlement does not depend on its bearer possessing any relevant power or capacity. To have rights or entitlements, it is only necessary for an individual to be a member of a group of rights-holding persons.[7]

Not everyone agrees, of course, that membership in a community entitles one to rights. Stanley Hauerwas, for example, in a critical response to Worsfold and Bartholome adopts a different position.[8] He objects to the concept of "rights" as essentially negative in form. In any case, Hauerwas finds the rights pertaining to children as, in fact, vested in the family and even these rights are not maintained without qualification by the state. In the final analysis Hauerwas wants us not to talk about the rights of children but the duties of adults.[9]

This is all too brief a précis of a serious, philosophical argument, but I offer it as illustration that there are different points of view here. I take my lead from Worsfold and Bartholome. For one thing, it seems to me that children are members of the human community by virtue of their birth, quite independently of any particular family unit of which they are a part. As members of that community, they have and are entitled to all the rights any other member of that community has or is entitled to. That they happen to be children is simply another temporary characteristic of their humanness.

To conclude that children have rights, the same rights adults have, does not simplify anything; on the contrary, it certainly complicates, for we must then deal with the crucial question of competence, or, in Rawls' terms, the extent to which capacity has been developed into capability. Of equal importance, in the absence of capacity, who is responsible for exercising the caretaker role in respect to the realization of rights? The language of duties places primary responsibility in the hands of the individuals exercising the duties. The language of rights places responsibility in the hands of the individual entitled to the rights. From the perspective of my overarching goal, which is a society of individuals able to achieve their own self-determined ends, conceiving of the locus of rights

---

[5]*Ibid,* pp. 152–3.

[6]William G. Bartholome, "Proxy Consent in the Medical Context: The Infant as Person," *Research Involving Children, Appendix,* U.S. Government Printing Office, DHEW Publication, No. (OS) 77-0005, 1977, pp. 3-23 to 3-54.

[7]*Ibid.,* p. 3-35.

[8]Stanley Hauerwas, "Rights, Duties, and Experimentation on Children: A Critical Response to Worsfold and Bartholome," *Research Involving Children, Appendix, op. cit.,* 5-1 to 5-27.

[9]*Ibid.,* p. 5-4.

and responsibilities in the individuals from the beginning seems consistent, even if difficult.

These observations suggest one more consequence. If children possess rights by virtue of their entry into the human condition, then it follows that adults do not have special rights when it comes to children, any more than they do with respect to one another. They may, of course, have special interests or duties. It would also follow that the State has no special claims on children that are not identical to those it has in respect to adults. In similar fashion the State's interests or duties may be different because of differing circumstances, but in respect to rights its posture is identical for all members of the society.

It is this position that we understand when we think back to John Holt's experience with the child/adult. The right of one's own space, the sanctity of one's own person, is something we clearly accord adults, but daily violate in respect to children. We do it very easily, and with the best of intentions (or so we argue), but without the permission of children, such adult behavior is clearly questionable.

COMPETENCE

Any person who seriously believes that children enjoy rights equally with all other members of the human community has to confront the issue of competence. After all, children cannot do the things adults can. They cannot operate complicated machinery, or be depended upon to behave consistently. They do not possess historical perspective, aren't strong enough to operate in a physical environment designed primarily by adults for adults, and so on. These differences are important. There is no rationalizing them away.

A question remains, however. To what extent are the competency differences we see a product of a priori conclusions? To what extent would the competency differences be as obvious if we believed other than we do?

Denzin, for example, in his chapter with the same title as my title, notes the problem with theories of learning which view the child in passive terms, theories which have been systematically translated into theories of education.

> Teachers, not children, are seen as experts on all matters. Children are thought to be unreliable objects, who must be actively controlled, tested repeatedly, never given a say in what they are taught, and rewarded for passive acceptance of the teacher's and the school's point of view. These theories of learning, then, complement and support the broader position that children are incompetent social beings.[10]

But suppose we were to look at children and ask what kinds of competencies they show us. Like many oppressed classes and castes, children might be said to be far

---

[10]Denzin, op. cit., p. 8.

more knowledgeable about their oppressors (adults) than adults are about children. That is a competence we give them little credit for; without it, how many fewer would survive. Children are skilled manipulators and sharp social observers of the adult world around them. They are as quick, certainly, and often quicker in understanding the interpersonal dynamics of emotional danger, in and out of the home, than we give them credit for. That children possess images of competence and standards of behavior that exceed their capacity is observed every time a child "dissolves" over frustration at her inability to complete a task in the fashion she desires, a fashion prized precisely because of the clarity possessed of the standard of adult performance in respect to the task.

In any case, some children are wiser than adults. Some are more coordinated. Most are more spontaneous, creative, and intuitive. Without lionizing children, these last three competencies, at least, are among those that children possess in greater degree than adults. Still, our images of children's incompetence, lead us to believe that they are less competent than they are. True, research and tradition argue that the capacity for reason develops approximately at age seven, and that the capacity for moral choice (that is, an understanding of personal responsibility) seems to emerge around age twelve. The problem that children face in respect to competence, however, is that they are always surrounded by adults who believe themselves to be competent. Adults who can do things better than children are often tempted to do these things for them. It is a natural tendency, and a dangerous trap, especially for the children. It is the classic problem of any natural elite. Is it better to do for others if you can do better than they, or better to let them do for themselves even if the end result for the doer is not as complete, fulfilling, or "accurate"?

I want to make one last comment about an aspect of competence that is especially troubling and which I will come back to later on. None of us has special competence when it comes to articulating the needs and interests of others. Each of us, on the other hand, possesses a special competence when it comes to expressing our own interests and purposes. That does not mean we are accurate in expressing them or necessarily choose what is best for ourselves. But no one is in a better position to articulate what each of us believes to be our own interest. Others may disagree with us, perhaps with what they believe to be our own best interests at heart, but none of us, adult or child, can access ourselves as we can. That kind of competence is vested in each of us; child or adult, we are the prime sources of data. As in Schumacher's anecdote of the child in the restaurant, recognition of that particular competence in turn may create the sense of, not just identity, but of existence itself.

POWER

Power, of course, is still the central element in the study of politics. In the interactive world of children and adults who has power?

At first glance it may seem a little strange to ask power questions about childhood, either by others in respect to children or, especially interesting, by children themselves. What kinds of answers might we get?

Clearly, adults have important powers in respect to children. Sheer physical size and strength, for example, are important. Language and conceptual development are important powers, especially with the "volume turned up." Some of these powers can seem even magical in the eyes of children. "How did you DO that, Daddy?" You can hear the wonder.

Physical coordination, the ability to work, to provide (or responsibly allocate the provisions of another) are important powers, too. The experience adults have of their own childhood, as Denzin points out in his paper in this volume, and the transition to and through adulthood, create the important power of perspective.

And what of the powers of children? Are there powers they have that adults do not? There is, first, the power of unbelievably rapid and multidirectional physical, mental, and emotional growth. It is a power not directly under the control of the child, and certainly not of any adult, although it can certainly be accommodated and supported. Learning and growing power is real and formidable, however deeply founded in genetics and ontogeny.

Second, there is the power of the clean slate. It is a power that can free society from imprisonment by its past. It can also doom us to unintended repetition of that same past. Perhaps this is not a power in the usual sense of capacity to act. Still, in the idea of the fresh start each infant represents to society, we can find an important resource for renewal that is vital to humanity and society. It is, incidentally, a power that none of us at this conference retains in any significant amount relative to what our children possess. Our slates are well-written upon. There is no way I can approach the 1980's with quite the perspective my children can; the newness and freshness they have is an important match to the memory and experience I bring. They are equal powers though very different. Mine is the power of performance; theirs, the power of promise.

This renewal power of children in human affairs is important, a vital ingredient to the development of society. Not all of us agree on its value, however. Cynics will argue (and with some justification) that the institution of schooling, whatever else its benefits, also moderates (if not stifles) the creativity of children and that at some level this is what we adults intend. Some adults and some institutions are threatened by innovation, surprise, and the new awareness which children display for us. But for others of us that is why we teach; working with children is a way of staying fresh, of remaining young, of tapping into energy sources and capacities—power—from which we would otherwise be removed. And for the society, that capacity of children to refresh and renew is a continuing source of inspiration and energy.

The main point of this exposition on power per se is the idea that power in the interaction between children and adults rests in both parties. Furthermore, the direction and consequences of power relations between children and adults can be constructive, destructive, draining, synergistic, or neutral. While children are at greater immediate risk in some of these interactions, as for example, in the case of physical and mental child abuse, it is not at all clear that adults and the larger society are not subject to risks of a different kind in the final outcomes of the power relations between children and adults. If adults obliterate the powers of children, society, that is, all of us, can be losers.

In any case, adults seem to be constantly surprised at the real powers that children of all ages display; witness my own sense of surprise at the perceptions and understandings of my 6-year-old. That children utilize their powers in often devasting ways—for example, creative civil disobedience, the "buy-or-cry" extortion racket in toy stores, the manipulation of adult fears of embarassment in public places—seems clear once we start asking what children *can* and *do* do instead of assuming that they cannot.

AUTHORITY

Power and authority are closely allied concepts. In many instances the words are used interchangeably. Here I want to make a distinction between the *power* or *capacity* to act and *formal permission* or *sanction* to act. I can say, for example, that I have more power than virtually all children, but authority over only my own or those in my charge by virtue of formal delegation. In the context of the politics of childhood and the conviction that the rights of children are coterminous with those of adults, the question is who has authority when it comes to children.

Like it or not, society vests a variety of different agencies and institutions with authority over children. As Jack Coons has so crisply put it, the law in our society "ordains the petty sovereignties of childhood," petty, he continues, "only in the sense that each of these infant hegemonies is itself subject to the overarching government."[11] Each of these sovereignties, however, has a scope that is anything by petty. Coons writes, for example, of the utter despotism of the infant waiting to be born subject to the mother's choice that he live or die. Parents have sweeping authority over the lives of children. The dominion of the public school begins at age six. Once a juvenile court assumes jurisdiction over a child, wide discretion exists in disposing of the child's freedom and treatment.[12] The importance of the dominion these sovereigns and others exercise over the lives of children is central to an understanding of the politics of childhood. For when we understand the extent of the sovereignty that various agencies and individuals exercise over children, we begin to understand some of their lives and something of the often terrible responsibilities we bear. Says Coons:

---

[11]John E. Coons, "Law and the Sovereigns of Childhood," *Phi Delta Kappan,* September, 1976, p. 19.
[12]*Idem.*

Children are small, weak, and inexperienced; adults are big, strong, and shrewd. One may liberate children from the law of man, but the law of nature is beyond repeal. There is no way to send an eight-year-old child out of the sovereignty of the parent and into a world of liberty. He will be projected instead into a new sovereignty of one kind or another.[13]

This, says Coons, is the practical, insuperable, and permanent obstacle to kids lib. Whatever the regime, it will be decided by big people, and the elements. Small children will be dominated, make no mistake about it.

If that is so, then what do we make of this matter of authority? Is there any hope for the child, the becoming adult? Is there escape from the exercise of external authority?

Many would find solace in the doctrine of *in loco parentis*. The evidence suggests there are real problems with this approach. Very often the various sovereigns over children seem to interpret the interest of children in terms which closely approximate the self-interest of the sovereigns. They tend to see the solutions for children's needs and aspirations in terms of the skills and capacities the sovereigns are responsible for exercising. Thus educators think in terms of schooling solutions. Corrections officials see corrections solutions. Welfare professionals see welfare solutions. And so on. Perhaps it is only human. It is probably not venal, but as professionals we do tend to see the *problems* as caused by other *sectors* (especially when we can't see our way clear to useful solutions in our own) and the solutions we *do* see we project from our *own* capabilities and resources upon the children rather than coming to them from the perspectives and needs emerging from the children themselves.

As Coons, Robert Mnookin, and Stephen Sugarman in the draft of their stimulating new book tentatively titled *Sovereigns of Childhood* point out, the critical question is not *whether* authority shall be exercised over the child, but *who* shall exercise it and under what kinds of constaints and incentives.

The question, of course, is not an open one. Society has, in fact, located that authority in many different institutions and agencies; there is momentum. There are establishments. What *is*, of course, need not be forever. The possibility of change, through careful thought, persuasive argument and effective organization, is always with us. One most interesting development, for instance, is the prospective HEW requirement that not only must parent or guardian consent to research but the assent of children over seven must also be secured.

KNOWLEDGE

Three separate issues may be raised here. How do we get knowledge about children that is useful in the political arenas in which they live and which affect

---

[13]*Ibid.*, p. 22.

their lives? The second question is the old Spencerian one, which knowledge is of most worth? Third, what criteria have to be met in order that we can lay claim to knowledge?

These are not easy questions. Indeed, they challenge quite fundamentally the ground on which we think we stand. I do not have neat answers, either, just some observations that I believe we all need to ruminate on.

First a word on formal inquiry as a source of knowledge. We all carry around in our heads images of formal inquiry as the process by which we seek to understand objective reality and formulate generalizations whose power extends beyond individual cases. Increasingly, however, scholars are beginning to wonder whether such images of science may in fact be getting in the way of understanding what we need to know in order to achieve human ends to which we individually and collectively may aspire.

The world of human affairs is tremendously complex. What matters to us greatly as individuals is not just how we are similar but precisely how we are different, not just the "freeze-frame" objective reality as defined (usually in jargon) by people external to us, but the subjective richness of meaning we individually encounter in life experience. Is there an unacknowledged tension between the knowledge produced by "science" and the different kind of knowledge each of us develops in the course of our day-to-day existence? Do we too easily allow ourselves to accept a parallel hegemony to that of adult over child when we uncritically accept the epistemological foundations of science over the epistemological foundations of our own direct experience in its richness, complexity, and inner meaning?

I don't want to be misunderstood here. I am not making an argument against formal inquiry about families, or child development, or the psychological traps that children and adults set for each other. It is not, I hope, a mushy-headed lionization of the individuality of each individual "flower." Rather what seems to me important is developing styles of inquiry which let our subjects speak to us, where the different knowledge of scientists and subjects interact cooperatively with one another, where ample opportunity is provided for the richness of individuals and their contexts to reveal themselves, which give individual stakeholders—not abstract groups—the opportunity to convey their reality, their knowledge, and their aspirations to achieve that which they would desire in definition of their own lives.

Spencer's question "What knowledge is of most worth?" raises the matter of values to view. A second question we might ask about knowledge, then, is how legitimate its claims to objectivity are. The objectivity of formal inquiry may be challenged on at least three grounds: the choice of problems and phenomena studied and not studied; second, the extent to which those engaged in the inquiry bring values to their work not immediately visible but still powerful in their influence; third, the extent to which the theories and structures of the disciplines from which inquiry springs themselves have values deeply imbedded which shape developing knowledge in subtle but powerful ways. Understanding the impact of values on formal inquiry is something we need to be much more explicit about, but more often they are the Edward T. Hall silent language whose messages are so hard to hear and whose "noise" blocks our hearing almost entirely.

There are basic problems in the appeal to science in the support of practice and policy in respect to children. Henry Levin has talked of the veil of science, the robes in which we wrapped our policy options. Coons, Mnookin, and Sugarman develop similar points in their draft book. They point to two barriers to the use of science in behalf of public policy for children. Ignorance is one of those barriers; there is a vast amount we do not know. Furthermore, it is likely we can never know it in time to act. More important, however, is the idea that the only scientific knowledge that can be used in support of policy is that portion of the knowledge on which there is wide consensus. Where there is conflict, they provocatively remind us, we are merely dressing our own views with the opinion of one scientist against the opinions of others. We are engaged at that point in argument rather than establishing the firm epistemological ground.[14]

FUTURES

One more piece remains in the puzzle box. I refer to the futures perspective and what it might contribute to a developed understanding of the politics of childhood.

Thinking of children in the context of the future is certainly not strange to us. We see bumper stickers, for example, saying "Put our Future to Work—Rent a Kid." We work to make the world a better place for our children. On the positive side, we can see our children as expressions of hope and aspiration and worry about the declining birthrate as an indicator of our own doubts and premonitions about the future.

There is an obvious sense in which children are of the future. That is when they will be adults. That is when their capacity will match ours and we will be relieved of the responsibilities of exercising authority on their behalf. It is the time when the destiny toward which they are heading as children becomes a working, playing, loving, achieving, losing, winning reality.

In this view, childhood is preparation and apprenticeship. But there is a problem here. Given the character and speed of social, technological, and political change in our era, what kind of preparation and apprenticeship do we provide? Who can say? The uncertainty is overwhelming.

This is where understanding a futures perspective can be helpful.

---

[14]John E. Coons, Robert Mnookin, and Stephen Sugarman, *Sovereigns of Childhood* (draft), Chapter 3, pp. 1–4.

First, a clear underlying condition leading to a vital interest in futures is the ubiquity of change; it is the perception and the reality of change which is the principal energizer behind the attempt to understand better that which is not yet! The point of looking to futures is not so much an academic concern for what is *to be* as it is out of a desire to do something *now*. In other words, we study futures in order to act in the present.

Second, one of the most important things that can be said about futures is that they are plural, not singular. That is to say, there are as many futures possible to us as there are real choices.

Third, the future, that particular future of many which becomes a present that we experience, does not just happen to us. It is something we invent.

From the notions of pluralism and invention we can extrapolate a fourth idea. Inventing the future is inherently an act of responsibility (or the reverse), one that requires attention to ethical and moral considerations. To choose is to express a value; the treatment of values is precisely the business of ethics and morality.

A fifth point we might make is that futures are unpredictable. The most surprising future of all would be one without any surprises. Sixth, futures work is characterized by long time frames—30 to 50 years. Seventh, futures emphasizes systems and holism; it attempts to see human phenomena in their complexity and interlinked nature. Futures emphasizes synthesis and de-emphasizes reductionism.

A last point worth mentioning is the concept of stakeholders. The recognition of the importance of values, choice, and the concept of invention requires us to ask who stands to gain or lose, in what ways, and to what degree. What future do we choose for children? Do we do it for them or with them? What future do we prepare them for, and by what right?

INTEGRATING THE ELEMENTS

That completes my attention to a half dozen pieces in the puzzle I have titled the Politics of Childhood. Let me summarize what I have said to this point:

1. The rights of children are the rights of any other member of society.
2. Competence is a central issue in childhood, one that has too often been approached in terms of adultcentrism or negative comparisons with adults.
3. Children have powers which should be viewed in balance with the different powers that adults have. I called two of these that children have the powers of growth and the clean slate.
4. Despite the balance of powers that might be seen in the interaction between children and adults, it is clearly the case that children will always be under the sovereignty of adults, although recognition of the identity of their

rights with those of adults might lead to considerably different interpretations of the exercise of those rights than we now allow.

5. The knowledge base on which we might rest different approaches to the politics of childhood is problematical for a variety of reasons having to do with the incompleteness of knowledge and the values and norms on which science is based.

6. The indeterminacy of the future coupled with our own responsibility for inventing it, suggests profound questions of legitimacy respecting how we approach the educational development of children.

What kind of synthesis can we make of all this? If individual self-determination and competence are the ends for children toward which we would lead, it becomes critically important that we pay careful attention to the individual articulation of the needs of infants, children, and adolescents. Three problems suggest themselves. How can the voice of children best be heard? Who cares for the children? Wherein do the bonds of accountability lie?[15] It is one thing to say that authority over children should be exercised so that from the earliest *their own* capacity for self-determination is given appropriate and ever-increasing exercise. It is another to discover who is most likely to want—and is in the best position—to do this. It is still a third to consider what incentives exist to keep adults attentive to these two matters.

Coons and Sugarman suggest three qualities that must inhere in the ideal chooser for children.[16] The first quality is the extent to which the chooser truly incorporates the voice of the child in the process. The second quality is the extent to which the chooser really cares about the child, or, as Bronfenbrenner would have it, the presence of irrational involvement with the child (translation: somebody has got to be crazy about that kid).[17] The third quality is accountability. The chooser must be closely linked to the welfare of the child so that what happens to the child directly affects the chooser.

Professional solutions, professionals as choosers, do not meet the criteria very well. Professionals do not have sufficient intimate knowledge of individual children to be able to "hear their voices" adequately. The cultural norms of all professions mitigate against the kind of caring that is called for. And professionals certainly do not live with their mistakes or their successes; they pass them on to the next grade or another institution entirely.

---

[15]Once again I am indebted to Coons and Sugarman's thinking in "A Case for Choice," *Parents, Teachers, and Children: Prospects for Choice in American Education*, Institute for Contemporary Studies, San Francisco, 1977, pp. 132-3.

[16]*Idem.*

[17]Urie Bronfenbrenner, "Who Needs Parent Education," *Teachers College Record*, May, 1978, p. 774.

Only one institution of the society appears to fulfill the criteria. That is the family. Parents are in the best position to be able to articulate the needs and concerns of children, especially since so many of them are articulated in essentially private languages that need translation if they are to be understood beyond the confines of the family itself. Second, it is the family where one is most likely to encounter the kind and degree of crazy caring that is so crucial to the interests of the children. Furthermore, it is there where whatever powers and competencies children have can be brought to bear. It is the one institution, in fact, where the political powers of children can be exercised most fully. Finally, it is the family that has to live with the consequences of the choices made. Living with the consequences of choices is the ultimate form of accountability. If the choices are good, the family is happy. If they are bad, the family is not. The built-in incentives for attentiveness, accuracy, and caring are doubly and triply reinforced.

I am personally persuaded of the power of Coons and Sugarman's argument. But it is also very troubling. For one thing, the so-called institution of the family is undergoing a transformation and diversification that is quite unprecedented. The values guiding family development are pluralistic and uncertain. What worked before seems inappropriate now for a host of reasons including changed mores, heightened expectations, the extention of equal rights, advancing technology, and so on.

If we are uncertain what the institution of the family is or what it means, it is not easy to contemplate how to support it externally, either by the creation of suitable incentives conceived to operate directly on family units or the invention and maintenance of professional services in assistance to children. How can we enrich parental choice in providing for their children? How do we cope with presumptions—or the reality—of inadequacy on the part of parents in making proper choices for their children, for example, on such things as nutrition, preventive health, physical and psychological shelter, and the like? If parents are in the best position to make choices, when and by what right do we intervene and over-ride? Do the consequences of over-ride undermine the institution of the family thus reducing still further its efficaciousness in representing the real interests of children and the likelihood of achieving desired social and political ends for children-become-adults?

I am as uncomfortable with the implications of the flow and logic of this presentation as I suspect some of you are. How do we increase choices for parents, for example, in respect to schooling? Are vouchers the logical conclusion, or are there solutions which retain the values of parental choice within the context of a public system of education? I share my concern and thoughts with you because they are issues that will not go away by failing to confront them. I am convinced we need to identify our values, clarify our assumptions, and creatively prepare options that will recognize why getting choices closer to parents (or instilling in others the characteristics of parents) is likely to have more beneficial effects for children and for society in the long run. Surely the professionals among us have to confront head-on the values underlying presumptions we may have or express that parents are *not* in a position to make good choices.

I close, then, with my opening questions. Who has power with respect to children? How is it exercised? By what right? To what ends? These are the central questions of the politics of childhood. In our answers to them I think we treat, in fact, a microcosm of the basic political and constitutional issues facing our society.[18]

[18]The critical acumen and assistance of Sarah Gideonse, Stephanie Feeney, Kathy Borman, and Joel Milgram are gratefully acknowledged. The stimulus in the Coons, Mnookin, and Sugarman draft materials *Sovereigns of Childhood* is once again acknowledged. The author is, of course, fully responsible for any continuing flubs that still remain.

Author Index

Numbers in *italics* indicate pages with complete bibliographic information.

Subject Index